BOOKS BY HERSHEL SHANKS

The City of David: A Guide to Biblical Jerusalem

Judaism in Stone: The Archaeology of Ancient Synagogues

The Dead Sea Scrolls After Forty Years (with James C. VanderKam,
P. Kyle McCarter, Jr., and James A. Sanders)

The Rise of Ancient Israel (with William G. Dever,
Baruch Halpern, P. Kyle McCarter, Jr.)

BOOKS EDITED BY HERSHEL SHANKS

*Ancient Israel: A Short History from Abraham to the Roman
Destruction of the Temple*

The Art and Craft of Judging: The Opinions of Judge Learned Hand

Christianity and Rabbinic Judaism: A Parallel History of Their Origins and Early Development

Understanding the Dead Sea Scrolls

Archaeology and the Bible: The Best of BAR, 2 vols. (with Dan P. Cole)

Feminist Approaches to the Bible (with Phyllis Trible, Tikva Frymer-Kensky,
Pamela J. Milne, Jane Schaberg)

Recent Archaeology in the Land of Israel (with Benjamin Mazar)

The Search for Jesus (with Stephen J. Patterson, Marcus J. Borg, John Dominic Crossan)

Jerusalem
An Archaeological Biography

HERSHEL SHANKS

Editor, *Biblical Archaeology Review*

RANDOM HOUSE NEW YORK

Copyright ©1995 by Hershel Shanks
All rights reserved under International and Pan-American Copyright Conventions.
Published in the United States by Random House, Inc., New York,
and simultaneously in Canada by Random House of Canada Limited, Toronto.

Grateful acknowledgment is made to HarperCollins Publishers, Inc.,
for permission to reprint four lines from "Ecology of Jerusalem"
from *Great Tranquillity: Questions and Answers* by Yehuda Amichai.
Copyright © 1983 by Yehuda Amichai.
Reprinted with permission
of HarperCollins Publishers, Inc.

Library of Congress Cataloging-in-Publication Data
Shanks, Hershel.
Jerusalem: an archaeological biography / by Hershel Shanks. — 1st ed.
p. cm.
Includes biographical references and index.
ISBN 0-679-44526-9
1. Jerusalem—History. 2. Jerusalem—Antiquities.
3. Excavations (Archaeology)—Jerusalem. I. Title.
DS109.9.S485 1995
933--dc20   95-24404

Manufactured in the United States of America
98765432 24689753 2346789
First Edition
Color separations by Hi-Tech Color, Boise, Idaho, U.S.A.

Contents

Acknowledgments   *ix*

Jerusalem Time Line   *x*

Introduction   *xiii*

I. Jerusalem Before the Israelites   1

A settlement is established about 2,500 years before the Israelites conquer the city. The Egyptians refer to Jerusalem in curse texts dating as early as 1850 B.C.E.

II. How David Conquered Jerusalem   11

David's general may have infiltrated the city through secret underground passages that can still be explored today.

III. The Fortress of Zion and the Puzzle of the *Millo*   25

A massive stone structure, preserved to over five stories high, may be the biblical Zion, a Canaanite term for a stronghold that defended Jerusalem.

IV. The Tombs of David and Other Kings of Judah   35

The Bible tells us just where King David was buried. Have archaeologists found the royal tombs of David and his Judahite successors?

V. King Solomon and the Lord's House   47

Although no trace of the Temple has been discovered, archaeological finds offer a vivid picture of what it and its lavish furnishings looked like.

VI. The Capital of the Kingdom of Judah   79

King Hezekiah builds his famous tunnel—which you can still walk through—to save Jerusalem from the Assyrian ruler Sennacherib's siege. As part of his religious reform, Hezekiah also centralizes worship in Jerusalem and destroys the bronze serpent from Moses' time. Jerusalem expands to the western ridge.

VII. The Babylonians Destroy the City and Burn the Temple   105

The flames that destroy Jerusalem ironically preserve clay bullae impressed with the seals of several people mentioned in the Bible, including the prophet Jeremiah's scribe.

VIII. Jerusalem During the Exile and Return 115

Some wealthy Jewish families continue to live quite luxuriously in the city after the Babylonian destruction. One of their tombs reveals the earliest biblical text ever discovered. Upon their return from Babylon, the exiles construct a much smaller city and rebuild the Temple on a more modest scale than Solomon's.

IX. Hellenistic and Hasmonean Jerusalem 125

An independent Jewish state emerges for the first time in 450 years. Jerusalem expands once again and flourishes—and becomes Hellenized.

X. Herodian Jerusalem 137

In a single generation, Herod transforms the city into a magnificent imperial capital, crowned by his rebuilt Temple. But Roman troops destroy it all in 70 C.E., leaving archaeologists to sift through the ash and rubble nearly 2,000 years later.

XI. The Jerusalem of Jesus 179

The Garden of Gethsemane, the Via Dolorosa, the Church of the Holy Sepulchre—which are authentic holy sites and which are not? And how do we know? Have the bones of the high priest Caiaphas, who presided at Jesus' trial, been found?

XII. The Second Jewish Revolt and Aelia Capitolina 215

Jews are barred from Roman Jerusalem, renamed Aelia Capitolina. 20th-century archaeologists create a new entrance to the Old City by clearing a recently discovered arch built by Hadrian in the 2nd century C.E.

XIII. Byzantine Jerusalem 225

The city thrives under Christian rule, as pilgrims flock to places touched by Jesus. A pagan emperor allows Jews to rebuild the Temple, but he is killed within a year. The famous Nea Church, lost for 1,600 years, is found by modern archaeologists.

XIV. Moslem and Crusader Jerusalem 233

Israeli archaeologists uncover an unknown chapter in the glorious Arab history in Jerusalem. Crusaders provide but a brief interlude to Arab hegemony, and Arab architecture continues to dominate the city.

Notes 245

Select Bibliography 249

Illustration Credits 251

Index 252

Acknowledgments

Above all, I would like to thank my teachers who, over the years, instructed me in the archaeology of Jerusalem—Yigael Yadin, of blessed memory; Dani Bahat, former District Archaeologist for Jerusalem; Gaby Barkay (Tel Aviv University); Jerry Murphy-O'Connor (École Biblique); Leen Ritmeyer; Phil King (Boston College); David Ussishkin (Tel Aviv University). I never took a class with any of them; I learned from them in the most marvelous manner; one on one, in the study, over bread and on the site. They taught me not only what there is to see, but how to reason archaeologically, how to think like a scholar.

On short notice I asked four of them—Jerry Murphy-O'Connor, Gaby Barkay, Phil King and Leen Ritmeyer—to read the manuscript of this book. They saved me from countless errors. But having been taught by their example to value a certain independence of mind, I have not always profited from their wisdom, or followed their direction. Thus, there may be errors of fact and judgment, of commission and omission. For these, I alone remain responsible.

Without the support of the staff of the Biblical Archaeology Society, this book would have been impossible. Suzanne Singer coordinated the team headed by Gabrielle DeFord, who supervised and refined design, acquired hundreds of illustrations and polished the text, and by Lauren Krause, who watched over the far-flung production elements. Judith Wohlberg ably assisted with production. Carol Arenberg provided helpful editing on the original manuscript. And from the first insightful read onward, Molly Dewsnap contributed editorial support in myriad ways along with Steven Feldman and Jack Meinhardt. Laurie Andrews meticulously copyedited every word and safeguarded consistency in both text and design; Eva Greene and Lisa Josephson assisted with correcting the early manuscript.

Rob Sugar designed the book and then passed production into the capable hands of Valerie Winer and Mark Colliton.

The deft touch of our Random House editor Jason Epstein is, to insiders, evident throughout. He was capably and pleasantly assisted by Joy de Menil. The elegant jacket is the work of Susan Shapiro.

Robert Barnett, Esq., relieved me of the burden of all contract negotiations. A lawyer, Bob also represents a fellow named Bill Clinton. Bob assures me, however, that all his clients are equally important to him. His attention to detail and follow-through, to say nothing of his negotiating skill, amply demonstrate the truth of that assurance.

To all, my heartfelt thanks.

Hershel Shanks
Washington, D.C.
June 1995

JERUSALEM TIME LINE

4500 B.C.E.   4000   3500   3000   2500   2000   1500

Chalcolithic Period (4500–3200 B.C.E.)

c. 3500 B.C.E
First settlement at Gihon Spring

Early Bronze Age (3200–2200 B.C.E.)

c. 2500 B.C.E.
First houses

Middle Bronze Age (2200–1550 B.C.E.)

c. 1850 B.C.E.
First mention of Jerusalem—
in Egyptian execration text

c. 1800 B.C.E.
First city wall

Late Bronze Age (1550–1200 B.C.E.)

c. 1400 B.C.E.
Mention of Jerusalem in
cuneiform Amarna letters

Iron Age I (1200–1000 B.C.E.)

Jerusalem is a Canaanite
(Jebusite) city.

Iron Age II (1000–586 B.C.E.)

c. 1000 B.C.E.
King David conquers
Jerusalem.

c. 960 B.C.E.
Solomon becomes
king, builds Temple.

c. 910 B.C.E.
Jeroboam sets
up competing
shrines at Dan
and Bethel.

c. 920 B.C.E.
Solomon dies.
Kingdom splits—
Israel in the north,
Judah in the south.

721 B.C.E.
Assyrians conquer Samaria,
ending northern kingdom
of Israel. Refugees flee to
Jerusalem. City expands
onto western hill.

715 B.C.E.
Hezekiah becomes king of
Judah, rules 28 years.

701 B.C.E.
Assyrian ruler Sennacherib besieges
Jerusalem—unsuccessfully.

639 B.C.E.
Josiah becomes king of
Judah, rules 31 years.

621 B.C.E.
Early form of Deuteronomy
found in Temple. Prophetess
Huldah declares it authoritative.

c. 610 B.C.E.
Date of oldest biblical
text, on silver amulets

c. 600 B.C.E.
Babylonians supplant Assyrians
as world's superpower.

586 B.C.E.
Babylonian destruction of
Jerusalem. First Temple period
ends. Babylonian Exile begins

Exilic Period (586–c. 539 B.C.E.)

c. 539 B.C.E.
Persian ruler Cyrus the Great
captures Babylon, permits
Jews to return to their land.

Persian Period (c. 539–332 B.C.E.)

c. 516 B.C.E.
Second Temple
built by returnees.

c. 445–425 B.C.E.
Nehemiah rebuilds walls; Ezra carries out
religious reforms. City confined to eastern hill.

332 B.C.E.
Alexander the Great conquers Judea.

Hellenistic Period (332–141 B.C.E.)

323 B.C.E.
Alexander dies.
Ptolemies and
Seleucids rule
Judea by turns
for 150 years.

168 B.C.E.
Led by the Maccabees,
Jews rebel against
Seleucid monarch
Antiochus IV.

164 B.C.E.
Jews capture the Temple.

Hasmonean Period (141–37 B.C.E.)

141 B.C.E.
Hasmonean dynasty begins. Jerusalem,
capital of an independent Jewish state,
again expands onto western hill.

63 B.C.E.
Roman general Pompey con-
quers Jerusalem. Jewish rulers
govern under Roman tutelage.

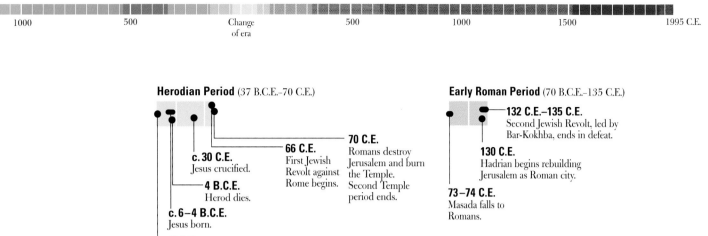

1000 500 Change of era 500 1000 1500 1995 C.E.

Herodian Period (37 B.C.E.–70 C.E.)

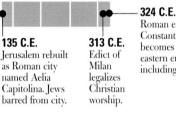

c. 30 C.E.
Jesus crucified.

4 B.C.E.
Herod dies.

c. 6–4 B.C.E.
Jesus born.

37 B.C.E.
Herod becomes ruler of Judea.
Rebuilds Second Temple.

66 C.E.
First Jewish
Revolt against
Rome begins.

70 C.E.
Romans destroy
Jerusalem and burn
the Temple.
Second Temple
period ends.

Early Roman Period (70 B.C.E.–135 C.E.)

132 C.E.–135 C.E.
Second Jewish Revolt, led by
Bar-Kokhba, ends in defeat.

130 C.E.
Hadrian begins rebuilding
Jerusalem as Roman city.

73–74 C.E.
Masada falls to
Romans.

Late Roman Period (135–324 C.E.)

135 C.E.
Jerusalem rebuilt
as Roman city
named Aelia
Capitolina. Jews
barred from city.

313 C.E.
Edict of
Milan
legalizes
Christian
worship.

324 C.E.
Roman emperor
Constantine
becomes ruler of the
eastern empire,
including Palestine.

Byzantine Period (324–638 C.E.)

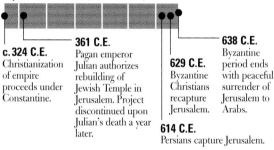

c. 324 C.E.
Christianization
of empire
proceeds under
Constantine.

361 C.E.
Pagan emperor
Julian authorizes
rebuilding of
Jewish Temple in
Jerusalem. Project
discontinued upon
Julian's death a year
later.

629 C.E.
Byzantine
Christians
recapture
Jerusalem.

614 C.E.
Persians capture Jerusalem.

638 C.E.
Byzantine
period ends
with peaceful
surrender of
Jerusalem to
Arabs.

Arab Period (638–1516 C.E.)

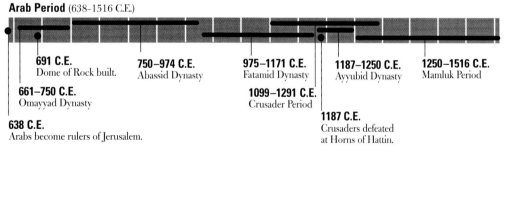

691 C.E.
Dome of Rock built.

661–750 C.E.
Omayyad Dynasty

638 C.E.
Arabs become rulers of Jerusalem.

750–974 C.E.
Abassid Dynasty

975–1171 C.E.
Fatamid Dynasty

1099–1291 C.E.
Crusader Period

1187 C.E.
Crusaders defeated
at Horns of Hattin.

1187–1250 C.E.
Ayyubid Dynasty

1250–1516 C.E.
Mamluk Period

Ottoman Period (1517–1917)

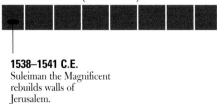

1538–1541 C.E.
Suleiman the Magnificent
rebuilds walls of
Jerusalem.

Modern Period (1918–)

1948
State of Israel established.
Jerusalem divided.

1924–1948
British Mandate

1967
Six-Day War. Israel captures
Old City of Jerusalem.

xi

Introduction

More than 40 years ago, I sat in a class at Harvard Law School studying the law of corporations. What was extraordinary about that year-long course was that it was confined to a single case. In—or through—that one case, Professor Baker was able to teach the entire law of corporations.

I am reminded of that now as I write about the archaeology of Jerusalem. Through the archaeology of Jerusalem, one can learn about almost everything even remotely connected to the ancient Near East: from Bible and ancient history, art and architecture, burial practices, languages and scripts to geography, water supply systems, chronology, theology, pottery typology, archaeological methodology, warfare and daily life. We can also learn about social divisions, ancient technology, a variety of cultures (from the Jebusites, Assyrians, Babylonians and Persians to the Greeks, Romans and Arabs). And, finally, we learn about divisions and debates among scholars—and even claims of altering evidence—as they try to reach conclusions on the basis of facts that are always incomplete.

The list could go on and on. Countless books have been written on each of these subjects and on their divisions and subdivisions. Obviously, we cannot pretend to any definitive treatment here. But from this book you will get a marvelous feel for the sweep of things—the big picture, as we like to call it at the Biblical Archaeology Society.

When you finish this book, you will understand a great deal about the 23 conquests of Jerusalem. You will see

- How the Israelites conquered the city from the Jebusites—three times (twice before King David managed to hold onto it).
- How the Assyrians devastated it after the Israelite confederation broke apart.
- How the Babylonians destroyed it.
- How the Persians defeated the Babylonians and ruled Jerusalem.
- How Alexander the Great conquered the world and Hellenized Jerusalem.
- How Alexander's heirs fought over the city until the Maccabees established an independent Jewish state once again, ruled by the Hasmonean dynasty.
- How King Herod ousted the Hasmoneans and killed their descendants.

- How, after Herod's death, Roman prefects and procurators exercised direct control over the city.
- How the Jews revolted against Roman rule and the Romans retaliated by destroying Jerusalem.
- How the Jews revolted again and the Romans banned Jews from Jerusalem and rebuilt it as a Roman city renamed Aelia Capitolina.
- How the city became Christian under Byzantium.
- How Arab Moslems ousted the Christians.
- How the Crusaders ousted the Moslems.
- How the Moslems ousted the Crusaders.

You will also participate in the debates and disagreements. Our aim is to give you enough of the evidence so that you can reach your own conclusions—or at least feel like a knowledgeable participant in the discussion—about whether King David's tomb has been found, where Jesus was buried, how David managed to capture such a well-fortified city or whether the city was emptied of all but poor Jews during the Babylonian Exile.

This book is part of the 1996 tri-millennium celebration of Jerusalem as the capital of Israel. That is certainly an occasion for celebration. Three thousand years is a long time. But that's only a little more than half its life. Jerusalem was already about 2,500 years old when David made it his capital. We have even tried here to sketch that earlier history.

That explains why this is a book, rather than the longish article that was originally intended. It all started when the staff of the *Biblical Archaeology Review* got together to discuss how the magazine would participate in the planned celebration. As part of our coverage, I agreed to write an article surveying the archaeology of Jerusalem.

As I wrote, ever compressing the material to the bone, it became apparent that any meaningful survey would be too long for an article. But I nevertheless plowed on and on, hoping that something could be done with the final manuscript. This is the result.

Hershel Shanks
June 1995

"Whoever has not seen
Jerusalem in its splendor has
never seen a lovely city."

Babylonian Talmud, *Succah* 51b

"Of the ten measures of beauty
that came down to the world,
Jerusalem took nine."

Babylonian Talmud, *Kidushin* 49b

I

Jerusalem Before the Israelites

THE YEAR 1996 MAY—OR MAY NOT—BE THE 3,000TH ANNIVERSARY OF Jerusalem as the capital of Israel. But one thing is sure: Jerusalem had a long history before David captured it and made it his capital in about 1000 B.C.E.*

We know this both from recent archaeological excavations and from ancient literary sources. Jerusalem is referred to in Egyptian execration texts, preserved in hieroglyphics dating to about 1850 B.C.E. (see photo, p. 2). There the city is called Rushalimum.

Jerusalem is also referred to as an important city in the cuneiform archive known as the Amarna letters from the 14th century B.C.E. (see photo, p. 2). In the Amarna letters the name is written Urusalim.

These are the earliest literary references to Jerusalem, but archaeologists take us back even further. In the early 1960s, British archaeologist Kathleen Kenyon found part of the earliest wall that enclosed the city. It was nearly six feet wide and preserved to about the same height. She dated the construction of this wall to about 1800 B.C.E. on the basis of pottery sherds found in the foundation trench.

*B.C.E. (Before the Common Era) and C.E. (Common Era) are the alternate designations for B.C. and A.D. often used in scholarly literature.

The ancient City of David, where Jerusalem began more than 5,000 years ago as a Canaanite settlement, is outlined by shadowed valleys south of the Temple Mount, seen at the top of the picture.

At one point, this wall has a right angle in it, indicating either that the wall consisted of an inset/outset construction or that the angle was part of a gateway.[1] Kenyon did not find other insets or outsets, so she concluded that the angle was once part of a gate tower (see photo and drawing, p. 4), although there is still some question about this.[2] If the angle does mark a gateway, it was probably the one people used to go out of the city to get water at the Gihon Spring, a gateway conveniently located just above the spring, on the path that leads down to it.

A settlement existed at the site even earlier than 1800 B.C.E. In the 1980s, Hebrew University archaeologist Yigal Shiloh found pottery dating to the Chalcolithic period (late 4th millennium B.C.E.). That's about 5,500 years ago. From the Early Bronze Age, Shiloh uncovered the remains of a house, dating to about 3000–2800 B.C.E. Then in about 1800 B.C.E., the city wall was built; this is the wall Kenyon uncovered. Shiloh found another hundred feet of this wall. Parts of the Shiloh extension were as much as ten feet thick.

When this city wall was built, Jerusalem was quite small, only about 10 or 11 acres, located on a spur, or ridge, extending south of what is known today as the Temple Mount (see map, p. 5). It surprises some to learn that earliest Jerusalem was located outside the present walls of the Old City, but that is the case. The Temple Mount was not included in the city until King Solomon's time.

Egypt's enemies are listed in hieratic script on this clay figurine, once shaped as a kneeling prisoner and destroyed in a ritual cursing those enemies. Egyptian execration texts like this one mention Jerusalem as early as the 19th century B.C.E.

A cuneiform tablet from Tell el-Amarna, in Egypt, dating to about the 14th century B.C.E. The archive found at the site consists of diplomatic correspondence between petty Canaanite rulers and their Egyptian overlords. The correspondence contains the second oldest reference to Jerusalem, nearly 400 years before King David captured the city.

Yigal Shiloh discovered part of an Early Bronze Age house, pictured above, dating to about 3000–2800 B.C.E. The pottery sherds at right are from an even earlier settlement, dating to the Chalcolithic period, about 3500 B.C.E.

Two keys to understanding the location of the original city of Jerusalem are geography and water. Imagine the present Old City wall as the squarish crown of a tooth from which two roots extend, each quite distinctive (see model, p. 6). The western root is high and broad and large. The eastern root is lower and narrower and much smaller. Both roots are surrounded on all sides but the north by deep valleys, so they are well situated for defensive purposes. The valley separating the two roots is known as the Tyropoeon Valley, or the Valley of the Cheesemakers. This valley was considerably deeper and more precipitous in ancient times, having since been filled with debris over the centuries.

West of the western root is the Hinnom Valley, which curves around south of the two roots to join the Kidron Valley, east of the eastern root. Reading from left to right, or west to east, it's the Hinnom Valley, the Tyropoeon Valley and the Kidron Valley.

The western root, or western ridge, as we will now call it, has several advantages over the eastern ridge. The larger, western ridge is higher and therefore receives cooler breezes. It is also easier to build on because the upper surface is flatter and the slopes are less steep. The western ridge is called Mount Zion (see photo, p. 5) because, until 20th-century archaeologists discovered otherwise,[3] it was thought that the original city of Jerusalem was located on this western ridge, because of all its natural advantages. Now, however, everyone agrees that the earliest city of Jerusalem was located not on the western ridge, but on the eastern ridge.

The angled wall at the bottom of the photo is part of the earliest city wall, constructed in about 1800 B.C.E. and excavated in the 1960s by British archaeologist Dame Kathleen Kenyon. If the angled part of this wall is part of a gate, this is what the gateway probably looked like (below), although it would have been covered with a mud plaster. The shaded part is extant; the rest is reconstructed. The Gihon Spring, the earliest city's water source, is a few yards away, outside the gate.

The reason for what may at first appear to be a poor choice is simple: water. Jerusalem's only regular source of fresh water—the Gihon Spring—is a spring low on the lower part of the eastern slope of the eastern ridge, near the floor of the Kidron Valley (see photo, p. 7). The eastern ridge is called the City of David because that is where the city David captured was located. His son Solomon extended the city northward to include the present Temple Mount area, which is also on the eastern ridge.

The Bible first mentions Jerusalem in Joshua's time, when the city was ruled by the Canaanite king Adoni-zedek (Joshua 10:1). He organized a coalition of five local rulers, or kings, to stop Joshua's advance, or, more specifically, to attack Gibeon, because the Gibeonites had agreed to let Joshua and the Israelites take the city peacefully and to serve thereafter as "hewers of wood and drawers of water" (Joshua 9). When the Gibeonites were attacked by the coalition organized by Adoni-zedek of Jerusalem, they naturally called on Joshua for help. Joshua, in a lightning advance at night, surprised the coalition forces and inflicted a "crushing defeat" on them (Joshua 10:10). Of course, Joshua had some help from the Lord. As he was chasing the coalition forces, "the Lord hurled huge stones on

them from the sky" (Joshua 10:11). That was the time the sun stood still to prolong the Israelite victory (Joshua 10:12–14). Joshua captured and impaled the five kings of the coalition on stakes (Joshua 10:26).

Even though the text tells us that "Joshua conquered the whole country" (Joshua 10:40), he apparently was unable to maintain his hold on Jerusalem. In Joshua 12, we are given a list of areas east of the Jordan that "the Israelites defeated and…took possession of." When it comes to areas west of the Jordan, however, the text tells us only that the Israelites "defeated" the local kings; it does not say they also possessed their cities. And then in Joshua 15:63 comes the confession: "But the Judahites could not dispossess the Jebusites, the inhabitants of Jerusalem; so the Judahites dwell with the Jebusites in Jerusalem to this day."

If, as some scholars contend, the stories in Joshua were essentially made up in the late 7th century B.C.E. and are of no historical value, I wonder why the text says the Jebusites occupy Jerusalem "to this day." It certainly sounds as if that sentence, at least, was written before David captured the city.

Jerusalem in David's Time

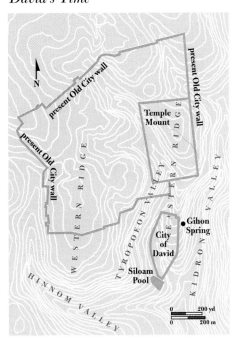

Extending south from the walled Old City (left) are the broad, high western ridge, known today as Mount Zion (in foreground), and, beyond it, the lower, narrower eastern ridge, known today as the City of David. The smaller, lower, less desirable eastern ridge was the site of Jerusalem's earliest settlement because of its proximity to the Gihon Spring.

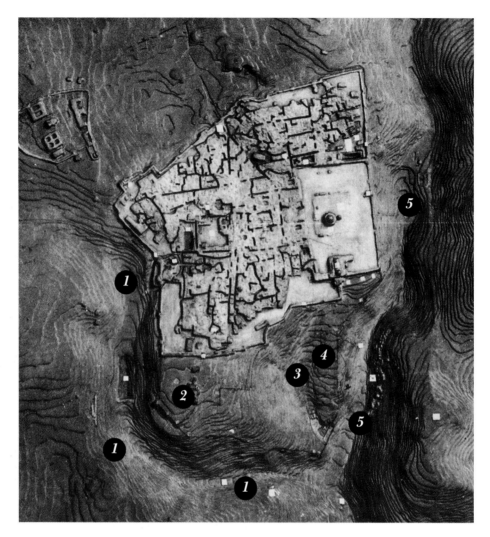

In this model, three valleys define ancient Jerusalem. On the east is the Kidron Valley (5); on the west, the Hinnom Valley (1), which curves around south of the city to meet the Kidron. The Tyropoeon Valley (3) separates the western ridge (Mount Zion) (2) from the eastern ridge (the City of David) (4).

In this natural cave, the Gihon Spring gushes forth from the opening beneath the steps, which descend from the Kidron Valley. This spring was early Jerusalem's only source of fresh water.

And if a 7th-century writer did make up the story, I wonder why he didn't simply say the Israelites conquered Jerusalem and occupied it. Who would have known the difference 375 years later, when Jerusalem had long been Israel's capital? Why preserve a record of Israel's inability to take possession of it if the story were made up? I suppose it can be argued that the writer created the story this way to glorify David's later capture of the city; after all, David is the hero of the tale. But if you're making up stories to glorify David, why not attribute more of Joshua's victories to him? (And why preserve so much that is derogatory about David, such as his affair with Bathsheba and the murder of her husband Uriah?)

I do not mean that the stories in Joshua are literally accurate or that they represent history as a modern historian would write it. But I would argue that there is a historical core, although the ancient writer was concerned not so much with recording history as with making a theological point. The biblical scholar's task is to sift and refine—to determine what is historically reliable and what isn't.

Unfortunately, scholars often divide into two camps—those who argue that the text is worthless as history and those who accept it as (nearly) literally true.

Jerusalem can be seen on the crest, the watershed line, in this view from the Judean desert east of the city.

A more nuanced approach is needed. Our commission must begin with the recognition that we can neither wholly reject nor wholly accept the biblical text as history. As historians of antiquity, our assignment is to identify the historical core of the text.

It seems clear that the early Israelites very much wanted to capture Jerusalem. In fact, they badly needed it. Again, geography explains why. Jerusalem lies on a narrow crest in the central part of the country along which all north–south traffic in central Canaan—both commercial and military—passed in ancient times. To the east and west of this crest, which is the watershed line, are deep wadis, or valleys, leading on the east to the Jordan Valley and the Dead Sea and on the west to the Mediterranean Sea. To travel in a north–south direction up and down these wadis would be incredibly difficult. The only feasible route in the central part of Canaan was—and is—to stick to the central crest. Traffic on this route did not compare with the international commerce that plied the Way of the Sea, along the Mediterranean, or the King's Highway, on the Transjordanian plateau, but to the early Israelites, it was of "utmost consequence."[4] In non-Israelite hands, Jerusalem separated Israelite territory in two.

Because of Jerusalem's obvious importance, the Israelites made another effort to conquer the city after Joshua's death, during the period of the Judges. According to the biblical record, the Judahites did conquer it: "The Judahites attacked Jerusalem and captured it; they put it to the sword and set the city on fire" (Judges 1:8). But either the biblical account is exaggerated or the Judahites were not able to hold the city, for shortly thereafter we learn that the Benjaminites, within whose territory Jerusalem lay (see Joshua 18:28), could not dislodge the Jebusite/Canaanite inhabitants of Jerusalem: "The Benjaminites did not dispossess the Jebusite inhabitants of Jerusalem; so the Jebusites have dwelt with the Benjaminites in Jerusalem to this day" (Judges 1:21). Later references to Jerusalem as a city of foreigners where Levites should not spend the night (Judges 19) confirm this interpretation.

It seems clear, therefore, that until David captured the city Jerusalem lay outside Israelite control.

II

How David Conquered Jerusalem

SCHOLARS HAVE BEEN MORE CONCERNED WITH *HOW* DAVID CAPTURED Jerusalem than with precisely *when* he captured it. The date must be computed by working backward, using biblical chronology, from a more-or-less known date fixed independently of the biblical chronology, such as Sennacherib's siege of Jerusalem in 701 B.C.E. Biblical chronology is sometimes ambiguous (reigns overlap, co-regencies are confusing and so on), so the date of David's conquest of Jerusalem, and the beginning of his reign in Jerusalem, is approximate—about 1000 B.C.E.

Some scholars have attempted to be more precise. I have seen dates ranging from 1109 B.C.E. to 995 B.C.E. How 1996 was chosen as the date of the tri-millennium celebration is not entirely clear. What is clear is that no one in the bureaucracy of modern Jerusalem correctly subtracted 3,000 from 1996 during the planning stage. I admit to having made the calculation incorrectly myself, which only added error to error and compounded the mistake.

The initial suggestion for the celebration came from then-Mayor Teddy Kollek. Someone apparently told him that David conquered Jerusalem in 996 B.C.E. Indeed, in a popular book on Jerusalem by the distinguished British archaeologist Dame Kathleen Kenyon, she gives the date of David's attack on Jerusalem as "*c.* 996."[5] On that basis, 1996 was chosen as the 3,000th anniversary of Jerusalem as the capital of Israel. When I pointed out that 3,000 subtracted from 1996 was not 996, but 1004, word came back that some scholars fixed the date of David's conquest at 1004 B.C.E., and publicists started using 1004 as the date.

A 20th-century tourist looks down Warren's Shaft, through which Joab, David's general, may have climbed to enter the city and surprise the Jebusites. Note the boundary line between two different types of rock in the middle of the picture— soft limestone above and harder dolomite below. Warren's Shaft is a natural sinkhole in the dolomite.

But I too erred. Because there is no year zero, 3,000 years before 1996 is 1005 B.C.E. As of this writing, we do not know if it is too late to change the official publicity and the calculation connected with it. Perhaps the organizers will rightly claim that no one knows the precise date of David's conquest, so 1996 is as good a year as any to celebrate it. Quite so.

If there is uncertainty about the date of David's conquest, there is even greater uncertainty as to how he did it—despite the fact that the Bible tells us how, in two places. The story is told in the Second Book of Samuel and retold in the First Book of Chronicles.

After David had reigned for seven years in Hebron (2 Samuel 5:5), he attacked the Jebusites in Jerusalem. The Jebusites, probably a Canaanite people, were confident that they could withstand the Israelite attack, however. The Jebusites shouted at David and his troops from the city wall, "You will never get in here" (2 Samuel 5:6; 1 Chronicles 11:5). The city was defended by something called the *Metsudat Tsion*, the Fortress of Zion (2 Samuel 5:7; 1 Chronicles 11:5). (Surprisingly, Zion is a pre-Israelite term, the name of the stronghold that defended Jebusite Jerusalem.) The Jebusites were apparently so sure they could defend the city that they taunted the approaching Israelites: "Even the blind and the lame will turn you back" (2 Samuel 5:6).

Then comes a sentence that the greatest biblical archaeologist of modern times, William Foxwell Albright, called "one of the most difficult exegetical problems in the historical books [of the Hebrew Bible]."[6] Translations of the passage (2 Samuel 5:8), although similar, nevertheless vary. We print three below (italics added):

> David had said on that day, "Whoever would strike down the Jebusites, let him get up the *water shaft* to attack the lame and the blind, those whom David hates." Therefore it is said, "The blind and the lame shall not come into the house."
>
> New Revised Standard Version

> That day, David said, "Whoever gets up the *tunnel* and kills a Jebusite…" [a note in this translation advises that the sentence breaks off] As for the blind and the lame, David hated them with his whole being. (Hence the saying: the blind and the lame may not enter the Temple.)
>
> New Jerusalem Bible

> On that occasion David said, "Those who attack the Jebusites shall reach the *water channel* and (strike down) the lame and the blind, who are hateful to David." That is why they say: "No one who is blind or lame may enter the House."
>
> New Jewish Publication Society

The Hebrew word translated above as "water shaft," "tunnel" and "water channel" is *tsinnor*. This puzzling word has also been translated many other ways, including dagger, hook, throat and penis.[7] If it means something like water shaft, tunnel or water channel, as the above translations indicate, then the text appears to be saying that David challenged his army to get into the Jebusite stronghold via the city's water system.

In this excavation photo, dig director Yigal Shiloh ascends Warren's Shaft with the help of a rope ladder.

In the description in Chronicles, David is quoted as offering to appoint as commander of his army the soldier who first smote the Jebusites ("Whoever shall first smite the Jebusites shall be chief and commander"). The next sentence in the Chronicler's account appears to support the idea that some sort of shaft or vertical tunnel had to be climbed to get into the city and surprise the Jebusites (italics added): "And Joab son of Zeruiah went *up* first, so he became chief" (1 Chronicles 11:6).

To summarize: The text seems to say that David offered command of his army to the first person to get up the Jebusite water shaft and that Joab successfully did this. It is clear that Joab was made commander, and the city was captured. David promptly renamed Jerusalem the "City of David" (2 Samuel 5:9; 1 Chronicles 11:5)—and that is what the eastern ridge, where David's city was located, is still called.

The reason the meaning of *tsinnor* is so important is that if it means "water shaft," as most translators say it does, then the *tsinnor,* or water shaft, through which Joab climbed to surprise the Jebusites may actually have survived and can be seen to this day.

This water shaft is known as Warren's Shaft, after its discoverer, British engineer Captain (later Sir) Charles Warren, who is famous for his excavations and explorations of Jerusalem in the 1860s. Warren's Shaft will introduce us to the complicated underground water system of ancient Jerusalem.

Incidentally, an early 2nd-century C.E. translator of the Bible from Hebrew into Greek, a Greek named Aquila, translated *tsinnor* as water shaft nearly 2,000 years before Warren made his discovery. Unlike later translators, Aquila could not have been influenced by knowledge of Warren's Shaft.

The starting place for understanding Warren's Shaft—and indeed, all of the ancient underground water systems of Jerusalem—is the Gihon Spring. One of the early explorers of the spring, the American orientalist Edward Robinson, reported that the Arabs living near the spring believed that a dragon lived beneath the cave from which the spring issues. This explained for them why the spring did not flow continuously but gushed forth intermittently (*gihon* means "gushing"). Modern scientists explain this phenomenon on the basis of an underground siphon system that has apparently been destroyed in recent decades; the Gihon Spring no longer gushes. But the legend about the dragon may be a very old one. When Nehemiah returned to Jerusalem after the Babylonian Exile and made his famous night tour around the city, he started near the "Dragon's Spring" (Nehemiah 2:13); this was probably the Gihon Spring.[8]

The cave from which the Gihon Spring issues is so low on the eastern slope of the City of David, so near the floor of the Kidron Valley, that it presents a problem for the defense of the city. In peacetime, it was easy enough for people to go out through the city gate, walk down a few steps to the level of the Gihon Spring, fill their buckets and come back inside. In wartime, however, when the city was under siege, it would have been extremely dangerous. Moreover, if the spring came under enemy control (because it was outside the wall), the city would quickly succumb to thirst—even if plenty of food was available. In a siege described in the Book of Judith (in the Apocrypha*), people were collapsing in the streets from thirst after only 34 days, even though there was no famine (Judith 7:6–22).

The obvious solution to the vulnerability of the Gihon Spring would be to include it within the city wall. The problem with this solution, however, is that the spring is so near the valley floor that the enemy on the opposite slope could easily hurl stones and arrows into the area of the spring from the other side, especially since the valley is narrow at this point, and the hill rises steeply.

*Bible-like books that were accepted as canonical by some faiths but not by others.

The early inhabitants of Jerusalem therefore devised another solution. They dug (or enlarged) a short tunnel from the spring to a nearby shaft that went straight up for a distance of 38 feet. From the top of the shaft, still underground, a long, sloping, curved tunnel led up to the surface—*inside the city wall*, higher up the hill. Thus, people could descend through the tunnel, from within the city, to the top of the vertical shaft (Warren's Shaft); from there, they could lower buckets to the bottom of the shaft, where the underground tunnel carried water from the spring (see drawings, p. 17). Voila! Water—available inside the city. A pile of rocks could easily camouflage the entrance to the spring.

The question, of course, is whether Warren's Shaft is the biblical *tsinnor*. Did Joab climb Warren's Shaft to get inside Jebusite Jerusalem and surprise the inhabitants, leading to David's capture of the city (and, incidentally, significantly advancing Joab's military career)? Warren's Shaft can still be explored, so readers can consider the possibility firsthand. Over the years, scholars have raised several objections to the Warren's Shaft = biblical *tsinnor* hypothesis. One is that *tsinnor* may not mean water shaft. There seems to be plenty of evidence, however, that water shaft is the most likely meaning—from Aquila's translation nearly 2,000 years ago to modern scholars who rely on related words in Ugaritic cuneiform.[9] But this is only the beginning of the

The gurgling Gihon Spring sends water through this tunnel, which leads to the bottom of Warren's Shaft. Thousands of years ago, Jerusalemites could lower a bucket on a rope to bring water up the shaft.

scholarly assault on the argument that Warren's Shaft is the *tsinnor*. Shiloh, who used South African mine workers to clear the shaft and its related tunnels, dated the shaft to the Israelite period, the time archaeologists call Iron Age II (c.1000–586 B.C.E.). If the shaft didn't exist in the Canaanite period, it could not be the key to David's conquest of the city.

This objection, however, has been blown to smithereens by Shiloh's own geological consultant. Unfortunately, Shiloh tragically died of stomach cancer at the age of 50—before his geological consultant wrote his definitive report. So we do not know what Shiloh's reaction would have been had he seen it. Shiloh's argument was that other underground water systems that can be dated—and there are several of them in Israelite cities (Gibeon, Megiddo, Hazor and others)[10]—were constructed in Iron Age II, the Israelite period, after David conquered Jerusalem. So, Shiloh argued, Warren's Shaft must also date to this period and not earlier.

Shiloh also relied on another argument, this one quite surprising. He knew that when his workers cleared the shaft, they found that it extended nearly ten feet below the level of the spring and below the tunnel that brought water from the spring to the bottom of the shaft. This meant the shaft was natural, not man-made. I do not know why Shiloh concluded from this that Warren's Shaft was not in existence during the Canaanite period.[11] The fact that it was a natural shaft suggests that it existed—probably for millions of years—before David captured Jerusalem. This fact also distinguished the Jerusalem water system from water systems at other Israelite sites that Shiloh relied on. All the other water systems were man-made from scratch. They didn't depend on natural openings that perhaps needed enlargement at most. Moreover, similar water systems in Greece have been dated as early as the 13th century B.C.E.[12]

The analysis of Shiloh's geological consultant, Dan Gill of the Israel Geological Survey, is brilliant.[13] Until Gill's analysis, most scholars had regarded the underground water systems of Jerusalem as man-made and had tried to explain them in terms of human intent—or error. For example, the semicircular course of the tunnel leading from the top of Warren's Shaft up to ground level was explained as necessary to moderate the slope. But if this were so, Gill asked, why is there a nine-foot scarp between the part of the tunnel where steps were carved and the part that is less steep and can be traversed without steps (see photos, pp. 18–19)? Negotiating this scarp required a rope or wooden ladder. The scarp, like many other features of the underground water systems, is unexplainable in terms of the builders' intention. This anomaly, and others like it, should have suggested that these underground water systems were built using naturally existing features. And that is what Gill showed. No doubt, man enlarged and shaped some of these natural features, but natural cavities in the rock were there before the water systems were created.

Beneath the City of David lie two strata of rock, the upper one comparatively soft and the lower one comparatively hard. The rock was deposited about 90 million years ago in what geologists call the Upper Cretaceous period. The soft upper layer is a form of limestone; the hard lower layer is dolomite. About a third of the relatively soft limestone is comprised of crushed fossil shells and some coral. As water seeps through the limestone, the fossil shells dissolve; the limestone becomes more and more permeable, but the underlying dolomite remains dense and hard—relatively impermeable.

Warren's Shaft Water System

Cross Section

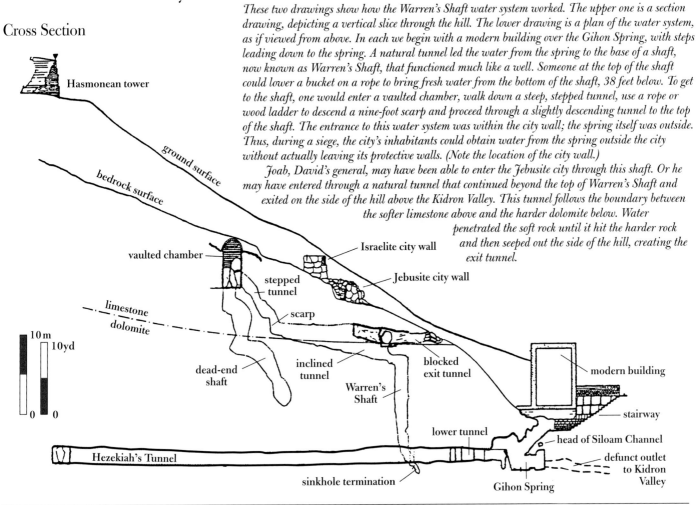

These two drawings show how the Warren's Shaft water system worked. The upper one is a section drawing, depicting a vertical slice through the hill. The lower drawing is a plan of the water system, as if viewed from above. In each we begin with a modern building over the Gihon Spring, with steps leading down to the spring. A natural tunnel led the water from the spring to the base of a shaft, now known as Warren's Shaft, that functioned much like a well. Someone at the top of the shaft could lower a bucket on a rope to bring fresh water from the bottom of the shaft, 38 feet below. To get to the shaft, one would enter a vaulted chamber, walk down a steep, stepped tunnel, use a rope or wood ladder to descend a nine-foot scarp and proceed through a slightly descending tunnel to the top of the shaft. The entrance to this water system was within the city wall; the spring itself was outside. Thus, during a siege, the city's inhabitants could obtain water from the spring outside the city without actually leaving its protective walls. (Note the location of the city wall.)

Joab, David's general, may have been able to enter the Jebusite city through this shaft. Or he may have entered through a natural tunnel that continued beyond the top of Warren's Shaft and exited on the side of the hill above the Kidron Valley. This tunnel follows the boundary between the softer limestone above and the harder dolomite below. Water penetrated the soft rock until it hit the harder rock and then seeped out the side of the hill, creating the exit tunnel.

Plan

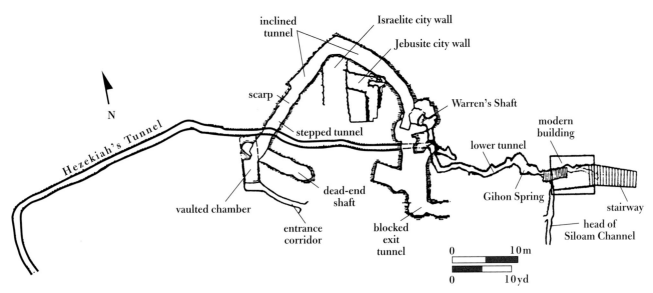

Modern stairs allow tourists to descend the steep, stepped tunnel that leads to the top of Warren's Shaft (right). In the excavation picture at left, we see the more moderate slope of the tunnel as it nears the top of Warren's Shaft.

Water that moves freely through the limestone is stopped at the dolomite and runs along the surface of the dolomite. Both layers of rock slope to the southeast. It is this action of the water running along the sloping upper surface of the dolomite that created the tunnel that leads from the ground surface to the top of Warren's Shaft. Man may have expanded the tunnel—originally it may have been just large enough for a boy to crawl through—and man certainly created the rock steps in the steeper part of the tunnel, but nature created the path and the original opening.

Geologists call tunnels and caves created in this way dissolution channels. Dissolution also occurs in the harder dolomite, but here it usually starts in faults, joints, cracks and fissures. Once an initial dissolution cavity is formed, it draws

more and more water and continuously enlarges, forming vertical shafts or sink-holes. That is how Warren's Shaft was created. It is a natural sinkhole that developed along a joint that Gill traced the entire length of the shaft. Toward the bottom, the shaft narrows to a funnel shape typical of such sinkholes. About ten feet of the sinkhole extend below the level of the short tunnel connecting the bottom of the shaft to the Gihon Spring. The irregular walls of the shaft are also typical of natural sinkholes, not man-made shafts.

Gill even tested the calcareous crust of Warren's Shaft by carbon 14 to determine its age.[14] The crust contained no carbon 14, indicating that the shaft was more than 40,000 years old, unequivocal evidence that it could not have been dug by man.

Another shaft, adjacent to Warren's Shaft but traveling in a slightly different direction, terminates at a higher point in a dead end. At one time, scholars tried to explain this dead-end shaft as an earlier attempt to reach the spring, an effort that was stymied when diggers hit rock too hard for them to penetrate. But this shaft, too, is simply a natural sinkhole. Furthermore, the rock that was supposedly too hard for diggers to penetrate is no harder than the rock surrounding Warren's Shaft.

Because the Warren's Shaft water system existed in the Canaanite period, it cannot be rejected as the *tsinnor* on the grounds that it was built too late to have provided an opening for David's general, Joab.

Another objection that is made is that it would have simply been too difficult for Joab to climb Warren's Shaft, which goes straight up for 38 feet. But the walls are not smooth (as they might have been if they had been excavated by man). The walls are rough and have ledges here and there. Warren himself, with the assistance of his colleague, Sergeant Birtles, managed to ascend the shaft by building platforms with a few six-foot-long boards. Here is Warren's description of the climb:

> We went down to the Fountain [Gihon Spring] shortly after sunrise [October 24, 1867]; we had some 12-feet battens 2 feet square, but were obligated to cut them in half, as 6-feet lengths could only be got into the passage; the water was unusually low, and we managed to crawl through on our bare knees without wetting our upper clothing very much, which was fortunate, as we had the whole day before us. After passing through the pool we had to crawl 50 feet, and then came upon the new passage, which is 17 feet long, opening into the shaft. The labor of getting up the scaffolding devolved on Sergeant Birtles and myself, the fellahin bringing in the wood and handing it to us.
>
> By jamming the boards against the sides of the shaft, we succeeded in getting up 20 feet, when we commenced the first landing, cutting a check in the rock for the frames to rest on, and made a good firm job of it. Then, with four uprights resting on this, we commenced a second landing.

Sergeant Henry Birtles, the loyal assistant to Captain Charles Warren, descends a shaft near the Temple Mount in this 19th-century painting from the archives of the Palestine Exploration Fund. Originally published in the Illustrated London News, *the painting shows Birtles making his way down a rope ladder with the aid of a solitary candle.*

On lighting a piece of magnesium wire at this point, we could see, 20 feet above us, a piece of loose masonry impending directly over our heads; and as several loose pieces had been found at the bottom, it occurred to both of us that our position was critical. Without speaking of it, we eyed each other ominously, and wished we were a little higher up.

The second landing found us 27 feet above the bottom of the shaft. The formation of the third was very difficult; and, on getting nearly to the loose piece of masonry, we found it more dangerously placed than we had imagined, and weighing about 8 cwt [8 hundredweight = 800 pounds]. So we arranged it that the third landing should be a few inches under this loose mass, so as to break its fall and give us a chance. This third landing was 38 feet above the bottom of the shaft. We floored it with triple boards. It was ticklish work, as an incautious blow would have detached the mass; and I doubt if our work would have stood the strain.

An alpine climber with modern rock-climbing equipment ascends Warren's Shaft. Joab, David's general, may have climbed this shaft to enter the Jebusite city.

About six feet above landing No. 3 the shaft opened out to the west into a great cavern, there being a sloping ascent up at an angle of 45 degrees, covered with loose stones about a foot cube. Having hastily made a little ladder, I went up; and very cautious I had to be. The stones seemed all longing to be off; and one starting would have sent the mass rolling, and me with it, on top of the Sergeant, all to form a mash at the bottom of the shaft.[15]

Many years ago, I talked to an Arab merchant selling coins near the Gihon

Spring about the possibility of climbing the shaft. He claimed to have climbed it in his youth, as did his friends, by working his way up with his back to the side of the shaft. Gill too reports that rock climbers of his acquaintance claim the shaft can be scaled with bare hands and legs.

Shiloh has described his successful effort to climb the shaft:

> One pleasant wintry day…I took a Sabbath stroll south of the city in an area where precipitous, rocky pillars rise above the valley …Alpine mountaineers were training on the steep rock faces. One was an Israeli named Ze'ev Bernstein; another was a recent Russian immigrant named Ilya Kantarovich; a third was Ken Evans from Ohio. They enthusiastically accepted my challenge to join our expedition and to climb Warren's Shaft.
>
> Early the next summer, we took our mountain climbers to the bottom of the shaft. All the necessary technical preparations were completed. For two hours, the climbers, using the most advanced equipment and climbing techniques, slowly progressed up the perpendicular shaft. When the first climber reached the top of the shaft, he lowered the ropes by which we archaeologists intended to ascend. Climbing with the aid of the lowered rope appeared to be relatively simple. However, here too we were surprised, for the climb up the shaft obviously demanded special abilities which we hadn't realized were needed. From among the entire team of archaeologists, only two reached the top of the dark shaft, even with the help of the rope—the author and the expedition's photographer, Itzhak Harari.[16]

So climbing Warren's Shaft may have been difficult, but it was not impossible.

Joab may have entered the city another way, however. The natural tunnel leading to the top of Warren's Shaft continues along the surface of the hard dolomite, exiting on the eastern slope of the City of David, outside the city wall. Scholars once explained this apparently anomalous tunnel as providing air to the tunnelers or a way of disposing of excavation waste. But it is simply another natural tunnel. If Joab entered Jebusite Jerusalem through this tunnel, he would have followed an easy horizontal path to the top of Warren's Shaft. This would have required none of the derring-do involved in climbing Warren's Shaft.

A final objection made by those determined to squelch the *tsinnor* theory is that even if Joab had successfully climbed the shaft, a host of Jebusite soldiers would have been waiting for him at the tunnel exit inside the city. Certainly, he could not have entered with a significant complement of troops, they argue.

At this point, we leave it for the reader to decide.

III

The Fortress of Zion and the Puzzle of the Millo

I T IS TANTALIZING TO SEE WHETHER, AMONG THE ARCHAEOLOGICAL EVIDENCE, we might be able to identify the *Metsudat Tsion*, the Fortress of Zion, the Canaanite structure that the Bible says defended the city when David and his general Joab attacked. Is there any chance that archaeologists have uncovered the Fortress of Zion? Surprisingly, the answer is yes, although, as usual, certainty eludes us.

Directly up the eastern slope from the Gihon Spring, near the summit of the hill, is the largest surviving structure from the Late Bronze Age (1550–1200 B.C.E.) or the Iron Age (1200–586 B.C.E.) in all of Israel. It is called the Stepped-Stone Structure because, from the outside it looks like a mountain of stones that can be easily ascended by climbing up gradually set-back stones. These stepped stones form a mantle covering the structure. Part of the mantle was originally underground. The part above ground was probably covered with a smooth plaster coating, so in its original condition, it would not have been as easy to climb.

Just south of this structure are the remains of a tower first uncovered in the 1920s by the Irish archaeologist R. A. S. Macalister. He dated all but the top four courses of this tower to King David's time. The tower was promptly dubbed the "Tower of David."[17] In fact, as later excavations showed, the tower dates much later, to about the 2nd century B.C.E.[18]

North of this tower is the Stepped-Stone Structure. Macalister also exposed the upper part of the Stepped-Stone Structure, which he identified as a Jebusite

The Stepped-Stone Structure, more than five stories high, is the largest Iron Age structure in Israel. In its original form, it may have been the Fortress of Zion, which protected the Jebusite city at the time David conquered it.

25

Stepped-Stone Structure

The inset drawing provides a detailed view of the Stepped-Stone Structure (blue). Originally built by the Jebusites (or Canaanites) as early as the 14th or 13th century B.C.E., the existing structure was reinforced by the Israelites when they conquered the city (it probably supported a building on top that is now lost). Houses were built into the side of the Stepped-Stone Structure in the 7th and 6th centuries B.C.E (tan). The towers on either side are later additions. The wall to the right of the right-hand tower was probably the city wall built by the exiles who returned from Babylonia in the 5th century B.C.E.

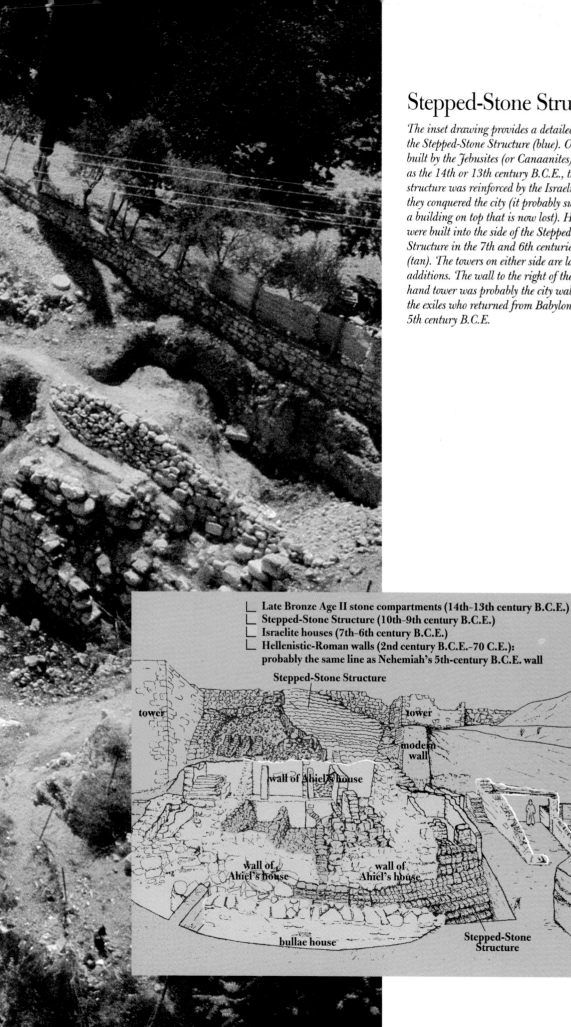

└─ Late Bronze Age II stone compartments (14th–13th century B.C.E.)
└─ Stepped-Stone Structure (10th–9th century B.C.E.)
└─ Israelite houses (7th–6th century B.C.E.)
└─ Hellenistic-Roman walls (2nd century B.C.E.–70 C.E.): probably the same line as Nehemiah's 5th-century B.C.E. wall

Stepped-Stone Structure

tower

tower

modern wall

wall of Ahiel's house

wall of Ahiel's house

wall of Ahiel's house

bullae house

Stepped-Stone Structure

rampart or bastion. He may have been right. This structure may be all that remains of the Jebusite Fortress of Zion. But Macalister surely had no solid basis for his dating of the structure.

In the 1960s, Kathleen Kenyon excavated beneath the "Tower of David" and removed part of the Stepped-Stone Structure adjacent to the tower. That is how the tower was redated to about the 2nd century B.C.E.; beneath the tower, she found pottery from the 2nd century B.C.E. As for the Stepped-Stone Structure, when she peeled away the stone mantle, or covering, she found the ruins of some 7th-century B.C.E. houses that had been destroyed in the Babylonian destruction of Jerusalem in 586 B.C.E. So, she reasoned, the Stepped-Stone Structure had to have been built later than the houses that appeared to lie beneath it.

But she was wrong, as Yigal Shiloh later showed. Shiloh followed the base of the Stepped-Stone Structure further down the hill and also exposed more of the area of the 7th-century houses uncovered by Kenyon. He found that the houses had been built *into* the Stepped-Stone Structure, which extended both below the houses and above them. Internally, the Stepped-Stone Structure consisted of terraced compartments that had been filled with rubble and soil.

Kathleen Kenyon, who dated these stone-filled terraces to the 13th century B.C.E., suggested that they supported buildings on the eastern slope of the city. They had to be repaired frequently lest the houses on top collapse. This terracing, she claimed, is what is referred to by the puzzling biblical word Millo, *which is customarily left untranslated.*

In the latest analysis made by archaeologists preparing the final report on Shiloh's excavations, the Stepped-Stone Structure is dated, based on the pottery, to the 14th (or 13th) century B.C.E., the Late Bronze Age II period (1400–1200 B.C.E.).[19] This was the time of the Jebusite/Canaanite occupation of the city. So the Stepped-Stone Structure may be a Jebusite bastion after all, and, as such, it is the best candidate we have for the Fortress of Zion.[20] Shiloh himself calls the Stepped-Stone Structure a "Jebusite citadel."

It is difficult to understand exactly how the Stepped-Stone Structure functioned. Shiloh is probably correct that it formed the base of a citadel built above it; in his own words, it probably "served as a sort of huge supporting wall for a superstructure rising at the top of the eastern slope of the city."[21]

The Stepped-Stone Structure has been preserved to a height of nearly 50 feet, approximately as high as a five- or six-story building. It is surely one of the most imposing ancient structures to have survived in Israel. Imagine the sight as David's forces approached the city with the Fortress of Zion rising at the top of the eastern slope and towering above the city—a grandiose and threatening sight indeed.

The Stepped-Stone Structure is also the key to resolving a textual crux in the Bible. According to the biblical account, as soon as David captured the city, he built around the *Millo* (2 Samuel 5:9; 1 Chronicles 11:8). But what is this *Millo*? The word is left untranslated and capitalized in English translations.

David was not the only one who built around the *Millo*. Solomon, the Bible tells us, used forced labor to build around the *Millo* and repair it (1 Kings 9:15). More than 200 years later, King Hezekiah, in anticipation of an Assyrian siege of Jerusalem (a matter we will hear a great deal about later), also repaired or fortified the *Millo* of the City of David (2 Chronicles 32:5). Apparently, Shechem also had a *Millo*, as we learn from the story of Abimelech in Judges 9.

Scholars generally agree that the word *Millo* is somehow related to the Hebrew for fill. (When drivers pull up to the pump in Israel, they say "*maleh*," "fill it up.") Some exegetes argue that the *Millo* was a tower; the Jewish Publication Society translation suggests in a footnote that it is a citadel. (For this reason, some scholars contend that the Stepped-Stone Structure is the *Millo*.)

According to Kenyon, however, *Millo* refers to stone terraces built by the Jebusites to support buildings on the eastern slope of the city. These terraces had to be constantly maintained lest the buildings they supported collapse. The summit of the eastern ridge is quite narrow. The buildable area was enlarged by extensive field-stone terraces built along the slope. Based on the terraces she excavated, Kenyon notes that the terraced extension was "almost as large as the level space on the summit of the ridge."[22]

According to a recent summary, "many biblical scholars have accepted Kenyon's suggestion" for the meaning of the biblical *Millo*, and Kenyon's suggestion "remains the most likely hypothesis."[23]

When David captured Jerusalem and built around the *Millo*, he also renamed Jerusalem the City of David ("David occupied the stronghold and renamed it the City of David" [2 Samuel 5:9]). He made it his own city— the capital of the country. After reigning for seven years in Hebron, he transferred the capital to Jerusalem, which was centrally located, and which had not been in the territory of any of the tribes. Like Washington, D.C., Jerusalem was a kind of federal enclave.

Making Jerusalem his capital was a stroke of political genius on David's part. It had the effect of uniting the tribes into a single political unit; no longer were

they expected to be subservient to a single ruling tribe whose territory included the capital. They were now subjects of a king who, symbolically at least, shed his Judahite tribal allegiance and moved his capital to a city that had never belonged to any one tribe.

Despite this, the Israelites managed to remain united for less than a century. When David's son Solomon died, in about 920 B.C.E., the tribes split apart again—along an old tribal line that crossed the country near Jerusalem. The royal Davidic line continued to rule in Jerusalem for more than 300 years (until the Babylonian destruction in 586 B.C.E.), but the area they ruled included only the territory of Judah (David's tribe) and the small adjacent territory of Benjamin.[24] The other ten tribes, in the north, became the kingdom of Israel.

Even the Temple at Jerusalem could not hold the tribes together after Solomon's death. But canny ruler that he was, David had also tried to unite the tribes religiously. Although they were apparently united ideologically in the worship of their God, Yahweh, David sought to reinforce the bond of religious allegiance. He did this by moving the Ark of the Covenant to Jerusalem from Kiriath-Jearim (in the territory of Judah), where it had lain for 20 years in a private

In King David's day a shekel was a weight, not a coin. When David bought the site where someday the Temple would stand, he paid Araunah the Jebusite 50 shekels of silver. Pictured at right is the Eshtemoa hoard in situ *at a site south of Jerusalem and at left after cleaning. This collection of silver pieces is probably much like the silver with which David paid Araunah. The Eshtemoa hoard included over 60 pounds of silver inserted into five jars. The jars date to nearly 200 years after David's time.*

house, since it was returned by the Philistines, who had captured it at the battle of Ebenezer (1 Samuel 4). The pomp and circumstance that accompanied the procession of the Ark to Jerusalem are described in glorious detail in 1 Chronicles 13–16. David commissioned a royal poet to compose a song of praise to the Lord, part of which reads:

> He is the Lord our God.
> His judgments cover the whole world.
> . . . .
> Sing to the Lord, all the earth.
> Proclaim his victory day by day.
> Declare his glory among the nations,
> His marvelous deeds to all the people.
>   1 Chronicles 16:14,23–24

If we can accept the biblical account, David's reign was marked by numerous military successes. His kingdom ultimately included a vast territory—from Egypt to the Euphrates—and Jerusalem became the capital of an empire.

David undertook considerable building in Jerusalem. In addition to repairing the *Millo* and building around it, he constructed a palace for himself (1 Chronicles 15:1). He also wanted to build a Temple for the Ark of the Covenant, which he had brought to Jerusalem (1 Kings 8:17), but the Lord spoke to David through the prophet Nathan, telling him that he, David, was not the one to build a house for the Lord (2 Samuel 7; 1 Chronicles 17). This was to be the task of his son Solomon. But David acquired the site on which Solomon was to build the Temple.

The story of David's purchase of the site is an interesting illustration of how biblical stories developed and changed even in ancient times. According to 2 Samuel 24, David purchased the site from Araunah the Jebusite for 50 shekels of silver (at the time the shekel was a weight, not a coin); according to a later account in 1 Chronicles 21, the Jebusite's name was Ornan and the price was 600 shekels worth of gold. Obviously, inflation has a long history.

The site is what we know today as the Temple Mount. It lay north of the City of David upon a height from which one could look down upon the city. Araunah (or Ornan) the Jebusite had used the site as a threshing floor—for which it was admirably suited, catching the winds that separated the wheat from the chaff as the grain was thrown into the air. David paid Araunah 50 shekels of silver for his threshing floor and his oxen. Then he built an altar on the site and sacrificed the oxen to the Lord (2 Samuel 24:24–25).

Of David's building activities in Jerusalem, virtually nothing has been recovered. Only a few potsherds survive from the time of his reign—and even these are not certain. Why? What happened to the Davidic buildings? Why, although we have so much archaeological evidence from before and after David's time, do we have so very little we can attribute to his time? The question is compounded when we add that the situation is much the same for Solomon's supposedly even more glorious reign. Why is so little left?

The answer archaeologists usually give is that later builders removed the earlier evidence; later builders wanted to construct on bedrock and often destroyed earlier strata. Another answer is that likely areas of exploration are not open to the archaeologist's spade. Digging on the Temple Mount, for example, is unthinkable; even an archaeological survey of the Temple Mount—just looking, not digging—is not permitted. The Temple Mount has not been scientifically surveyed since the 1860s, more than 125 years ago. On the summit of the City of David are some prime areas for archaeological excavation, but private homes now occupy these sites.

But these explanations provide only a partial—and not a particularly satisfying—answer to the question of the puzzling paucity of archaeological remains from the first half of the 10th century B.C.E. If the reader has a better explanation, I would like to know it.

IV

The Tombs of David and Other Kings of Judah

EVEN THOUGH WE HAVE FOUND VERY LITTLE ARCHAEOLOGICAL EVIDENCE FROM the time of David, we may have found his tomb. And it is not the site known as David's Tomb on Mount Zion. We have already seen that Mount Zion is inappropriately named, if the name is meant to indicate the area where the City of David was located. Thus there is some kind of symmetry in inaccurately locating David's tomb on this inaccurately labeled location.

According to the most recent, and probably the best reasoned argument,[25] the room where the cenotaph of David is located belonged to the Christian community of Jerusalem and was originally a 2nd-, 3rd- or 4th-century C.E. building that was turned into a church (see photo, p. 36). In the fighting during Israel's 1948 War of Independence, a shell exploded in the building, ironically providing the opportunity for archaeologist Jacob Pinkerfeld to excavate part of the building in the course of repairs. No one questions Pinkerfeld's conclusion that the building was originally built in the 2nd to 4th century C.E. But Pinkerfeld also concluded that the building had originally been a synagogue.

Pinkerfeld based his conclusion on the existence of a niche, or apse, behind the cenotaph, which he said was for the Torah ark, and on the orientation of the apse, which pointed exactly toward the Temple Mount. Later investigations, however, have shown that the apse does not point *exactly* toward the Temple Mount. Indeed, it points more nearly toward the Church of the Holy Sepulchre, where Jesus was thought to be buried. Moreover, the apse appears to have been a later Byzantine addition.

A view of the Jerusalem hills, seen from inside of what may be the tomb of King David.

The traditional tomb of King David on Mount Zion. But this isn't his tomb and the hill isn't Mount Zion. Ironically, the building was once a Christian church.

But the *coup de grace* for Pinkerfeld's argument is the historical situation of Jews in the 2nd, 3rd and 4th centuries C.E. They were banned from Jerusalem after the suppression of the Second Jewish Revolt against Rome (132–135 C.E.). As Father Jerome Murphy-O'Connor put it, "Even if individual Jews occasionally took the risk of living in Jerusalem, it is impossible that there should have been a functioning synagogue."[26] So the traditional site of the tomb of Israel's most revered king, which is visited by thousands of tourists each year, is in a building that was once a church. Upstairs is the traditional site of the Last Supper.

What may in fact be David's tomb, or the tomb of one of his successors, is located in the City of David. To understand why this might be the case, we must go back to the Bible, where we are told that David "was buried in the City of David" (1 Kings 2:10). Subsequent kings were also buried there, beginning with Solomon and going on to Ahaz, in the 8th century B.C.E. Thereafter, Judahite kings were no longer buried within the city.

In a site as small as the City of David—an area of just 11 or 12 acres—it should not be hard to find this burial site, if it existed. We can pinpoint the location even further, however. Nehemiah tells us that the royal tombs were in the southern part of the City of David (Nehemiah 3:16).

Following these directions, French archaeologist Raymond Weill commenced excavations in this area before World War I (and continued digging for a short time after the war). Weill uncovered the remains of what he believed were nine tombs right where the Bible said they would be. One of these, perhaps the most monumental, might be the tomb of King David.

This tomb, which Weill labelled T1, is shaped like a tunnel, or an artificially excavated cave, 52.5 feet long and more than 8 feet wide. The open end

is more than 13 feet high. About halfway back, the floor rises to form a kind of shelf, reducing the height between floor and ceiling to about six feet. Just in front of the back wall is a four-foot-long rock-cut depression for a body or, perhaps, a magnificent sarcophagus, or coffin.

The original appearance of the tomb is difficult to imagine because the entrance, together with much of one side, was hacked away long ago. In addition, the long tunnel was altered to provide a second, lower level at the front end. Grooves were cut in the inner walls on either side of the tunnel, creating slots into which wooden supports for a floor could be fit. In this way, a lower level could have been created beneath the floor where someone else, perhaps, could have been buried. In front of the tomb, several steps lead down to another opening that appears to be the entrance to a later tomb chamber for someone who wanted to be buried as close as possible to whoever was buried in the main chamber.

The other tombs Weill identified vary. One is a smaller version of T1. Others are so quarried away that it is impossible to make any sense of the remains. Still others are squarish caves in the side of the slope or remnants of what appear to have been shaft tombs.

Ancient tombs within the City of David. The largest and most elaborate (on the left), designated T1 by the excavator, may be David's Tomb. Unfortunately, the entrance to the tomb has been hacked away, perhaps as a result of quarrying.

King David's Tomb?

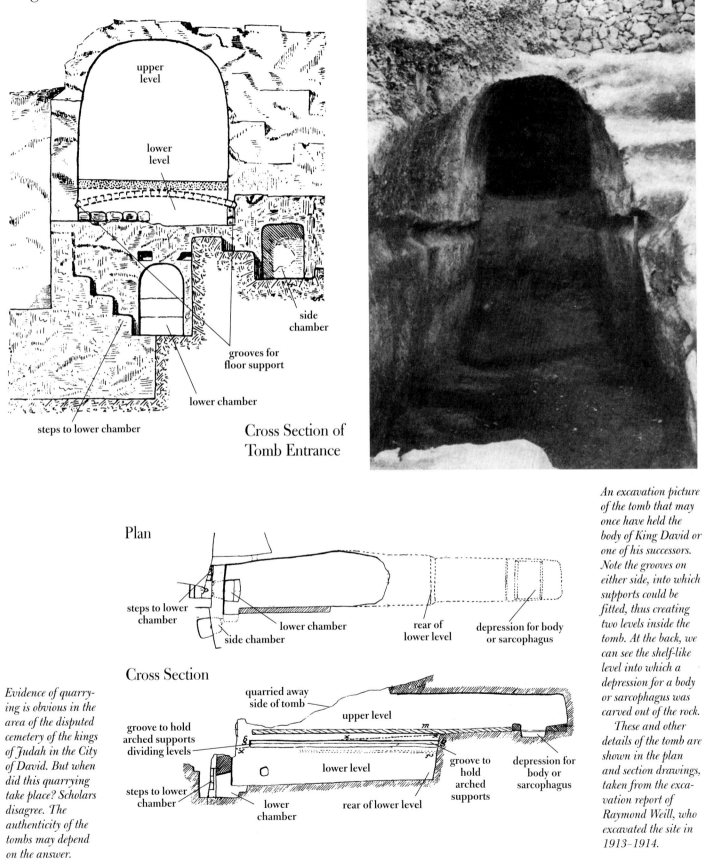

upper
level

lower
level

side
chamber

grooves for
floor support

lower chamber

steps to lower chamber

Cross Section of
Tomb Entrance

Plan

steps to lower
chamber

side chamber

lower chamber

rear of
lower level

depression for body
or sarcophagus

Cross Section

Evidence of quarrying is obvious in the area of the disputed cemetery of the kings of Judah in the City of David. But when did this quarrying take place? Scholars disagree. The authenticity of the tombs may depend on the answer.

quarried away
side of tomb

upper level

groove to hold
arched supports
dividing levels

lower level

steps to lower
chamber

lower
chamber

rear of lower level

groove to
hold
arched
supports

depression for
body or
sarcophagus

An excavation picture of the tomb that may once have held the body of King David or one of his successors. Note the grooves on either side, into which supports could be fitted, thus creating two levels inside the tomb. At the back, we can see the shelf-like level into which a depression for a body or sarcophagus was carved out of the rock.

These and other details of the tomb are shown in the plan and section drawings, taken from the excavation report of Raymond Weill, who excavated the site in 1913–1914.

The most elegant First Temple period tombs in Jerusalem, located on the grounds of the École Biblique. Some scholars believe these are the tombs of the later kings of Judah. Israeli archaeologist Gabriel Barkay discusses the tomb decorations with a Dominican father.

For many years after Weill's discovery, prominent scholars supported his conclusion that this was the burial ground of the kings of Judah, as specifically located in the Bible. Today, however, the pendulum has swung in the opposite direction. Standard works like *The New Encyclopedia of Archaeological Excavations in the Holy Land* and the *Anchor Bible Dictionary* reject Weill's hypothesis.

It is hard to avoid seeing an anti-Bible bias just beneath the surface of these recent rejections, especially when one examines the reasons for them. The discussion has focused on T1, without really looking at the other tombs. (A new scientific study is badly needed; the tombs have not been seriously studied in the last 75 years.) The arguments against the contention that T1 is a royal tomb, perhaps the tomb of King David himself, fall into two categories: (1) it is not a tomb; and (2) if it is a tomb, it can't be shown to be of the Davidic period.

Kathleen Kenyon argued that T1 is really a cistern, not a tomb. On the face of it, this seems absurd. How could the back of this tunnel hold water? And

École Biblique Cave Complex 1

A plan of one of the cave-tomb complexes at the École Biblique, showing the entrance, the entrance chamber and the tomb chambers. Four bone repositories were carved beneath burial benches. In the innermost chamber (7), approached by steps, is an unusual sarcophagus, perhaps reserved for the most revered of the people buried here.

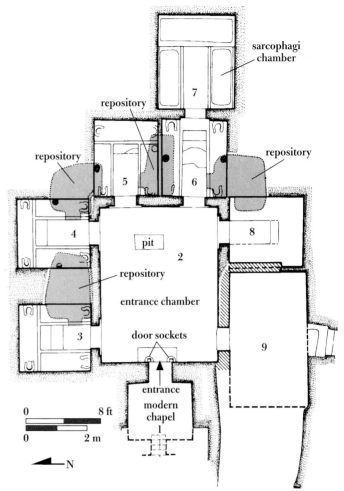

what was the small depression at the back for, if not to accommodate a coffin or a body? Even Kenyon admits that if T1 was a cistern, it was a cistern "of rather unusual form."[27]

Another argument is that the tomb cannot be dated to the Israelite period. We know what tombs from the 8th century B.C.E. look like. They have been found in abundance around Jerusalem, as we will see. And none of them looks like T1. But we don't really know what 10th-century B.C.E. Israelite tombs (when David was buried) looked like. Surprising as it may seem, among the hundreds of ancient tombs in and around Jerusalem, not a single one can be securely dated to the 10th century B.C.E. So we really have nothing with which to compare T1. That it may not look like a tomb dating 200 years later seems hardly relevant. (And in some respects, it can be argued, T1 does resemble these later tombs, with a kind of rock-cut burial shelf in the back and a slight depression in the shelf.)

Moreover, we really don't know what T1 originally looked like. The entrance is completely gone. There aren't even hints to help us. A complete, original plan cannot be drawn. And it appears to have been altered from time to time.

In short, we can't demonstrate that T1 is a 10th-century tomb; but neither can it be demonstrated that it is *not* a 10th-century tomb. It simply cannot be dated securely by its characteristics as a tomb, if it is a tomb at all.

David Ussishkin, a prominent Israeli archaeologist who has scientifically surveyed many Jerusalem tombs (but not these), rejects the identification of T1 as a royal tomb because the quality of the architecture is poor.[28] But in private conversations with me, Ussishkin has called my attention to other royal burials within cities; there, too, the architecture is poor, although the sarcophagi and grave goods are elegant and of the highest quality.[29]

The case has not been made beyond a reasonable doubt that T1 is the tomb of King David, or even that it is a royal tomb of the House of David. But it does remain a reasonable—and tantalizing—possibility.[30] And no one has come up with another satisfactory explanation for these unusual installations, located right where the Bible says the early kings of Israel were buried. If they are not tombs, what are they?

Tombs in the City of David are not the only Jerusalem tombs that have been identified as royal tombs. Another set of cave tombs is said to belong to the kings of Judah who reigned *after* the kings buried in the City of David. A reasonable assumption, which is universally accepted, is that at some point the City of David cemetery was too crowded for any more kings to be buried there. At that point, the Bible no longer tells us they were buried in the City of David. They were obviously buried somewhere else.

Amos Kloner, a leading Israeli archaeologist, believes he can identify these later tombs.[31] They are on the grounds of the French archaeological school in

First Temple period tombs are characterized by burial benches adjacent to the walls of the tomb chamber, like the ones pictured at left from the École Biblique tombs. Note the fine parapet at the edge of the burial benches. Beneath some of the burial benches, bone repositories were carved. About a year after the original burial, the bones were removed from the burial benches and placed in the bone repositories to make room for additional burials.

The picture at right is a close-up of the bone repository seen at lower right in the photo at left.

Jerusalem, officially named the École Biblique et Archéologique Française, and are known as the École Biblique tombs.

Unlike the contenders in the City of David, the École Biblique tombs do have the characteristics we have come to expect of royal tombs, and they unquestionably date to the First Temple period. In a word, they are the finest First Temple period tombs that have been found anywhere in Jerusalem—or in Israel, for that matter.

There are actually two cave complexes in the École Biblique tombs, one with six tomb chambers and the other with seven. Each tomb complex is entered through an impressively large, high-ceilinged entrance chamber. Where the rock walls meet the ceiling, elaborate double cornices have often been carved. Some of the rock walls have been made to imitate wood paneling (see photos, p. 44).

The typical characteristics of First Temple tombs in the École Biblique tombs include rock-cut burial benches on three sides of the burial chambers and bone repositories below some of the benches. After the flesh decomposed, the bones of the deceased were placed in repositories to make room on the

Some burial benches feature headrests carved into the stone, like this one from the École Biblique tombs (below).

Israeli archaeologist Gabriel Barkay (above) points to an elegant ceiling cornice carved into the rock of a chamber in one of the École Biblique tombs.

A sunken panel (at left) carved into the rock of one of the École Biblique tomb chambers imitates woodwork and shows off the stonemason's artistry.

burial benches for later burials. (This may explain biblical phrases such as "slept with his fathers" and "gathered unto their fathers"—bones were literally gathered into repositories with the bones of immediate ancestors.)

Another characteristic of First Temple tombs is a headrest carved into the rock-cut burial bench. In the École Biblique tombs the headrests are unusually fancy, shaped like the Greek letter omega (Ω), or a horseshoe. The head of the deceased was placed in the headrest, a kind of embracing pillow.

Even the burial benches in the École Biblique tombs are special. Some of

them are edged with low parapets. The workmanship has been described as "expert" and "highly skilled."[32]

The most elaborate—and innermost—tomb chamber is approached by steps leading up from another tomb chamber. This innermost chamber is especially beautifully carved and contains, instead of burial benches, three sarcophagi carved out of the bedrock. Narrow shelves to support the lids of the sarcophagi are also carved into the rock, but the lids themselves have long since disappeared.

Kloner does not rest his case that these are the tombs of the later kings of Judah on elegance alone. Josephus, the 1st-century Jewish historian, Kloner notes, refers to some "royal caverns" in the area of the École Biblique tombs. Kloner argues that the Greek word translated as "caverns" may also mean "burial caves." Thus the reference would be to "royal burial caves."[33] In other words, in Josephus's time these burial caves were regarded as "Burial Caves of the Kings." As such, they may well have been the final resting place for the later kings of Judah.

We've gotten a little ahead of our story, however, with the tombs of the later kings of Judah. So let's go back to where we left off—the death of King David.

The innermost room of cave complex 1, approached by the steps shown in the photo on p. 42, contained a sarcophagus carved out of the living rock, a rare feature in First Temple period tombs. Perhaps it was permanently reserved for an especially revered leader.

V

King Solomon and the Lord's House

THE THRONE DID NOT PASS EASILY UPON DAVID'S DEATH. EVEN DURING David's lifetime, the palace was rife with intrigue. Witness the rebellion led by his son Absalom, who had previously murdered his half-brother Amnon, David's eldest son (2 Samuel 13–19). The rebellion ended with Absalom's death.

The royal son conceived in adultery by David and Bathsheba (2 Samuel 11:4–5) had died for his father's sin (2 Samuel 12:1,14). Bathsheba, now David's wife, conceived again and bore Solomon, who, David promised Bathsheba, would succeed him.

When David lay old and dying, however, his eldest surviving son, Adonijah, had himself acclaimed king by the priest Abiathar. When David was told of this, he ordered the priest Zadok and the prophet Nathan to accompany Solomon, who was to ride on a mule, down to the Gihon Spring and there anoint him king over all Israel. And it was done.

The Bible does not explain why David directed Nathan the prophet and Zadok the priest to take Solomon to this particular place for the anointing.* But the place is identified with certainty: Gihon. Perhaps the old king recalled that by capturing the Gihon Spring he was able to take Jerusalem and thereby, for a time, forge Israel into a unified country. Or perhaps the intermittently

*Perhaps water was an integral part of the ritual. As Jerome Murphy-O'Connor has noted in a personal communication, Adonijah, too, was consecrated king at a spring, En Rogel, south of the City of David.

Two-dimensional cherubim decorated the walls of Solomon's Temple and three-dimensional cherubim hovered over the ark. Mythical creatures, cherubim combine attributes of several species, including, like the one pictured here, the strength of a lion, the fecundity of a bull, the swiftness of an eagle and the wisdom of a human being. This cherub likely comes from ancient Arslan Tash, in Syria.

Solomon's Temple

Solomon's Temple consisted of three rooms laid out on an east–west axis: a portico (ulam), an outer sanctum or main hall (hekhal) and a shrine or Holy of Holies (debir). The entrance was in the short eastern wall. Two bronze columns, called Jachin and Boaz—each 27 feet tall—stood in the ulam, *or portico.*

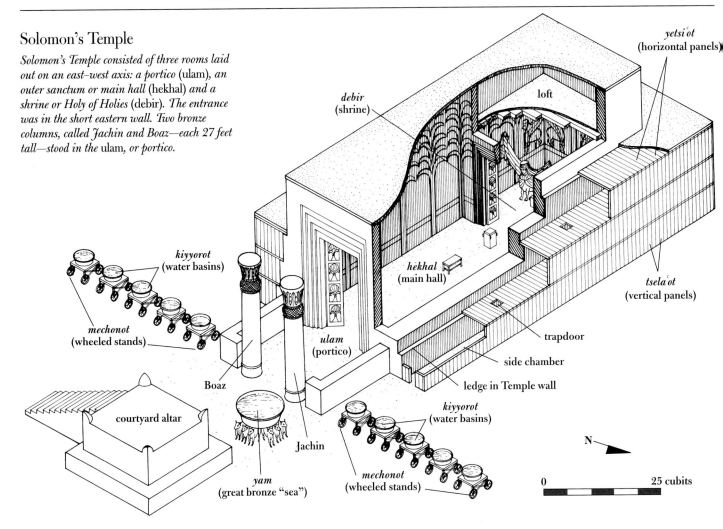

yetsi'ot
(horizontal panels)

debir
(shrine)

loft

kiyyorot
(water basins)

mechonot
(wheeled stands)

hekhal
(main hall)

tsela'ot
(vertical panels)

Boaz

ulam
(portico)

trapdoor

side chamber

ledge in Temple wall

kiyyorot
(water basins)

courtyard altar

Jachin

mechonot
(wheeled stands)

yam
(great bronze "sea")

N

0   25 cubits

gushing waters of Gihon were considered sacred even then. Or perhaps the life-giving waters of the spring represented to the dying old king the continuity of Israel and its God:

> So Zadok the priest and Nathan the prophet…went down and mounted Solomon on King David's mule, and escorted him to Gihon. There Zadok the priest took the horn of oil from the Tent of the Lord, and anointed Solomon. Then they blew the ram's horn, and all the people shouted, "Long live King Solomon!" Then all the people went up after him in procession, playing on pipes, and rejoicing with great joy, so that the very earth was split with the noise.
>
> 1 Kings 1:38–40

The gateway through which the procession entered the city after this joyous coronation may have been the gateway uncovered in Kenyon's excavation, which continued in use down to this time.

Solomon promptly had Adonijah killed, as well as a general who had sided with Adonijah—none other than Joab, whose bravery and ingenuity, years

earlier, had enabled David to conquer Jerusalem. Joab was buried "at his home in the wilderness" (1 Kings 2:34).

The highlight of Solomon's reign, at least from the perspective of the biblical author, was the construction of the Temple of the Lord, Yahweh's dwelling place. It took Solomon seven years to build the Temple (it took him 13 years, however, to build his palace).

Not a stone of Solomon's Temple has survived. It was destroyed by Nebuchadnezzar in 586 B.C.E. Later in the same century, it was succeeded by the Second Temple, built by returnees from the Babylonian Exile. The Second

The Temple of Tell Tainat

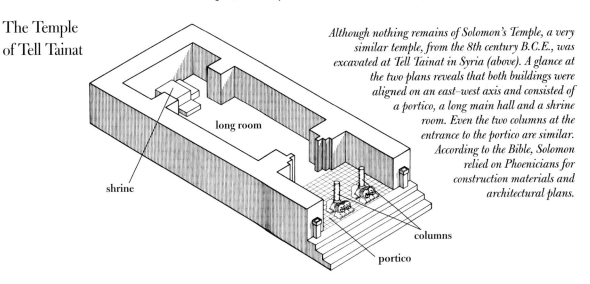

shrine

long room

columns

portico

Although nothing remains of Solomon's Temple, a very similar temple, from the 8th century B.C.E., was excavated at Tell Tainat in Syria (above). A glance at the two plans reveals that both buildings were aligned on an east–west axis and consisted of a portico, a long main hall and a shrine room. Even the two columns at the entrance to the portico are similar. According to the Bible, Solomon relied on Phoenicians for construction materials and architectural plans.

Temple was rebuilt from the ground up by Herod the Great in the 1st century B.C.E.[34] It was Herod's temple that the Romans destroyed in 70 C.E. The Dome of the Rock now occupies the site, making archaeological excavation of the area unfeasible.

The Bible, however, does give a fairly detailed, although sometimes ambiguous, picture of Solomon's Temple. And by using analogous archaeological evidence, we can reconstruct both the Temple and its furnishings.

The Temple was a surprisingly small building—less than 100 feet long, a little more than 30 feet wide and approximately 50 feet high. We can be more precise in biblical terms—60 cubits long, 20 cubits wide and 30 cubits high (1 Kings 6:2). (At this time, a cubit measured approximately 52.5 centimeters [20.5 inches]).[35]

The building, or house (*bayit*), was divided into three parts: (1) a portico or porch (*ulam*), which was 10 cubits long; (2) the main hall (*hekhal*), which was 40 cubits long; and (3) the inner sanctuary (*debir*), or Holy of Holies (*kodesh ha-kodashim*), which was 20 cubits long (1 Kings 6:2–3,17,20). This of course adds up to 70, not 60, cubits. Perhaps the biblical writer did not include the porch, or portico, when computing the length of the Temple; if so, the house

Ten wheeled stands made of bronze, called mechonot *(singular,* mechonah*), stood in the courtyard in front of Solomon's Temple. On top of each stand was an offering bowl. Several such stands, though not from Solomon's Temple, have been recovered. The one at right, from Cyprus, is an extraordinary example. Like the* mechonot *at Solomon's Temple, this bronze stand is decorated with cherubim. A similar, though less complete* mechonah, *above, is in the Bible Lands Museum in Jerusalem.*

(bayit) refers only to the main hall and inner sanctuary.[36] In the portico were two free-standing pillars named Jachin and Boaz (1 Kings 7:21). Their significance is a mystery.

A temple from the 8th century B.C.E. discovered at Tell Tainat in ancient Syria (now in Turkey) bears a remarkable resemblance to Solomon's Temple. Like Solomon's Temple, it was a "long-room," with a porch, a main hall and a small shrine room at the back. The Tell Tainat temple, and a host of other temples archaeologists have discovered, help us trace the origins of the architectural form and give us confidence in the basic reliability of the biblical description. The long-room temple as an architectural form appears to have been imported to Canaan from Syria sometime in the 2nd millennium B.C.E.

This is consistent with the Bible's recognition that Solomon built the Temple with the help of Hiram, king of Tyre, who supplied the cedar and cypress timber for the building (1 Kings 9:11). Solomon paid Hiram for these supplies by giving him 20 cities in the Galilee. But Hiram wanted more, so Solomon threw in 120 talents of gold.

It appears that the architect was also from up north—another fellow from Tyre, also named Hiram, although his mother was from the Israelite tribe of Naphtali before she married his Tyrian father (1 Kings 7:13-14). (There was intermarriage even in those days; Solomon, of course, had many foreign wives.) The architect Hiram was "endowed with skill, ability and talent for executing all work in bronze" and was responsible for many of the appurtenances of the Temple.

Like all traces of the building, the appurtenances of Solomon's Temple have disappeared. But archaeology

These iron incense shovels recently excavated in an 8th-century B.C.E. shrine at Tel Dan are similar to the incense shovels used in Solomon's Temple.

helps us create a picture of them. For example, Hiram fashioned ten bronze wagonlike stands, called in Hebrew *mechonot* (singular, *mechonah*). They are described as having four wheels and standing three cubits high and four cubits square. The *mechonot* had insets (perhaps openwork) and were decorated with lions, oxen and cherubim. They were arrayed five on each side of the Temple entrance in the outside courtyard (1 Kings 7:27–39). Yet, even with the detailed description of the *mechonot* (there is more said in the Bible than I have given), it is difficult to picture them. In this case, a picture would truly be worth a thousand words. Archaeologists, however, have uncovered several offering stands similar to the ones described in the Book of Kings—even down

A horned altar recovered at Tel Beer-sheba is similar to the animal-sacrifice altar that must have stood in the court-yard in front of Solomon's Temple. The animal-sacrifice altar pictured here dates from the 9th or 8th century B.C.E., stands over five feet high and measures nine feet on each side, exactly the dimensions of the altar the Israelites built in Sinai, according to the Bible.

to the material of which they were made (bronze). Offering bowls were placed on top of the stands.

The incense shovels (*machtot*; singular, *machtah*) mentioned in 1 Kings 7:50 we can easily picture. Recently, near an altar at Tel Dan, some iron incense shovels dating to the 8th century B.C.E. were found, the oldest incense shovels ever discovered. They have loops at the end so they can be hung on wall hooks.

Oddly enough, the large altar in front of Solomon's Temple is not explicitly mentioned in the text of Kings and can only be inferred. We are told that 22,000 oxen and 120,000 sheep were sacrificed, apparently at the center of the court-yard, when the Temple was consecrated.* Approximately 200 years later, King Ahaz replaced this altar with a large new altar modeled after one he had seen in Damascus (2 Kings 16:10–17).

In 2 Chronicles 4:1 we are told that Solomon built an altar 20 cubits on each side and 10 cubits high. The account in Kings, however, which is older and probably more reliable, makes no mention of this altar. We can get a won-derful idea of what the altar probably looked like from a 9th- or 8th-century B.C.E. four-horned altar that was found dismantled at Beer-sheba. This altar was

---

*1 Kings 8:62–64 mentions in passing a bronze altar that was "too small."

This 4-inch-high and 7-inch-long bull suggests what the bigger Temple bulls that held the yam, *or sea, might have looked like. It was discovered near Mount Gilboa by an Israeli soldier; later excavations revealed that the site was an open-air cult enclosure complete with an altar. The bull dates to about the 12th century B.C.E.*

Small altars (at left and below) excavated at Megiddo are similar in size to the incense altar in Solomon's Temple.

The lamp stands in Solomon's Temple probably looked more like this (at right) than like the seven-branched menorah that later became such a popular Jewish symbol. The bowl on top was filled with oil that fed one or more lighted wicks. The example shown here comes from Megiddo and dates approximately to Solomon's time.

The walls of Solomon's Temple were ornately decorated and included palmettes like this ivory example (above) dating to the 8th century B.C.E. excavated at Samaria.

more than five feet high and almost nine feet (five royal cubits) square, exactly the dimesions of the Tabernacle altar erected by the Israelites in the wilderness.

Archaeology can also help us picture the 12 bronze bulls, three facing in each direction, whose hindquarters supported the great bronze basin (*yam*, literally, "sea"), which also stood in the courtyard before the Temple. Look at the bronze bull recently discovered—accidentally, by a soldier—at an otherwise unknown site near Mount Gilboa, now called the Bull Site. The area was excavated by Hebrew University archaeologist Amihai Mazar and was discovered to have been an early open-air sanctuary.[37]

Inside Solomon's Temple, in the main hall, probably in front of the doors of the inner sanctuary (the Holy of Holies), stood a golden incense altar. Numerous altars of similar size have been recovered from archaeological excavations. Although none of these is made of gold and, at least according to one prominent scholar, they were used for meal offerings rather than incense,[38] they do give us a realistic picture of the incense altar in the main hall of the Temple.

Also in the main hall of the Temple were ten lamp stands, five on each side of the hall (1 Kings 7:49). Most people reading this passage immediately imagine seven-branched candelabra called menorahs. But no mention is made of branches, let alone seven branches.

A seven-branched menorah *is* described, however, as having been in the portable Tabernacle the Israelites carried through the desert on their way to the Promised Land (Exodus 25:31–40, 37:17–24). Some scholars believe that the authorial strand of Exodus in which the menorah is described (the so-called Priestly source, called P) is late and reflects conditions in the post-Exilic period after the return from Babylonia. Other scholars disagree and argue for a pre-Exilic date—and therefore a more reliable text—for the composition of P.

But even Duke University professor Carol Meyers, the leading scholar who argues for a seven-branched menorah in the desert Tabernacle, says that seven-branched menorahs are quite improbable in Solomon's Temple.[39] The principal reason is that we have numerous lamp stands from the Iron Age, and none of them gives any indication of having branches. Moreover, the description of the Solomonic lamp stands in Kings does not mention branches—a curious omission in light of the detailed description in Exodus of the Tabernacle menorah.[40] As Professor Meyers notes, "If 'branches' were a prominent aspect of these ten Solomonic lamp stands, it is difficult to imagine that their presence would be unnoted in the text."

The lamp stands in Solomon's Temple were probably decorated like the ones found in excavations and surmounted with a bowl for the oil and wicks. A number of these bowls with pinches for seven wicks have been found, and it may well be that this kind of bowl was also used on top of the lamp stands in Solomon's Temple.

The back wall of the main hall was decorated differently and more ornately

An ivory cherub found at Nimrud, like the example on page 46, suggests what the cherubim in Solomon's Temple looked like. Both cherubim wear an Egyptian-style wig and crown, although this example appears facing forward rather than in the usual Egyptian profile.

than the other three walls, for behind it was the Holy of Holies. This wall was decorated with palmettes and cherubim. The palmettes could well have looked like those found in 9th- to 8th-century B.C.E. ivory decorations from Samaria.

Cherubim decorated other walls of the Temple as well, and two huge, three-dimensional cherubim made of gold-plated olive wood filled the Holy of Holies, hovering over the Ark of the Covenant. The wings of the cherubim touched each other over the Ark and the other wings extended to the walls (1 Kings 6:23–28). The wings of the cherubim spread out over the Ark, "so that the cherubim shielded the Ark…from above" (1 Kings 8:7).

What did these cherubim look like? Despite more than 90 references in the Bible to cherubim, we never get a very precise description. They have wings; that much is clear (for example, see 1 Kings 6:24). Ezekiel describes what appear to be cherubim in his visionary temple as having characteristics of human beings, lions, eagles and bulls (Ezekiel 1:5–12; see also Ezekiel 10:1–5).

Once again archaeology comes to the rescue. Several of these composite mythical creatures have been found in archaeological excavations. They vary somewhat but clearly include human and animal features. They are intended, as one scholar has noted, "to express something beyond human limitations." One of the most beautiful examples is an openwork ivory cherub from the Bible Lands Museum in Jerusalem. As we see in the illustration on page 46, it combines characteristics of the same creatures mentioned in Ezekiel. The ivory cherub has a human face, an eagle's wings, the forequarters of a lion and the hindquarters of an ox or bull. The face is shown in typical Egyptian profile, revealing the strong influence of Egyptian culture in Phoenicia, from which Israel borrowed the iconographic tradition of the cherubim.[41] Another cherub, not nearly as beautiful, may be seen in the bronze openwork of the stand (*mechonah*) pictured on page 50, which is also in the Bible Lands Museum. You will recall that the Bible describes the *mechonot* as incorporating cherubim (1 Kings 7:29).

The cherub is meant to embrace the lion's strength, the eagle's swiftness and ability to soar into the heavens, the bull's fecundity and the human being's wisdom and reason. Before philosophy, this was how omnipotence and omniscience were portrayed.

But what is the function of the cherubim in the Holy of Holies? They appear to have a double function: first, as protectors and guardians (cherubim were placed at the entrance to the Garden of Eden after Adam and Eve were expelled [Genesis 3:24]); and, second, to create a throne, or resting place, for God's invisible presence. The psalmist sang of "You who are enthroned on the cherubim" (Psalm 80:2). When King Hezekiah prays, he addresses the "Lord of Hosts, enthroned on the cherubim" (2 Kings 19:15; Isaiah 37:16; see also 1 Samuel 4:4 and 2 Samuel 6:2).

When the Temple was completed, King Solomon ordered a great feast that lasted for 14 days (1 Kings 8:65). The Ark of the Covenant was brought from the City of David into the Temple (1 Kings 8:1). Solomon himself offered a long, moving prayer, only part of which we quote here:

> Praised be the Lord, the God of Israel, who has fulfilled with deeds the promise He made to my father David. For He said, "Ever since I brought My people Israel out of Egypt, I have not chosen a city among all the tribes of Israel for building a House where My name might abide; but I have chosen David to rule My people Israel."
>
> Now my father David had intended to build a House for the name of the Lord, the God of Israel. But the Lord said to my father David, "As regards your intention to build a House for My name, you did right to have that intention. However, you shall not build the House yourself; instead, your son, the issue of your loins, shall build the House for My name."

And the Lord has fulfilled the promise that He made: I have succeeded my father David and have ascended the throne of Israel, as
the Lord promised. I have built the House for the name of the Lord,
the God of Israel; and I have set a place there for the Ark, containing the covenant which the Lord made with our fathers when He
brought them out from the land of Egypt....

But will God really dwell on earth? Even the heavens to their
uttermost reaches cannot contain You, how much less this House
that I have built! Yet turn, O Lord my God, to the prayer and sup-
plication of Your servant, and hear the cry and prayer which Your
servant offers before You this day. May Your eyes be open day and
night toward this House, toward the place of which You have said,
"My name shall abide there"; may You heed the prayers which Your

servant will offer toward this place. And when You hear the suppli-
cations which Your servant and Your people Israel offer toward this
place, give heed in Your heavenly abode—give heed and pardon. Ren-
der to each man according to his ways as You know his heart to be—
for You alone know the hearts of all men—so that they may revere
You all the days that they live on the land that You gave to our fathers.

Or if a foreigner who is not of Your people Israel comes from a
distant land for the sake of Your name—for they shall hear about
Your great name and Your mighty hand and Your outstretched arm—
when he comes to pray toward this House, oh, hear in Your heavenly abode and grant all that the foreigner asks You for. Thus all the
peoples of the earth will know Your name and revere You, as does
Your people Israel.

*The Western Wall of
the Temple Mount, the
focus of Jewish
prayer, was once
thought to be the
remains of Solomon's
Temple or at least of
his Temple Mount. In
fact, even the lower
courses date nearly a
millennium later.
The builder was
Herod the Great
(37–4 B.C.E.).
Solomon's Temple
Mount is buried
beneath Herod's much
larger replacement.*

> Praised be the Lord who has granted a haven to His people
> Israel...[M]ay these words of mine, which I have offered in suppli-
> cation before the Lord, be close to the Lord our God day and night,
> that He may provide for His servant and for His people Israel, accord-
> ing to each day's needs—to the end that all the peoples of the earth
> may know that the Lord alone is God; there is no other.
>
> 1 Kings 8: 15–21, 27–30, 38–43, 56, 59–60

Many pages ago, I said that not a stone of Solomon's Temple has survived. But what about the Western Wall, formerly called the Wailing Wall, the place where Jews have come for centuries to mourn the destruction of their Temple, first by the Babylonians and then by the Romans—the holiest Jewish site? Ever since I can remember, newspapers have identified the Western Wall as the only remaining relic of Solomon's Temple.

First of all, this is the wall of the Temple Mount, not the wall of the Temple itself. In order to build on the irregular height we know as the Temple Mount, it was necessary to create a level construction site. This was done, as was customary, by building an enclosure wall that was filled in to create a platform that could support the construction.

But more significant, the Western Wall is not the wall of *Solomon's* Temple Mount. The lower courses were built by Herod the Great in the 1st century B.C.E. (the upper courses have frequently been replaced, most recently in the 19th century). It is easy to distinguish the Herodian masonry, which has carefully cut margins and flat central bosses, from the cruder, smaller masonry above. That's one way to tell that the Western Wall is Herodian and not Solomonic.

But there is also another way. Herod nearly doubled the size of the Temple Mount before rebuilding the Second Temple originally built by Zerubbabel and the exiles who returned from Babylonia in the late 6th century B.C.E. Herod extended the Temple Mount on three sides—north, south and west. So the Solomonic Temple Mount wall is buried under the Temple Mount, somewhere east of the Herodian Western Wall.

Ironically, Judaism's holiest shrine was built, not by Solomon, as people no doubt supposed when the Western Wall attained sacred status, but by Herod, who was one of the most hated kings ever to rule the Jews. Although he regarded himself as Jewish, Herod was of Idumean stock. His forebears had been converted to Judaism a generation or two earlier. Moreover, according to the Jewish historian Josephus, Herod's mother was Arabian (a Nabatean), and thus presumably not Jewish. In biblical times, the child's status was determined by the status of the father. Under later rabbinic law it was—and is—determined by the Jewishness of the mother. If rabbinic law was already in force in Herod's day, he would not have been Jewish.

Although no longer associated with King Solomon, the Western Wall has been sanctified by centuries of Jewish tears and prayers.

The emperor Augustus is supposed to have punned that he would rather be Herod's pig (*"hus"* in Greek) than Herod's son (*huios*). The reason: Herod murdered three of his sons but abstained from eating pork in accordance with Jewish dietary restrictions. This, then, was the builder of the venerated Western Wall. Modern scholarship cannot detract from the sanctity of the Western Wall, however, hallowed as it is by generations of Jewish tears and by the blood of the Israeli soldiers who recaptured it in 1967.

The mistaken identification of the Western Wall as the Temple of Solomon is the third false attribution we have noted. I have already mentioned David's Tomb on Mount Zion, as well as Mount Zion itself. Now for a fourth.

Under the southeastern corner of the Temple are some immense vaultings known as Solomon's Stables. Getting permission to see them is difficult. It depends on luck and on the goodwill of the Moslem authorities at the time you apply, but it is well worth trying. In a word, they are magnificent.

Eighty-eight pillars of characteristic Herodian masonry (although sometimes rebuilt) divide the huge area into 12 long, vaulted aisles. In the 12th century, Crusader knights actually stabled their horses among these pillars. They had already given the name "Templum Salomonis" to the Al-Aqsa mosque that stood above their "stables," so they naturally attributed construction of the underground vaults to King Solomon as well. And if the Crusaders used the area as a stable, why not suppose that King Solomon had? The name stuck, and the area is still known as Solomon's Stables although it has nothing to do with Solomon or his time. Indeed, the Temple Mount did not extend this far south until King Herod's time.

But there is construction on the Temple Mount that might be Solomonic. It can be found in two places.

I noted earlier that Herod enlarged the Temple Mount to twice its previous size by extending it on the north, south and west (see p. 66). He did not extend it on the east, however, because the original Temple Mount wall on the east sat on the edge of the hill, which descended precipitously into the Kidron Valley. For the same reason, later builders and repairers of the walls of the Temple Mount always kept to the eastern line established by Solomon. On the east face of the Temple Mount wall, 106 feet north of the southeastern corner, is the famous "Straight Joint" at the bottom of the wall. This Straight Joint was first noticed by Charles Warren, the same explorer for whom Warren's Shaft is named. A straight joint, or seam, is found in masonry where an addition has been made; otherwise, courses of masonry overlap each other. The masonry south of this Straight Joint in the bottom courses (the higher courses are later repairs) is clearly Herodian, with narrow margins and carefully drafted flat bosses in the center. This telltale design and the fine craftsmanship—each large block snugly aligned with the adjoining block without a knife blade of space between them—identifies the masonry south of the Straight Joint as Herod's southern extension of the prior Temple Mount (see photos, p. 64).

But what about the masonry north of the Straight Joint?

Scholarly suggestions as to the date of the thick-bossed, somewhat more crudely cut wall north of the Straight Joint have ranged widely—from Solomonic to Persian to Herodian. The least likely of these suggestions is Solomonic. It would be difficult to find an archaeologist at the end of the 20th century who would defend a Solomonic date for the masonry north of the Straight Joint.

But no one has ever looked at the base of the wall north of the Straight Joint.[42] In the 1960s Kathleen Kenyon excavated the area on either side of the Straight Joint. It is still easy to see where her excavation ended—the ground slopes up precipitously. But for some unknown reason, she did not dig down to bedrock north of the Straight Joint. Why she stopped is hard to say, because it would have been easy to continue the excavation straight down. If we were to excavate down to bedrock in this area (or somewhat to the north), we might well find Solomonic masonry.

Although there is a Moslem cemetery east of the Temple Mount, the graves do not come up to the wall at this point, and a new excavation could be confined to the area Kenyon already excavated. But politically, this is impossible. So we will have to wait for a better time to see whether Solomonic masonry still exists at the base of the wall somewhere north of the Straight Joint.

A bit of the Solomonic Temple Mount wall may well be exposed at another point, however—on the Temple Mount itself. It looks like a step. It's barely visible. But it may be part of the original Temple Mount wall built by King Solomon.

A magnificent vaulted hall beneath the southeastern corner of the Temple Mount is known as Solomon's Stables. But it has nothing to do with King Solomon. Like the Western Wall, it was constructed by Herod the Great nearly ten centuries after Solomon reigned. (For more on this vaulted chamber, see chapter 10.)

The "Straight Joint," or seam (above, lower right at arrow, close-up in photo at right), which runs part way up the eastern wall of the Temple Mount, indicates that an addition to the wall was attached here. (The seam does not extend upward to the later repairs of the wall.) The portion of the wall left of the Straight Joint was added by Herod the Great. The Herodian ashlars are easily identifiable. Scholars disagree as to who constructed the wall to the right (north) of the Straight Joint. But the eastern wall line is probably the one that King Solomon built upon, so the base of the wall to the right of the Straight Joint might be Solomonic masonry.

The discovery was made by Leen Ritmeyer, the architect attached to the excavations south of the Temple Mount led by Hebrew University professor Benjamin Mazar in the late 1960s and 1970s. The key to Ritmeyer's discovery is a statement in *Middot*, a tractate of the Mishnah, the earliest rabbinic* text, compiled by Judah ha-Nasi (known in Jewish tradition simply as "Rabbi") in the late 2nd century or early 3rd century C.E. The statement reads as follows: "The Temple Mount measured 500 cubits by 500 cubits." That's all.

Ritmeyer put this together with a curious fact first noticed by his predecessor at the dig, Irish architect Brian Lalor. The golden Dome of the Rock, which is now the central feature on the Temple Mount, sits on a platform that itself sits on the Temple Mount. This Moslem platform can be ascended by eight different sets of steps—on all four sides. At the top of each flight of steps is an arcade that architecturally marks the entrance to the Moslem platform.

The steps in each of these stairways are all parallel to the adjacent wall of the Moslem platform—except for the steps of one stairway. The stairway at the northwest corner of the western wall of the Moslem platform is different (see pp. 66–69). The steps in this stairway are not quite parallel to the wall of the Moslem platform that the steps ascend. Moreover, the bottom step is different from the others. The bottom step is made of a single line of large, beautifully polished ashlars,** in contrast to the other steps, which are composed of many smaller stones. Lalor pointed out these anomalies to Ritmeyer. Ritmeyer put them together, with the help of the tractate from the Mishnah, to locate an earlier Temple Mount.

When examining a plan of the Temple Mount, Ritmeyer noticed that this bottom step, which is not precisely parallel to the western wall of the Moslem platform, is precisely parallel to the eastern wall of the Temple Mount. Could this unusual bottom step be part of the western wall of the original Temple Mount?

Ritmeyer next measured the distance from the eastern wall of the Temple Mount (which, as we have seen, has always been located on the same line because the slope falls steeply down to the Kidron Valley east of this line) to the telltale bottom step of the stairway. Using the precise measurement of the Royal Cubit— 20.67 inches instead of 20.5 inches—the distance was exactly 500 cubits, the measurement of the Temple Mount as recorded in the Mishnah.

If Ritmeyer had found the east and west walls of the original Temple Mount, could he locate the north and south walls of the 500-cubit-square Temple Mount referred to in the Mishnah? Several clues enabled him to fix the northern line of this square Temple Mount. The first bit of help came from Charles Warren, who had meticulously examined the Temple Mount in the 1860s on behalf of

---

*Rabbinic Judaism refers to the Judaism developed by the rabbis after the Roman destruction of the Temple in 70 C.E. All modern forms of Judaism are forms of rabbinic Judaism.

**An ashlar is a rectangular block of hewn stone.

The
Growth of
the Temple
Mount

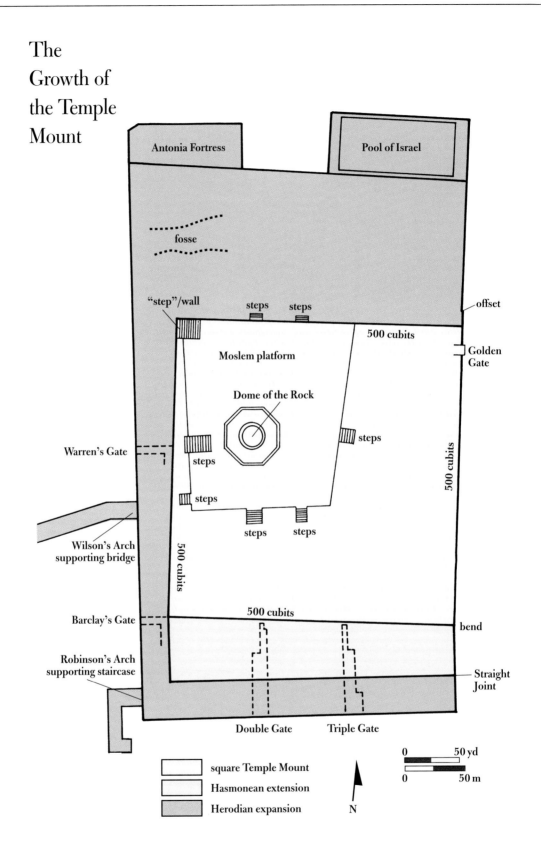

Antonia Fortress

Pool of Israel

fosse

"step"/wall

steps   steps

offset

500 cubits

Golden
Gate

Moslem platform

Dome of the Rock

Warren's Gate

steps

steps

500 cubits

steps

Wilson's Arch
supporting bridge

steps

steps   steps

500 cubits

Barclay's Gate

500 cubits

bend

Robinson's Arch
supporting staircase

Straight
Joint

Double Gate   Triple Gate

0   50 yd

0   50 m

☐ square Temple Mount

☐ Hasmonean extension

☐ Herodian expansion

N

The plan at left illustrates the development of the Temple Mount. The original Temple Mount, 500 cubits square, is shown in yellow. A Maccabean (Hasmonean) addition in the 2nd century B.C.E. is in blue on the plan. The area Herod the Great added in the 1st century B.C.E. is in brown. The platform on which the Dome of the Rock now sits is outlined on the area of the original Temple Mount. Eight sets of steps now lead up to this Moslem platform. Only one is not perpendicular to the platform wall that it ascends—the staircase in the northwest corner. This observation led to the discovery of what may be the only exposed First Temple period remains of the Temple Mount.

the London-based Palestine Exploration Fund, even digging deep shafts and lengthy underground tunnels outside the Temple Mount to understand the construction and architecture.

Remember that Jerusalem is protected by deep valleys on all sides except the north, which is the direction from which conquering armies have almost always come. Jerusalem's defenders have always had to pay special attention to the northern line of defense. Warren discovered that a dry moat, or fosse, had been dug 52 feet north of the line of the Moslem platform (and 52 feet north of the northern end of the step/wall that may have been the western wall of the original Temple Mount). Warren called this moat an "excavated ditch," which protected the city from an attack from the north. Both the Greek geographer Strabo (64 B.C.E.–21 C.E.) and Josephus refer to this moat. Josephus tells us that it was filled in by the Roman general Pompey in 63 B.C.E. to enable his soldiers to storm the towers of the pre-Herodian Temple Mount. So the northern wall of the Temple Mount must have been south of this moat, somewhere between the edge of the moat and the present Moslem platform.

The next clue also came from Warren, who had explored the underground structures, such as cisterns, tunnels and rooms, that could be entered from the top of the Temple Mount. One of these underground structures, No. 29 in his plan, was a vaulted room built along the northern edge of the Moslem platform. Warren described the southern wall of this chamber as a "quarried rock scarp." Ritmeyer concluded that this rock scarp was probably cut to hold the foundation for the northern wall of the earlier Temple Mount. The 52 feet from this wall to the dry moat was just enough room for the towers that extended from the wall, as described by Josephus.

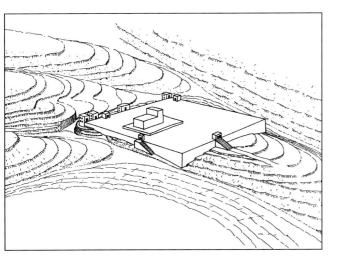

This schematic drawing shows how the original, square Temple Mount might have looked.

Tentatively assuming that this scarp fixed the northern line of the earlier Temple Mount, Ritmeyer extended the line to the line of the step/wall and found that the two lines formed a right angle—the presumed northwestern corner of the earlier, square Temple Mount. Extending the scarp line east to the eastern wall of the Temple Mount enabled Ritmeyer to fix the northeastern corner of the earlier Temple Mount. Only one wall was now missing—the southern wall.

Ritmeyer then measured 500 cubits south on the eastern Temple Mount wall, again examining Warren's plans. He found that Warren had recorded a slight bend in the eastern wall at precisely that point. Ritmeyer noted that "Warren observed this slight bend with his surveying instruments. Presumably it could be confirmed by remeasurement today. However, for political reasons, it is not feasible to undertake this exercise now."

Warren suggested that at the point of the bend the style of the masonry changed—south of this slight bend the masonry was Hasmonean, indicating an Hasmonean extension of the Temple Mount some time before the Herodian extension. But the important point is that this bend fixed the southern wall of the square Temple Mount and tended to confirm the identification of the northern line.

Although the Mishnah does not say that the 500-cubit-square Temple Mount refers to the Solomonic Temple Mount, archaeological evidence does indicate that it probably was square. Professor Avraham Biran of Hebrew Union College in Jerusalem has excavated a *temenos*, or sacred enclosure, at Tel Dan, which,

although much smaller than 500 cubits, is nearly square (see p. 70). The Dan *temenos* was, in all likelihood, built by Jeroboam I, ruler of the northern kingdom of Israel in the 10th century B.C.E., shortly after Solomon's death (1 Kings 12:28–31), probably in conscious imitation of the Temple Mount in Jerusalem with which the Dan *temenos* was intended to compete. The visionary temple described in Ezekiel 40–43 also forms a square—of exactly 500 cubits to a side.

Ritmeyer has other, technical reasons for concluding that he has identified the Temple Mount referred to in the Mishnah.[43] He is careful, however, to call the square Temple Mount he has located the "First Temple period" Temple Mount and not the Solomonic Temple Mount. But there is no reason to believe that the Solomonic Temple Mount was changed in the First Temple period. The

This stairway leads up to the Moslem platform on which the Dome of the Rock stands. Unlike the seven other stairways leading up to the platform, this one is not exactly parallel to the adjacent wall of the platform. Instead, it is precisely parallel to the eastern wall of the Temple Mount. The bottom step, seen in the close-up, consists of very large polished ashlars; it was formerly part of a wall, possibly the western wall of the original Temple Mount. If so, it is the only surviving section of the original Temple Mount that has been exposed.

The temenos *at Tel Dan, as reconstructed at the site, functioned much like the Temple Mount in Jerusalem and was probably built by the northern kingdom of Israel in imitation of the Jerusalem shrine. That the Tel Dan* temenos *was nearly square (60 by 62 feet) suggests that the original Temple Mount platform was also square.*

First Temple was destroyed by the Babylonians in 586 B.C.E. When the exiles returned to rebuild the Temple, they were in no position to enlarge the Temple Mount; they doubtless simply repaired the old one.

If all this is true, the bottom step on the northwestern stairway leading to the Moslem platform may be part of the western wall of the Solomonic Temple Mount.

Looking at this step today, which is level with the adjacent walkway, it appears that it might be composed of street paving stones. The adjacent walkway, however, was only recently laid down by Moslem religious authorities, without approval of the Israel Antiquities Authority. Unfortunately, the new pavement covered the small part of the side of the step/wall that had been exposed. Ritmeyer located a photograph taken before the pavement was laid showing the top of a small, hewn margin on the *side* of the ashlars that make up this step, indicating that they were part of the outside of a wall and not simply paving stones.

Incidentally, if Ritmeyer is correct—and most scholars think he is—his conclusion is inconsistent with a popular recent theory advanced by Hebrew University physics professor Asher Kaufman as to where the Temple was located. Kaufman contends that the Temple was located about 330 feet (100 meters) northwest of the Dome of the Rock.[44] He notes that there is no eastern gateway in the Temple Mount that would lead directly to the Temple if it were located where the Dome of the Rock now stands. Kaufman locates the Temple opposite the Golden Gate, the only gate in the eastern wall that serves the Temple Mount directly.

The Golden Gate is north of the Dome of the Rock. If you enter through the Golden Gate and walk due west, perpendicular to the eastern wall of the

Map of Solomon's Jerusalem

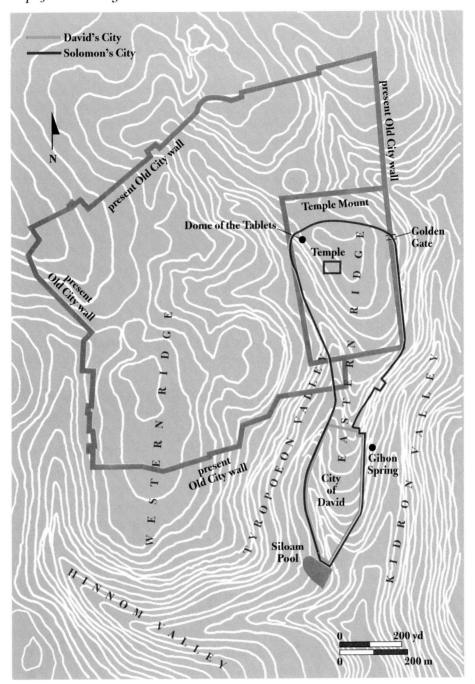

Temple Mount, you come to a little cupola over a flat rock. In Arab tradition, this cupola is known as the Dome of the Tablets (see photo, p. 72), presumably commemorating the site of the Tablets of the Law in the Holy of Holies. The stone is just one meter lower than es-Sakhra ("the Rock" in Arabic), the rock mass sheltered in the Dome of the Rock, the highest point on the Temple Mount.

Kaufman notes the difficulty with placing the Ark of the Covenant on the uneven surface of es-Sakhra, compared to the flat surface under the Dome of the

The Dome of the Tablets on the Temple Mount, where Hebrew University physics professor Asher Kaufman argues the Holy of Holies was located. This theory would place Solomon's Temple north of the Dome of the Rock. However, if placed where Kaufman suggests, part of the Temple compound would have fallen off the original, square Temple Mount identified by Leen Ritmeyer.

Tablets. According to ancient rabbinic sources, the Ark of the Covenant rested on the supposedly flat Foundation Stone (*Even ha-Shetiah*) in the Holy of Holies. By means of careful measurements of certain rock surfaces, rows of stones, the remains of walls and sections of pavement (some of which, unfortunately, have since been covered by the Moslem religious authorities), Kaufman believes he can identify the precise location and design of the Second Temple compound, which he envisions as trapezoidal. The First Temple, that is, Solomon's Temple, was almost surely built on the same spot—north of the Dome of the Rock.

Kaufman has convinced few, if any, archaeologists or biblical scholars of his theory, however. If Ritmeyer is correct regarding the 500-cubit-square Temple Mount, Kaufman must be wrong, because Kaufman's Temple complex, with its adjacent cells and courts, would fall off the northern end of Ritmeyer's square Temple Mount. And the Temple building itself would be perilously close to the edge of the square Temple Mount.

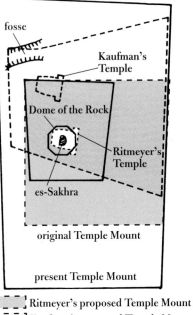

Another bit of probable Solomonic construction takes us back to the Gihon Spring in the City of David, the source of the city's water supply. The Warren's Shaft system was used primarily in time of danger. Ordinarily, it was easier to walk down to the spring outside the wall to get fresh water. But water was also used for irrigation, to increase the yield in the adjacent fields in the Kidron Valley and the King's Garden at the southern end of the City of David. Water from the gushing spring would naturally flow in this direction, but when this happened the flow was largely uncontrolled. It went where it went.

To control and direct the flow, a channel, called the Siloam Channel, was built from the Gihon Spring south, along the eastern slope of the City of David near the valley floor. The Siloam Channel is partly an exposed, rock-hewn, stone-covered channel and partly a rock-hewn tunnel, extending for about 1,300 feet. The channel is about a foot and a half wide and varies in height from about four feet to nine feet. Only about half of the channel has been explored; the rest awaits some enterprising young archaeologist. It is this Siloam Channel that the prophet Isaiah probably refers to when he speaks of "the gently flowing waters of Siloam" (Isaiah 8:5).

In the eastern wall of the Siloam Channel, facing the valley, are windowlike apertures; small dams regulated the water flowing through these windows to agricultural plots in the valley. In addition, these openings captured runoff from exposed rock surfaces higher up on the slope.

The Siloam Channel was useful in another way. It carried water from the Gihon Spring to reservoirs at the southern end of the City of David. These

Most scholars place the Temple on the site of the Dome of the Rock. A widely publicized alternative position is held by Hebrew University professor Asher Kaufman, who places the Temple north of the Dome of the Rock. Kaufman contends that the Temple Mount was a trapezoid that included his location of the Temple. Few, if any, scholars agree with him.

Solomon's Jerusalem

Guided by archaeologists' fragmentary discoveries, an artist has recreated Jerusalem as Solomon would have seen it. The view is from the east, as if one was standing on the Mount of Olives looking over the city to the still barren western hill now called Mount Zion, and north to the Temple Mount. At the far right, on the exposed bedrock of the Temple

Mount, stands Solomon's Temple (1). To its left is the royal palace complex (2) and the Citadel (3), supported by the Stepped-Stone Structure (4). The Gihon Spring (5), outside the city wall, flows underground to Warren's Shaft (6), which makes water available inside the city through the use of a bucket lowered on a rope. The water from the Gihon Spring was also

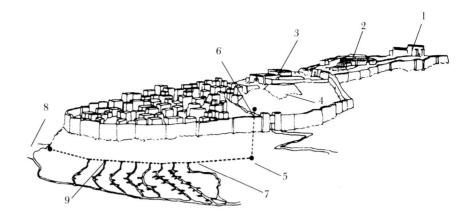

carried through a conduit called the Siloam Channel (7) south along the eastern flank of the hill to a storage pool (8) at the southern end of the city. "Windows" (9) in the channel allowed water to be released into the agricultural plots in the Kidron Valley.

75

The King's Garden was probably located on this site at the southern end of the City of David. In season, it is still fresh and green.

reservoirs were especially important because of the nature of the water flow. Until recent times, the Gihon Spring did not flow constantly, but gushed intermittently. Also, the spring does not lie below a water table. Reservoirs at the southern end of the City of David meant fresh water was conveniently available at any time.

How did the channel operate in conjunction with the Warren's Shaft system? Adjusting small dams near the Gihon Spring's source could determine whether the water flowed through the short tunnel to the base of Warren's Shaft or down the valley through the Siloam Channel.

The Siloam Channel probably dates to King Solomon's reign, according to Shiloh and other scholars. But this is at best just an educated guess that illustrates how difficult it is to date water systems. There are no stratified potsherds by which to date the Siloam Channel. Thus, the first step in dating the Siloam Channel is based on its relationship to the Warren's Shaft system and to a third water system that also begins at the Gihon Spring, the famous Hezekiah's Tunnel.

Hezekiah's Tunnel can be securely dated to the late 8th century B.C.E. by an unusual confluence of biblical texts and an ancient inscription, as we shall see when we examine this third underground water system in some detail in chapter 6. Like the Siloam Channel, Hezekiah's Tunnel carried water from the Gihon Spring to a pool at the southern end of the City of David; but Hezekiah's Tunnel carried water underground, a safe route even in wartime. In some ways,

To irrigate the crop gardens in the Kidron Valley, east of the City of David, King Solomon built a channel that directed the water of the Gihon Spring south. Part of the channel was open and part underground. "Windows" in the channel, like the one pictured here, allowed the water to be periodically diverted to the adjacent valley. The rest of the flow was fed to a pool at the southern end of the city, where it watered the King's Garden.

Hezekiah's Tunnel made the Siloam Channel inoperable. For this and other reasons, scholars have concluded that the Siloam Channel was constructed before Hezekiah's Tunnel—some time before the late 8th century B.C.E. The Siloam Channel also appears to date later than the Warren's Shaft system.

That's the archaeological evidence. To determine more precisely the date of the Siloam Channel, we must turn to history—that is, the Bible. The most likely time of its construction within this historical framework seems to be the reign of King Solomon. If that seems a little wobbly to you, welcome to the club.

VI

The Capital of the Kingdom of Judah

WHEN SOLOMON DIED THE NATION SPLIT APART, AND THE PERIOD known as the Divided Monarchy began. Judah, with the small tribe of Benjamin, formed the southern kingdom of Judah, with its capital in Jerusalem. The ten northern tribes became the northern kingdom of Israel, with its capital first at Shechem, then at Tirzah and finally at Samaria.

Judah, led by Solomon's foolhardy son Rehoboam, fought several bloody wars with Israel, led by Jeroboam (1 Kings 12:24, 14:30; 2 Chronicles 12:15). Challenging the religious centrality of Jerusalem, Jeroboam set up shrines featuring bulls at Bethel and Dan, at opposite ends of the northern kingdom. Some scholars suggest that the bulls were not meant to be worshiped, but were pedestals for the deity, comparable to the cherubim in Solomon's Temple, which appear to have served as the resting place for God's invisible presence.

As the capital of Judah only, Jerusalem declined in significance. Gradually, Solomon's empire was hacked away by internal dissension, secession, revolt—and by the rising imperial power of Assyria. In 721 B.C.E., the expanding Assyrian empire finally snuffed out the northern kingdom of Israel. The inhabitants were deported and became the "ten lost tribes," whose descendants are in far-flung places.

Some of the northerners, however, sought refuge with their brothers in the south, and many of them settled in Jerusalem. At least this is the speculation by experts trying to explain the expansion of the city at about this time.

An ivory pomegranate dating to the 8th century B.C.E. may be the only relic to survive from Solomon's Temple. A hole in the bottom indicates that it was originally the head of a small priestly scepter. An inscription in Old Hebrew carved on the shoulder reads, "Holy to the priests, belonging to the T[emple of Yahwe]h." Yahweh is the personal name of the Israelite God.

79

The archaeological evidence of this expansion resolved a long-standing scholarly disagreement about the size of Jerusalem. The debate was between so-called minimalists and their opponents, the so-called maximalists. The minimalists maintained that Jerusalem was confined to the eastern ridge (east of the Tyropoeon or Central Valley) until the 2nd century B.C.E. The leading proponent of this view was the influential Kathleen Kenyon, who dug several excavation squares on the western ridge and found no walls or buildings earlier than the 2nd century B.C.E. Her views were opposed by some Israeli scholars, who were often viewed skeptically and suspected of harboring nationalist aims that affected their historical conclusions. On the other hand, Kenyon's anti-Israel political views were well known, and her position, too, was suspect.[45]

The argument was finally settled by Israeli excavations after 1967. Digging in the Jewish Quarter of the Old City, Hebrew University professor Nahman Avigad discovered—on the western hill—remains of houses with plastered walls, dating as early as the 8th century B.C.E. The date of the walls was established by abundant potsherds, and even whole vessels, associated with the houses. In other excavations on the western hill, remains from this period have also been found, complementing Avigad's finds in the Jewish Quarter.

The *coup de grace*, however, was Avigad's discovery of a massive wall 23 feet thick, known as the "Broad Wall" (see photo, p. 82). (According to Avigad, this is the Broad Wall referred to in Nehemiah 3:8, where it is said that the wall was *repaired* after the Babylonian Exile.) A wall this thick could only be a city wall. Avigad uncovered more than 210 feet of this wall in his Jewish Quarter excavation; fortunately, the segment he found included an angle, so he could safely reconstruct the wall in two directions. Although the general orientation was north–south, the southern part of the wall contained an angle pointing southwest, indicating that the wall almost surely enclosed the western hill. The maximalists were right. The city had expanded to the western hill by the 8th century B.C.E.

Interestingly, the part of the wall that turned west cut through and destroyed some houses that had been built before the wall. Yet these houses also dated to the 8th century B.C.E. This means there must have been an unwalled settlement on the western hill earlier in the 8th century, before the wall was built. With the exception of a few isolated sherds, no pottery before the 8th century has been found on the western hill, so the westward expansion of the city did not begin until this time; perhaps the inhabitants of the unfortified settlement were mostly refugees from the deteriorating situation in the north. Then in the late 8th century, a new city wall was built on the western side to include residents on the western hill. To build this massive new wall, some of the houses built outside the old wall earlier in the century had to be destroyed.

Evidence from another area confirms that the expansion of the city did not begin until sometime in the 8th century B.C.E. A major excavation led by

For decades scholars were divided between the minimalists, who argued that Jerusalem was confined to the eastern ridge until the 2nd century B.C.E., and the maximalists, who contended that the city spread onto the western ridge as early as the 8th century B.C.E. The argument was finally settled by the discovery of 8th-century B.C.E. houses and a city wall on the western ridge. British archaeologist Kathleen Kenyon, who led the minimalists, was loath to concede, however. Forced to recognize that there was some expansion in the 8th century B.C.E. to the western hill, Kenyon nevertheless maintained that only part of the western hill was inhabited at that time. Strangely, she insisted that the Siloam Pool, which was designed to provide a secure water source inside the city, remained outside the city wall.

Professor Benjamin Mazar south and southwest of the Temple Mount extended as far as the slope of the Central Valley, where Mazar found some cave tombs, which he dated to the 8th century B.C.E. Tombs within the walls would have polluted the city and were forbidden (with the exception of royal tombs); therefore, this area must have been outside the city until the 8th century B.C.E.*

The picture we get is that until the 8th century, Jerusalem was confined to the eastern hill. At that time, it began expanding west, mostly with refugees from the northern kingdom of Israel. Toward the end of the century, the western hill was enclosed within a new city wall.

The Bible tends to confirm this interpretation. In 2 Chronicles 32, we are told of Hezekiah's preparations for Sennacherib's 8th-century siege of Jerusalem. Hezekiah rebuilt the part of the city wall that had a breach in it, he raised some towers on the wall, and *"outside it he built another wall"* (2 Chronicles 32:5, italics added). The Broad Wall, then, is Hezekiah's new wall.

There may even be biblical confirmation that Hezekiah had to demolish some Israelite houses to build this new wall. In one of Isaiah's visions, in which he probably refers to Sennacherib's siege of Jerusalem ("They stormed at Judah's gateway" [Isaiah 22:7]), the prophet says, presumably of Hezekiah's administration, "You took note of the many breaches in the City of David...you counted the houses of Jerusalem and *pulled houses down to fortify the wall"* (Isaiah 22:9–10, italics added).

After the fall of the northern kingdom in 721 B.C.E., the Assyrians advanced

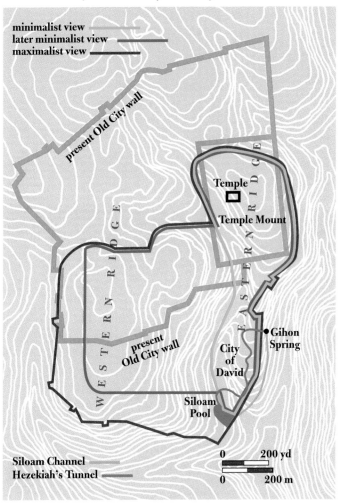

Three Views of 8th-Century B.C.E. Jerusalem

minimalist view
later minimalist view
maximalist view

present Old City wall

Temple

Temple Mount

WESTERN RIDGE

EASTERN RIDGE

present Old City wall

City of David

Gihon Spring

Siloam Pool

Siloam Channel
Hezekiah's Tunnel

0   200 yd
0   200 m

down the Mediterranean coast all the way to the Egyptian border. By Hezekiah's time, the southern kingdom, Judah, was already paying tribute to Assyria. But Hezekiah was not without his military successes. He had driven the Philistines in the southwest back to the coastal area along the Mediterranean. Perhaps encouraged by this success, he formed an alliance with Egypt and attempted to throw

*Tombs are often helpful in establishing the bounds of a city because the tomb can be presumed to be outside the city.

The Broad Wall,
built by King Heze-
kiah in the 8th
century B.C.E. and
mentioned in the
Bible, is 23 feet wide
and probably stood to
a height of about 27
feet. It enclosed the
expanded areas of the
city with a protective
wall. At the photo's
bottom left corner are
the remains of an
8th-century B.C.E.
house, partially
destroyed to construct
the Broad Wall.

off the Assyrian yoke. With more chutzpah than caution, he refused to pay the required Assyrian tribute. Hezekiah surely must have known that his little mountain kingdom was no match for the Assyrian hordes. Nevertheless, he was apparently successful in defying Assyrian power for a time. But when the inevitable Assyrian counterattack came, it burst forth with terrifying force.

In 701 B.C.E., the great Assyrian ruler Sennacherib devastated the major Judahite city of Lachish, about 30 miles southwest of Jerusalem. In fact, many Judahite cities—46, according to an Assyrian cuneiform account—were destroyed. Hezekiah sued for peace and agreed to pay Sennacherib whatever tribute he imposed if he would withdraw from the land. Hezekiah stripped the silver and gold from the Temple as booty for the Assyrian monarch (2 Kings 18:13–16). But even then, the Assyrians did not withdraw their armies. Flushed with victory, Sennacherib laid siege to Jerusalem.[46]

The prophet Isaiah, who had advised against Hezekiah's alliance with Egypt, inveighed against the land with some of the most powerful words ever uttered by a prophet:

> O sinful nation, people loaded with iniquity…
> Your country is desolate, your cities lie in ashes;
> Strangers devour your land before your eyes…
> Only Zion [Jerusalem] is left…
> Your countless sacrifices, what are they to me?
>   says the Lord.
> I am sated with the whole-offerings of rams and
>   the fat of buffaloes…
> Though you offer countless prayers,
> I will not listen…
> Put away the evil of your deeds,
>   away out of my sight.
> Cease to do evil and learn to do right,
> Pursue justice and champion the oppressed;
> Give the orphan his rights, plead the widow's cause…
> Then though your sins are scarlet,
> They may become white as snow…
> Then I will secure a respite from my foes
>   and take vengeance on my enemies…
> Then…you shall be called
>   the home of righteousness, the faithful city.
> Justice shall redeem Zion
>   and righteousness her repentant people.
>   Isaiah 1:4–27

This cuneiform prism contains an account of the siege of Jerusalem by the Assyrian ruler Sennacherib in 701 B.C.E. Although Sennacherib boasts that he made Hezekiah "a prisoner in Jerusalem, his royal residence, like a bird in a cage," Sennacherib does not claim to have conquered the city.

The Assyrian siege of Jerusalem was unsuccessful; and although we don't know for sure what broke the siege, we do know how the Israelites inside the city managed to hold out.

We have already looked at the wall Hezekiah built to protect the new settlement on the western hill outside the old wall. But Hezekiah did a great deal more to prepare for the siege he clearly saw coming. He organized the city militarily, appointing battle officers; he collected a large quantity of weapons and shields (2 Chronicles 32:5–6). And with words, the Judahite king encouraged and inspired his people. In a biblically recorded speech, he addressed them:

> Be strong; be brave. Do not let the king of Assyria or the rabble he has
> brought with him strike terror or panic in your hearts. We have more on
> our side than he has. He has human strength. But we have the Lord our
> God to help us and to fight our battles.
>
> 2 Chronicles 32:7–8

Before the siege, Sennacherib's emissaries to Jerusalem delivered a message to Hezekiah's people. The core of the message was this: "Hezekiah is misleading you into risking death by famine and thirst when he tells you that the Lord your God will save you" (2 Chronicles 32:11). Sennacherib obviously intended to capture the city by starving the Jerusalemites and depriving them of water. Thirst was the threat Sennacherib considered to be most fearsome. So in addition to laying up vast stores of food, Hezekiah had ingeniously made available to the besieged city the life-giving waters of the Gihon Spring—a fact of which Sennacherib was apparently unaware.

In addition to his other preparations, Hezekiah constructed a new 1,750-foot tunnel underneath the City of David, so that the Gihon Spring now flowed into the Pool of Siloam at the southwestern corner of the city (see map, p. 81). Sennacherib's taunt that the Judahites would die of thirst proved, in the end, to be mere braggadocio.

Jerusalem may well have been saved by Hezekiah's extraordinary tunnel, a remarkable engineering feat for its time and clearly recognized as such. The biblical description is vivid:

> When Hezekiah saw that Sennacherib intended to attack Jerusalem, he
> planned with his civil and military officers to stop up the water of the
> springs outside the city; and they supported him. They gathered together
> a large number of people and stopped up all the springs and the stream
> which flowed through the land [perhaps a reference to the Siloam Channel]. "Why should the kings of Assyria come here and find much water?"
> they asked...Hezekiah closed the upper outlet of the waters of Gihon
> and directed them down to the west side of the City of David.
>
> 2 Chronicles 32:2–4, 30

Hezekiah's Tunnel, which brought the water of the Gihon Spring, outside the city, to a reservoir within the city, played a crucial role in breaking Sennacherib's late-8th-century B.C.E. siege of Jerusalem. The tunnel was doubtless a major engineering feat for its time and is referred to in the Bible.

The account of Hezekiah's reign in the Second Book of Kings concludes:

> The rest of the deeds of Hezekiah, his exploits and how he made the [Siloam] Pool and the conduit and brought water into the city are recorded in the Book of Chronicles of the Kings of Judah.
>
> 2 Kings 20:20

Obviously the tunnel was one of Hezekiah's major accomplishments.

The tunnel starts, as would be expected, at the Gihon Spring and incorporates the short, irregular tunnel leading to the bottom of Warren's Shaft (this use of part of the Warren's Shaft system shows that Hezekiah's Tunnel is later). Hezekiah's Tunnel then veers off at a 90 degree angle to the left, following its own serpentine path under the city and debouching a third of a mile away, on

The Siloam Pool, where the water from Hezekiah's Tunnel debouches.

the other side of the hill, into the Pool of Siloam (not to be confused with the Siloam Channel).

The tunnel was dug by two crews digging in opposite directions. We know this from what is considered the most important ancient monumental Hebrew inscription ever found, the Siloam inscription. The inscription was carved into the wall of Hezekiah's Tunnel about 20 feet from the exit into the Siloam Pool, where the tunnel is almost 15 feet high. It commemorates the dramatic moment when the two crews of tunnelers met.

The letters are in Old Hebrew (sometimes called Paleo-Hebrew), the kind used before the Babylonian Exile. When the Jews returned from the Babylonian Exile, they brought with them the square Aramaic letters used to write Hebrew to this day. The only exceptions are texts that use the old-style script in an archaizing manner, as on coins of the First and Second Jewish Revolt (1st and 2nd centuries C.E.), where the old script was used for nationalistic reasons. Another example is in texts among the Dead Sea Scrolls, where the name of God (YHWH) is often written in Old Hebrew letters. But before the Babylonian Exile, Hebrew was always written in these Old Hebrew letters, as is the case with the Siloam inscription.

The Siloam inscription was discovered in 1880 by some boys swimming in the Pool of Siloam. Soon thereafter vandals recklessly chiseled the inscription out of the rock. The pieces ended up in the shop of an antiquities dealer, where Ottoman authorities discovered them. They were then shipped to Constantinople (now Istanbul). I have argued in *Biblical Archaeology Review* that the inscription should be returned to Jerusalem,[47] at least on loan. As of this writing, the Israel Museum is trying to arrange to have the inscription on loan for the 3,000th anniversary celebration. The most recent word is that the Turkish authorities have agreed.

The rock panel on which the inscription was carved was carefully prepared and smoothed (see photo, p. 88). The inscription was written only on the bottom half, however. We can only wonder what the intended beginning of the inscription was. The part that was engraved begins in the middle of a sentence. It reads:

> ...breakthrough. And this was the account of the breakthrough. While the laborers were still working with their picks, each toward the other, and while there were still three cubits to be broken through, the voice of each was heard calling to the other, because there was a *zdh** in the rock to the south and to the north. And at the moment of the breakthrough, the laborers struck each toward the other, pick against pick. Then the water flowed from the spring to the pool for 1,200 cubits. And the height of the rock above the heads of the laborers was 100 cubits.

Interestingly enough, the inscription does not mention Hezekiah's name. Perhaps the upper part of the inscription was never completed, and Hezekiah's name would have been mentioned there. But there is also another possibility. The Siloam inscription is written, not from the viewpoint of the king, as royal inscriptions are, but from the viewpoint of the workmen. "While the laborers were still working..." The highlight of the description is the dramatic breakthrough, the moment when the workmen met: "At the moment of the breakthrough, the laborers struck each toward the other..."

---

*Perhaps "split," "crack" or "overlap"; the etymology and meaning of *zdh* are still disputed.

The Siloam inscription, carved in the wall of Hezekiah's Tunnel and chiseled out by vandals, memorializes the meeting of the two teams of tunnelers who dug from opposite directions. Carved in Old Hebrew letters, the inscription is now in the Istanbul Archaeological Museum.

The inscription celebrates the sheer scale of the project and includes details of the measurements and a tribute to the engineering achievement. Remember, too, that this inscription was not meant for public display. It was located 20 feet into the tunnel, where it was barely visible. One scholar has insightfully suggested that the inscription was sponsored by the engineers of the project, not by the king—which might explain why Hezekiah is not mentioned.[48]

Scholars have long wondered how the two teams of tunnelers, starting from different sides of the city and following such a circuitous route, managed to meet. Somehow, without any of the tools used by modern engineers, without even a magnetic compass, they miraculously did meet. Another anomaly: If they had dug in a straight line, the distance would have been 1,050 feet instead of 1,750 feet. By following an S-shaped route underground, they increased the distance by more than 65 percent. Why?

Long ago it was suggested that the large southern curve was made to avoid desecrating the royal tombs above. But what about the northern curve? Most of the other suggestions that have been offered make even less sense. But Dan Gill, the geologist who explained Warren's Shaft, also explained the route of Hezekiah's Tunnel: It too started as a natural opening. No doubt, the tunnel had to be enlarged and shaped, but the route was already there.

If Hezekiah's Tunnel started as a natural fissure, that not only explains the circuitous route and how the two teams of tunnelers managed to meet, but it also solves another puzzle unnoticed by previous investigators: How did tunnelers working at the blind end of a narrow passage get enough air to survive, especially using oil-burning lamps?

Several telltale signs in the tunnel indicate that it started out as a natural fissure: The height varies from 4.75 feet in some places in the northern half to 16.5 feet at the southern end. Obviously, no one would have deliberately dug a tunnel with such irregular heights (see photos, p. 90). The tunnelers certainly had no reason to excavate an area with such an unnecessarily high ceiling. Where the channel's original opening was too low, the tunnelers raised the ceiling; this is clear from their pick marks on the smoothly hewn rock plane. Where the ceiling is high, however, the ceiling is irregular, rough bedrock, the original natural dissolution channel.

The fact that the ceiling at the southern end is so high indicates something else: The dissolution channel originally flowed to the north. The height of the ceiling at the southern end shows that the floor was originally much higher at this end. After enlarging the natural dissolution tunnel, the tunnelers no doubt discovered that the channel ran in the wrong direction. They therefore had to "straighten down," which they did with extraordinary precision. The floor of Hezekiah's Tunnel now proceeds down a smooth but very slight slope from the Gihon Spring to the Pool of Siloam, descending just 12.5 inches in the course of 1,750 feet. Having demonstrated the precision with which the floor was executed, it is difficult to attribute anomalies like the varied height of the ceiling or the circuitous route to incompetence or carelessness.

It would be nice if that were the end of the story: Everything would be wrapped up so neatly. But at least two difficulties remain that are not explained by the natural fissure theory. At my urging, Gill discussed them in an article in *Biblical Archaeology Review*, although they appear only in a footnote at the end.

The Siloam inscription seems to celebrate the "breakthrough," when the two teams of tunnelers met. It suggests that they were able to find each other when one crew heard the voices of the other. If they were already connected by a dissolution channel, what was the big deal?

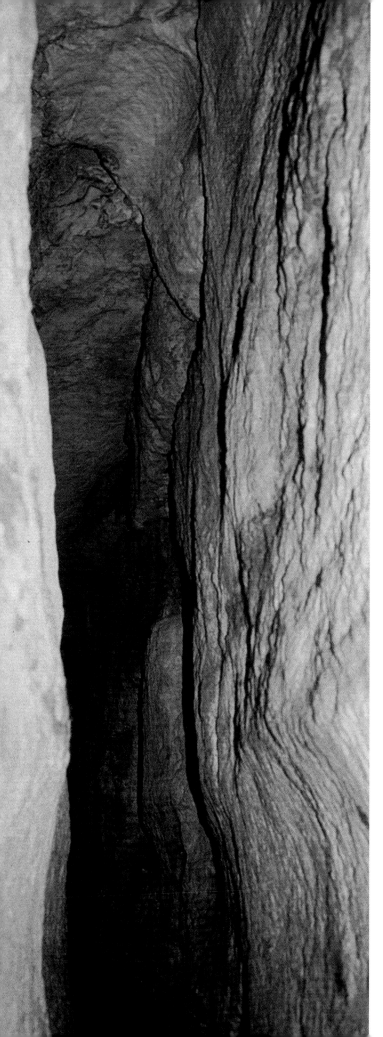

The ceiling in Hezekiah's Tunnel, seen at left, is more than 16 feet high at the southern end. The ceiling at this point is in its natural condition, without pick marks. The tunnelers would never have dug a tunnel over 16 feet high. All this supports the theory that the tunnelers exploited a natural fissure when they began the tunnel.

A false tunnel that the tunnelers quickly abandoned (above) suggests that they had difficulty meeting those who were digging from the opposite end. The frenzied effort of the two teams of tunnelers to meet in the middle is reflected in the twists and turns of the pick marks near the point of meeting (near left). If the way was marked by a natural fissure in the rock, why were the tunnelers so uncertain of their direction?

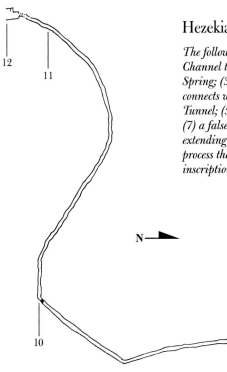

Hezekiah 's Tunnel

The following points are indicated: (1) The beginning of the Siloam Channel to irrigate fields in the Kidron Valley; (2) the source of the Gihon Spring; (3) the opening of a passage of unknown purpose to the south that connects with the Siloam Channel; (4) the beginning of Hezekiah's Tunnel; (5) Warren's Shaft water system; (6) the point of meeting; (7) a false tunnel; (8) a false tunnel; (9) a false tunnel; (10) a sinkhole extending from the ceiling up to ground level caused by the same natural process that created Warren's Shaft; (11) the place from which the Siloam inscription was removed; (12) the Pool of Siloam.

The Siloam inscription is not the only indication that it was not easy for the tunnelers to meet; the tunnel itself reveals this. We can tell where the tunnelers met by the change in direction of the pickax marks. On both sides of the meeting point are what appear to be short, one might even say frenzied, twists and turns in the direction of the tunnel, seemingly efforts to locate the tunnelers on the other side. These twists and turns start when the tunnelers were about 100 feet apart.

How can we explain these zigzags just before the point of meeting? Here is Gill's answer: "Another problem is the frequent meandering near the meeting point. This may simply be the course of the original karst (an irregular limestone region with sinks, underground streams and caverns) conduit. That is the best answer I can think of."[49] It's not a very satisfying answer.

There is yet another problem. There are three beautifully chiseled "false tunnels" about three feet long, two with flat ceilings and straight walls. All three are near the meeting point. It looks like these were simply mistakes, places where tunnelers went off in the wrong direction, perhaps misled by echoes. What purpose could these "false tunnels" have served if the natural channel connected before the tunnelers met? Gill suggests that the tunnelers may have been misled by a fork in the original channel and that they may have enlarged the wrong fork before discovering their mistake. Alternatively, he suggests the false starts may have been intentionally created to allow two-way traffic for maintenance personnel who periodically cleaned the tunnel of debris. To me, both explanations seem a bit forced, and no better one has been offered.

There is no question, however, that the two sides did meet, and this tunnel probably saved Jerusalem from destruction by Sennacherib.

The Bible records both Hezekiah's military prowess and his religious devotion. He is even compared to King David (2 Kings 18:3). Hezekiah's religious convictions may well have been influenced by his contemporary, the prophet Isaiah. Several passages from Isaiah were appropriated word-for-word in passages in the Second Book of Kings relating to Hezekiah. And when Hezekiah fell ill, Isaiah promised him he would be healed—and he was.

Hezekiah was also responsible for instituting a religious reform that scholars regularly refer to as Hezekiah's Reform.

As part of this reform, Hezekiah destroyed a bronze serpent that had been in existence since the time of Moses, to which people offered sacrifices (2 Kings 18:4). Archaeology gives us a pretty good idea of what this serpent looked like, as several have been found in excavations. One of the most beautiful—even the gilding on the head has survived—was discovered by Beno Rothenberg in a Midianite shrine at Timna, near Eilat. It dates to the 13th or 12th century B.C.E.—the very time of Moses.

Hezekiah also "smashed the [sacred] pillars [to pagan gods] and cut down the sacred post" (2 Kings 18:4). But his most important measure was to centralize worship in the Jerusalem Temple, outlawing shrines elsewhere in the kingdom. As the Bible puts it, he "abolished the shrines" (2 Kings 18:4).

Hezekiah's religious reform thus had two sides: First, he sought to purify the cult by removing pagan deities and their paraphernalia. And second, he attempted to establish control over the priests and to curtail their political power by confining religious devotion to the Jerusalem Temple.

That Israelite religious devotion badly needed purifying is amply demonstrated by the archaeological record. Kenyon found what she called a *favissa*, a repository of vessels and other objects, mostly broken, that had been deposited in a sanctuary (see drawing, p. 95). The *favissa* was located just outside the eastern wall of the City of David. Among the 1,300 objects in the *favissa*, she found 429 human and animal figurines. Most of the human figurines were so-called pillar figurines, small statuettes of women with flaring pillar-like bases and exaggerated breasts. These figurines are frequently interpreted as fertility figurines, perhaps similar to the *teraphim* Rachel stole from her father, Laban, when she left with Jacob for the Promised Land (Genesis 31:19).

The animal figurines in the *favissa* were mostly horses, sometimes with riders, and are more difficult to interpret. They are certainly not toys, as some have suggested. They date to about the 8th century B.C.E.

In Nahman Avigad's excavations in the Jewish Quarter of the Old City, he found numerous female figurines dating to the same period (see photo, p. 94). In short, these figurines were not uncommon. Hundreds have been recovered, even in the holy city of Jerusalem. In fact, they have been found all over Judah, often in private houses.

Some scholars have argued that with the help of archaeology we can get a picture of "popular" religion, as opposed to the "elite" religion reflected in the Bible. The figurines and other evidence of non-monotheistic and anthropomorphic aspects of religious observance are supposed to represent what really went on, as opposed to what the Bible suggests.

This analysis is faulty on several scores. First, the Bible itself tells about the transgressions of the people. But more importantly, a sharp division between popular religion and elite religion is overly simplistic. To understand Israelite religion, we must appreciate two things. First, at any given time, Israelite religious understanding embraced a range of conceptions, just like modern Christianity and Judaism, from the highly elevated to the pagan, with many conceptions in between. A sharp dichotomy between elite and popular religion is artificial.

Second, Israelite monotheism developed over time. Moreover, the biblical text often reflects religious beliefs of the period of composition (or later editing), rather than the period being written about. For example, in a passage noted earlier from Solomon's prayer upon the dedication of the Temple, Solomon asks: "But will

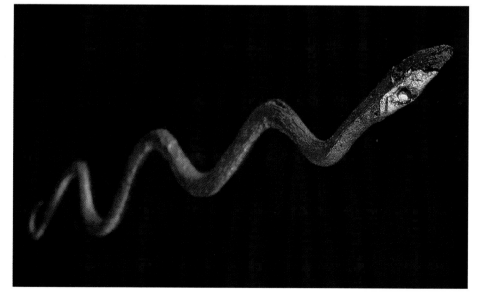

As part of his religious reform, Hezekiah destroyed a bronze serpent that had existed since Moses' time. Serpents were commonly featured in religious rituals, as illustrated by the ceramic snake on this contemporaneous offering stand from Beth Shean (at left) and a copper snake with a gilded head (at right) from the 13th–12th century B.C.E. (the time of Moses) found in a Midianite shrine near Eilat.

Female figurines from the 9th to the 7th centuries B.C.E. were abundant in Jerusalem. Probably fertility figurines, they may represent the pagan goddess Asherah, frequently condemned in the Bible. The head, made from a mold, was attached to a flaring base with exaggerated breasts.

God really dwell on earth?" (1 Kings 8:27). The prayer is obviously intended to negate the idea that God dwells in the Temple, as pagan gods are supposed to do. Even heaven and earth cannot contain the Israelite God, Solomon's prayer tells us, for he is everywhere.

The ideology embedded in this prayer probably dates from later than Solomon's time. When the Temple was built, it was probably thought of as God's dwelling place. At least this part of Solomon's prayer may be a later, 7th-century B.C.E. composition inserted by an editor usually identified by scholars as the Deuteronomist.* Israelite theology was highly developed by Hezekiah's time, as is reflected by great 8th-century literary prophets like Isaiah, Amos and Micah. Hezekiah, no doubt, meant to proclaim their theology. But he was not entirely successful, as we know by the fact that King Josiah, nearly a century later, undertook another religious reform, in many respects similar to Hezekiah's. But more of that later.

A unique relic of priestly religiosity has survived from Hezekiah's time. It is a tiny ivory pomegranate that was once the head of a scepter used by the priests in the Solomonic Temple (see photo, p. 78). Unfortunately, this artifact was not recovered from a scientific excavation (unless it was stolen from one), but surfaced in the antiquities market, where French scholar André Lemaire found it in a Jerusalem antiquities shop. No one knows where it came from. At first some scholars suspected it was a fake. But doubts evaporated when experts examined

*The deuteronomistic history is composed of Deuteronomy and the books of Joshua, Judges, Samuel and Kings.

the Hebrew letters carefully carved on the shoulder of the pomegranate under a microscope (see photo, p. 96).

The inscription is the key to identifying the pomegranate. Unfortunately, one side of the ball of the pomegranate is missing, so part of the inscription is also missing and must be reconstructed. The part of the inscription that has survived is clear, however, and there is no question about the reading. It reads as follows, with the reconstructed part in brackets: "Holy to the priests, belonging to the T[emple of Yahwe]h."

The Hebrew word for "temple" (incidentally, the same as the word for "house") is *beyt*. The first letter of this three-letter word (in Hebrew, written without consonants) is clearly there, as are parts of the other two letters. Scholars all agree that the word must be reconstructed as *beyt*.

Beyt Yahweh is not quite as certain, however. Only the last letter of the name of the Israelite God Yahweh (YHWH) has survived. A few scholars suggest that it could be something else that ends in "h," for example, the pagan goddess Asherah ('ŠRH). But this is a distinctly minority view. (There is no record, archaeological or literary, for example, of a temple to Asherah). Most scholars who have studied the problem agree that the inscription refers to the Israelite God Yahweh.

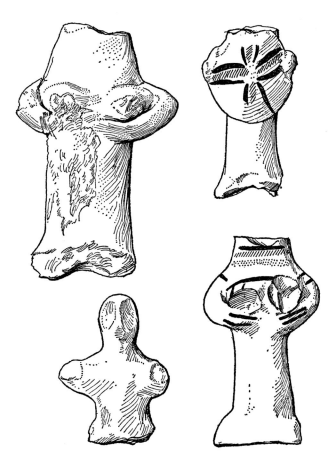

Three of the world's greatest paleographers—experts in the study of the development of script—agree that the shape and form of the letters in the inscription indicate that it dates to the mid- or late 8th century B.C.E. They are Frank Cross of Harvard, the late Nahman Avigad of Hebrew University and André Lemaire of the College de France and the Centre National de la Recherche Scientifique, in Paris. Thus attribution to Hezekiah's time is reasonably assured.

We know that the ivory pomegranate was once the head of a scepter because it is similar to a number of other scepter heads, some of them pomegranate scepters, and because of the small hole in the bottom of the pomegranate where the scepter rod fit in. This ivory pomegranate, now on exhibit in the Israel Museum, is the only surviving relic from Solomon's Temple.

Some of the more than 1,300 objects found in a Jerusalem favissa, *a repository of usually broken objects that had been used at a sanctuary, perhaps as votive offerings.*

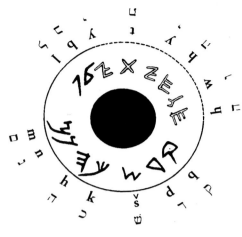

The inscription around the shoulder of the ivory pomegranate, also pictured on page 78, is written in Old Hebrew letters, the kind used before the Babylonian Exile. It reads as follows: "Holy to the priests, belonging to the T[emple of Yahwe]h." (The part in brackets was destroyed and has been reconstructed.) The pomegranate has been dated by the shape and stance of these letters to the 8th century B.C.E. In the drawing, existing letters and parts of letters are in solid black; reconstructed letters are outlined. On the outer rings, the Old Hebrew letters are identified in Roman and in modern Hebrew letters.

According to the Bible, Hezekiah's son Manasseh reversed many of the religious reforms his father had instituted. Manasseh rebuilt the altars of Baal, served Asherah, practiced witchcraft, sacrificed infants and "worshiped all the host of heaven" (2 Chronicles 33:1–9).

Manasseh's grandson Josiah was apparently raised by a tutor in the religious tradition of Hezekiah. Josiah ascended the throne at the age of only eight and reigned for 31 years, from about 639 to 608 B.C.E. By the time he was 16, he was already abolishing the "high places" and destroying pagan pillars, Baal altars, and carved and cast idols (2 Chronicles 34:3–4). And indeed, Josiah is best known for his religious reforms—Josiah's Reform, scholars call it.

A critical event in Josiah's reign occurred when, during repairs to the Temple, a "book of the Law" (or scroll of Teaching, according to the New Jewish Publication Society translation) was "found" by the high priest Hilkiah (2 Kings 22:8; compare 2 Chronicles 34:14–15). The scroll was read to Josiah, who appointed a five-*man* committee, including the high priest, a scribe and the prime minister, to determine the authority of the scroll. The prophets Jeremiah, Zephaniah and Nahum all lived nearby at the time, but this all-male committee didn't take the scroll to any of them for authentication. Instead, they took it to a woman, a prophetess from Jerusalem named

Huldah, whose judgment was that the scroll was authentic and that it reflected divine authority.

And this judgment was thereafter accepted by everyone. This is the first recorded instance of Scripture being declared of divine origin. The remarkable thing about this episode is that the male-female aspect of the story was completely unremarked. No one considered it the least bit inappropriate that an all-male committee took the Scroll of the Law to a woman to determine its status. When she declared it the word of the Lord, no one questioned her authority to determine the issue. This episode is often overlooked by scholars assessing the role of women in ancient Israel.[50] Incidentally, the southern gates of the Temple Mount—the Double Gate and the Triple Gate—are named for Huldah the prophetess.

Most scholars agree that the book "found" during Josiah's repairs of the Temple was an early form of the Book of Deuteronomy, which consists of a retelling of Israel's history in the words of Moses and includes large legal sections binding on the people.

The name Hilkiah, the high priest credited with finding the book of Deuteronomy, appears on a beautiful ancient seal that is especially unusual because it is still in its finger ring. It is not Hilkiah's own seal, but it may be that of his son. It is a typical seal of the period, written in the same Old Hebrew letters as the Siloam inscription. Engraved in blue agate, it reads: "Belonging to Hanan, son of Hilkiyahu, the priest." As is standard, the inscription is engraved in mirror image so that when impressed in the clay bulla used to seal documents it would read correctly. Like many seals from this time, this one is aniconic (that is, with no figures, human or animal) and the lines of script are separated by thin double lines.

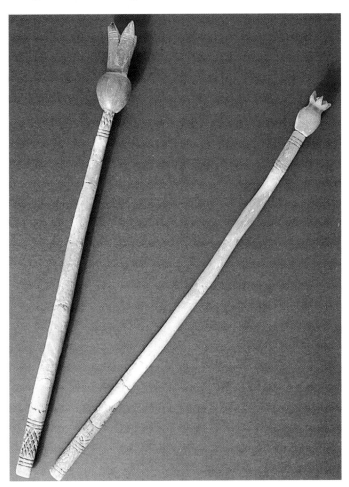

These ivory-headed pomegranate scepters with extant rods found in other excavations dispel any doubt that the ivory pomegranate was once the head of a small scepter.

Hilkiyahu is the Hebrew form of the name translated in English Bibles as Hilkiah. Whether "the priest" refers to the owner of the seal or his father is not clear from the text alone. But from other seals, we know that the priest referred to in the seal is Hanan, not Hilkiah; whenever a title or position is included in a seal inscription, it is the title of the owner.

97

This typical and remarkably preserved seal (top left) mentions Hilkiah. This may be the same Hilkiah who found an early form of the Book of Deuteronomy during King Josiah's 7th-century B.C.E. religious reform, as described in the Book of Kings. The three lines of script are in Old Hebrew letters. The letters on the seal are in mirror image so they will be readable when impressed into a clay bulla, as appears in the drawing (top right). The clay bulla at lower left (drawing, lower right), found in a recent excavation in the City of David, bears an impression of the seal of "Azariah son of Hilkiah." Azariah, a high priest in the 7th century B.C.E., was the grandfather of Ezra.

But if Hanan was a priest, his father was also a priest, perhaps even a high priest. There are several reasons to believe that this Hilkiah is the high priest who "found" the Book of Deuteronomy in addition to the fact that the name is right and the time is right. Although we don't know where the seal and ring were discovered—like the ivory pomegranate, it surfaced on the antiquities market rather than in an excavation—in all probability it came from Judah. The suffix *-yahu* (-YHW) in personal names is typical of the southern kingdom of Judah. In the northern kingdom of Israel, the same name would be Hilki*yo* (suffix -YW, instead of -YHW). Because Josiah had abolished all veneration of Yahweh outside of Jerusalem, Hanan (and his father) probably served as priests in the Jerusalem Temple.

One problem with this identification, however, is that 1 Chronicles 5:39 and 9:11 list Azariah, not Hanan, as the son of Hilkiah. Perhaps Azariah was Hilkiyahu's eldest son and Hanan was a younger son.

But even if this isn't the famous Hilkiah, we have another artifact that may refer to him. In his excavations in the City of David, Yigal Shiloh found a hoard of bullae that date to this same period. One of these bullae was impressed with the seal of "Azaryahu [Azariah], son of Hilkiyahu [Hilkiah]." We don't have the designation "priest" or "high priest" on this seal, but the name of the father and son are right and the time is right. It is quite likely that the Hilkiyahu mentioned on at least one of these seals is the Hilkiah credited with finding the Book of Deuteronomy.[51]

After the Scroll of the Law (Deuteronomy) was authenticated by Huldah, Josiah himself went to the Temple and read the scroll to all the people. He then solemnized a new covenant with the Lord—that the people "would follow the Lord and observe His commandments, His injunctions, and His laws with all their heart and soul; that they would fulfill all the terms of this covenant as inscribed upon the scroll. And all the people entered into the covenant" (2 Kings 23:3).

Hilkiah and the other priests then removed from the Temple all the objects made for Baal and Asherah, burning them in the Kidron Valley. Josiah also shut down all the other shrines in Judah, once again to centralize worship of Yahweh in Jerusalem.

Finally, Josiah "did away with the horses that the kings of Judah had dedicated to the sun, at the entrance of the Temple of the Lord" (2 Kings 23:11). We have some idea what these horses dedicated to the sun actually looked like. In Kenyon's excavation in the City of David, she found a miniature horse with a sun-disc on its forehead. In short, the biblical writer was not simply making things up.

Before leaving First Temple Jerusalem, we should look briefly at some remarkable tombs of the period—across the Kidron Valley from the City of David on the slope below the Arab village of Silwan. Tel Aviv University archaeologist David Ussishkin surveyed these 50 cave tombs and was able to trace their rather extraordinary history: Initially, they were cut out of the rock as tombs for the wealthy and influential in the 9th to 7th centuries B.C.E. Each tomb has an exceptional view of the city across the valley. Many bear the

King Josiah removed statues of horses dedicated to the sun from the Temple entrance as part of his religious reform. This small clay horse, with a sun-disc between his ears, was excavated in the City of David and illustrates the reality of what King Josiah opposed.

Silwan villagers have now incorporated this First Temple period tomb chamber into their home.

stylistic marks of the First Temple period, including stone burial benches carved in the bedrock and some curved and horseshoe-shaped headrests. One of these First Temple tombs was remodeled in the style of a Second Temple tomb—with loculi (*kochim*), long narrow niches for interment, carved into the walls of the burial chambers.

When the Romans rebuilt Jerusalem in the 2nd century C.E. as a Roman city named Aelia Capitolina, they used this area as a quarry and destroyed many of the tombs. Later, in the Byzantine period, Christian monks lived in the caves. Still later, homeless Moslems inhabited the caves. Today, they sometimes form the basements of Arab homes.

The Tomb of the Royal Steward (below). The inscription (above and at left), originally over the tomb entrance, is now in the British Museum. Although found in 1874, the inscription defied decipherment until 1953, when Hebrew University professor Nahman Avigad succeeded in translating it. The prophet Isaiah castigated a high-ranking official (literally one "who is over the house") for preparing an extravagant burial site for himself. Isaiah was probably referring to this tomb that was made, according to the inscription, for a high official "who is over the house."

In 1870, the great French scholar Charles Clermont-Ganneau discovered a Hebrew inscription over the entrance to one of these tombs. The inscription was already badly mutilated, and to prevent further destruction, it was removed. It is now in the British Museum in London.

For nearly 80 years, scholars tried unsuccessfully to decipher the inscription. Only in 1953 was the impossible accomplished—by Hebrew University professor Nahman Avigad. His brilliant decipherment is now conceded on all sides—and the tomb has very probably been identified as belonging to a high official named Shebna in the service of King Hezekiah (8th-7th centuries B.C.E.). Both Shebna and this very tomb are apparently referred to by the prophet Isaiah. Nearly a century before Josiah's reform, Isaiah castigated Shebna for preparing too elegant a tomb for himself in the Silwan cliff:

A First Temple period toilet seat in situ *above a cesspit (at left); the cesspit disclosed to excavators much about the diet of the inhabitants. The close-up reveals a separate hole in the toilet seat apparently for male urination. The bowl next to the toilet seat might have been used for water as a flushing agent or to pour a liming agent into the cesspit.*

> Thus said my Lord God of Hosts: "Go in to see that steward, that Shebna in charge of the palace [literally, who is over the house]:
>> 'What have you here, and whom have you here,
>> That you have hewn out a tomb for yourself here?—
>> O you who have hewn your tomb on high;
>> O you who have hollowed out for yourself an abode in the cliff!
>> The Lord is about to shake you.' "
>
> Isaiah 22:15–17

Because this passage identifies Shebna as the royal steward in charge of the king's house (or palace), the inscription has become known as the Royal Steward inscription. As deciphered by Avigad, it reads as follows:

> This is [the sepulchre of] -*yahu* who is over the house. There is no silver and no gold here, but [his bones] and the bones of his *amah* (probably wife) with him. Cursed be the man who will open this.

Unfortunately, only the last part of the man's name, -*yahu*, has survived in the inscription. This is a common suffix in Judahite personal names and refers

to Yahweh, the personal name of the Israelite God. Presumably the full name was Shebnayahu. The title, *asher al ha-bayit*, literally, "who is over the house," is identical in this 8th–7th century B.C.E. inscription and in Isaiah.

On a more mundane level, City of David excavators found a First Temple period bathroom, complete with an elegant stone toilet seat, set in the floor above a cesspit. The toilet seat has a separate hole in the front for male urination. A ceramic bowl was found next to the toilet seat. Archaeologists are not sure whether this was used to hold water, as a kind of flushing agent, or a liming agent to be thrown into the cesspit.

With no respect for the privacy of the ancient occupants, archaeologists even studied the remains in the cesspit. The toilet was apparently last used during the Babylonian siege of the city, in the 6th century B.C.E. The contents of the cesspit indicate that even the wealthiest Jerusalemites suffered from famine and were eating wild plants. It is this Babylonian attack on the city that forms the subject of the next chapter.

VII

The Babylonians Destroy the City and Burn the Temple

NOT LONG AFTER JOSIAH'S UNTIMELY DEATH (IN A BATTLE WITH THE Egyptians near Megiddo), a new world superpower, Babylonia, supplanted Assyria. From Judah's viewpoint, Babylonia was no better than Assyria. Moreover, with the decline of Assyria, Egypt reasserted its influence, and Judah was once more caught in the middle, between a resurgent Egypt and the new whirlwind from Mesopotamia, Babylonia. Judah hoped to resist the Babylonian onslaught by allying itself with Egypt.

For some time, the prophet Jeremiah had condemned reliance on Egypt and predicted destruction at the hands of the Babylonians. In the fourth year of the reign of King Jehoiakim (c. 605 B.C.E.), the Bible tells us (Jeremiah 36:1), the Lord spoke to Jeremiah and instructed him to write his prophecies on a scroll. "Perhaps," Yahweh told Jeremiah, "when the House of Judah hear of all the disasters I intend to bring upon them, they will turn back from their wicked ways, and I will pardon their iniquity and their sin" (Jeremiah 36:3). "So Jeremiah called Baruch son of Neriah; and Baruch wrote down in the scroll, at Jeremiah's dictation, all the words which the Lord had spoken to him" (Jeremiah 36:4).

Jeremiah himself was in hiding, so he told his friend and confidant Baruch to take the scroll and read it aloud in the Temple on a fast day. "Baruch son of Neriah did just as the prophet Jeremiah had instructed him, about reading the words of the Lord from the scroll in the House of the Lord" (Jeremiah 36:8).

When Baruch did this, it was reported to high officials at the king's palace not far away, and Baruch was sent for and told to read the scroll to the palace

Arrowheads from the Babylonian siege of Jerusalem, lying in situ in a layer of charred wood and ash at the base of an Israelite tower that defended the city.

officials. The officials, showing some courage, advised him to go into hiding with Jeremiah. His life might be in danger, they told him, if the king reacted unfavorably to the message of the scroll.

The scroll—apparently confiscated from Baruch at the palace—was then taken to King Jehoiakim himself. Each time a few columns were read to the king, he took them and burned them in the winter fire that was warming him. Then he ordered three courtiers, including Yerahme'el, his "son," to "arrest the scribe Baruch and the prophet Jeremiah." But the courtiers could not find the pair: "the Lord hid them" (Jeremiah 36:26).

When Jeremiah heard that the king had burned the scroll, he dictated a second copy to Baruch (Jeremiah 36:32). Then the Lord instructed Jeremiah to prophesy to King Jehoiakim:

> Thus said the Lord [to Jehoiakim]: You burned that scroll, saying, "How dare you write in it that the king of Babylon will come and destroy this land and cause man and beast to cease from it?" Assuredly, thus said the Lord concerning King Jehoiakim of Judah: He shall not have any of his line sitting on the throne of David; and his own corpse shall be left exposed to the heat by day and the cold by night. And I will punish him and his offspring and his courtiers for their iniquity; I will bring on them and on the inhabitants of Jerusalem and on all the men of Judah all the disasters of which I have warned them—but they would not listen.
>
> Jeremiah 36:29–31

In 1975 a hoard of more than 250 bullae impressed with Hebrew seals appeared on the antiquities market. No one knows how, when or where they were discovered. They may have been stolen promptly on discovery from an archaeological excavation. They date from the period just before the Babylonian destruction of Jerusalem in the 6th century B.C.E. and probably came from an administrative storeroom where important documents were filed. The documents sealed by the bullae would have burned in the destruction of the city.

A bulla impressed with the seal of Baruch, the secretary, friend and confidant of the prophet Jeremiah. The bulla is baked hard, suggesting that it may have been caught in the fiery destruction of the city in 586 B.C.E. The flames destroyed the document to which it was attached but assured the preservation of the clay bulla.

In the mid-1970s a hoard of bullae appeared on the antiquities market. The lumps of clay were originally used to seal the strings tying important documents. Bullae both secured the documents and served as a kind of signature of the senders.

Among the more than 250 bullae in this hoard, one is impressed with the seal of Baruch, son of Neriah—secretary, confidant, faithful companion and political ally of the prophet Jeremiah. The seal impressed in the bullae looks much like the seals mentioning Hilkiah that we already looked at. Like those seals, Baruch's seal is written in Old Hebrew script, its lines of script are separated by two narrow parallel lines, and the seal contains no images. It reads simply: "Belonging to Berekhyahu [Baruch's Hebrew name], son of Neriyahu [Neriah's Hebrew name], the scribe." As on one of the Hilkiah seals, the occupation (scribe) refers to the owner of the seal, not to the father of the seal's owner.

Seldom do we find archaeological artifacts with written references to people actually mentioned in the Bible. This is one of those rare instances. The experience leaves one with a sense of awe, a closeness to the text that gives it a different kind of reality. "Here is the seal of Jeremiah's scribe!" one feels the urge to exclaim.

In 1995 the world learned that another bulla with Baruch's seal impressed in it had survived. This bulla, now in the hands of an Israeli collector living in London, is even better preserved and the seal impression even clearer than the bulla with the same seal in the Israel Museum. On the back of the London bulla, impressions of the papyrus fibers of the document that was secured with the bulla can still be seen. And on the edge, the fingerprint of Jeremiah's scribe is impressed in the clay.[52]

Another bulla in the hoard of 250 was impressed with the seal of King Jehoiakim's "son" Yerahme'el, who was sent by the king on the unsuccessful mission to arrest Baruch and Jeremiah. Yerahme'el's seal, in two lines of Old Hebrew script separated by a thin double line, reads: "Belonging to Yerahme'el 'son' of the king."[53] I have put "son" in quotation marks because it is not clear

whether the term denotes a biological son. Scholars are of three minds—at least: (1) the word means what it says; (2) "son" refers to a royal official unrelated by blood to the king; (3) "son" refers to any male scion of the royal family.

Five people in the Bible are referred to as "son of the king"; three of them have functions related to police and security, as was the case with Yerahme'el. Perhaps this was not a sufficiently elevated position for the king's blood son. Or perhaps, on the contrary, police and security matters could more easily be entrusted to family members. Many male members of the royal family could have held this title. This at least outlines the argument.[54]

A hoard of 51 bullae from the same period was found in Yigal Shiloh's excavation in the City of David. One of the bullae in that hoard also belonged to a person specifically mentioned in the Bible. After God had instructed Jeremiah to write his prophecies on a scroll, you will recall, the prophecies were read to the people by Jeremiah's scribe, Baruch. The day was declared a fast day in the hope that people would repent. So the scroll was read to people assembled in the Temple courtyard. Baruch himself stood "in the chamber of Gemariah son of Shaphan the scribe, in the upper court, near the new gateway of the Temple

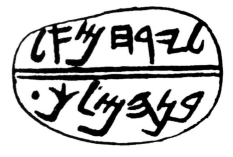

The seal impression of Yerahme'el, the king's son (either figuratively or literally), who was sent to arrest Jeremiah for publicly reading his prophecies of Jerusalem's doom.

of the Lord" (Jeremiah 36:10). Among the bullae in the hoard uncovered by Shiloh was one impressed with the seal of "Gemaryahu son of Shaphan."

We have mentioned six seals or seal impressions with the names of four people mentioned in the Bible—Hilkiah, Baruch, Yerahme'el and Gemariah. The names of two other people mentioned in the Bible have also been found on bullae or seals: Baruch's brother Seraiah, who is mentioned in Jeremiah 51:59; and Azaliah, son of Meshullam, mentioned in 2 Kings 22:3.[55]

Seraiah accompanied King Zedekiah to Babylon when the king went there to assure Nebuchadnezzar of his allegiance. Before they left for Babylon, Jeremiah told Seraiah, "When you get to Babylon, see that you read out all these words. And say, 'O Lord, You Yourself have declared concerning this place that it shall be cut off, without inhabitant, man or beast; that it shall be a desolation for all time'" (Jeremiah 51:61–62). Seraiah's seal is another one that has survived the ages.

In the late 7th century B.C.E., the Babylonians defeated the Egyptians in two crucial battles in northern Syria. The Babylonians then turned toward Judah, which became a helpless vassal. In 597 B.C.E., Nebuchadnezzar, the fearsome Babylonian ruler and general, looted the Temple and even took the Judahite king Jehoiachin (not to be confused with Jehoiakim) to Babylon as a hostage. A Babylonian chronicle records:

This beautiful seal belonged to Seraiah, who accompanied King Zedekiah of Judah when he journeyed to Babylon to assure Nebuchadnezzar of his loyalty. When in Babylon, Seraiah prophesied the city's doom.

> [T]he King of Akkad [Nebuchadnezzar] mobilized his army...Over against the city of Judah he encamped. On the second of Adar he captured the city and took the king prisoner...He took heavy tribute and brought it to Babylon.

Cuneiform tablets from Babylonia also record that Jehoiachin, identified as the "king of Judah," was provided with food at the Babylonian king's table.[56]

The Babylonians put their own puppet king on the throne of Judah, Jehoiachin's uncle Zedekiah. Ignoring both his Babylonian master and Jeremiah's warnings, however, Zedekiah again allied Judah with Egypt and at one point withheld Babylonian tribute. Nebuchadnezzar responded by systematically devastating the land, much as Sennacherib had done a century earlier. A letter (actually an inscribed potsherd) found at Lachish describes the desperate situation shortly before the Babylonian attack on Jerusalem (Lachish Letter No. 4).[57] The beacon at Azekah, southwest of Jerusalem, could no longer be seen; apparently

Part of a hoard of ostraca (inscribed potsherds) found at Lachish and written shortly before the Babylonian destruction of Jerusalem. This one, known as Lachish Letter No. 4, describes a desperate situation: The sender of the letter can no longer see the beacon of Azekah. He is tending (or watching) the signal of Lachish. Shortly after this letter was written, Lachish fell. Jerusalem was next.

it had already fallen to the enemy. Jerusalem's turn could not be far behind.

In January 588 B.C.E., Nebuchadnezzar laid siege to Jerusalem. Egypt attempted to relieve the siege and succeeded for a while, but, as Jeremiah had predicted, the Babylonians soon returned. When the situation became hopeless, King Zedekiah fled Jerusalem with his family. The Babylonians captured him at Jericho, however. They promptly put Zedekiah's sons to death before his eyes and then blinded him, so that the last thing he would ever see was the murder of his sons. Then Zedekiah was taken to Babylon in chains.

Meanwhile, Nebuchadnezzar broke through the walls of Jerusalem on the 17th day of the month of Tammuz; less than a month later, on the 9th day of Av, he burned the Temple.[58] Observant Jews still mark these dates with mourning and fasting.

Jerusalem had been able to hold out for nearly two and a half years, however—surely a tribute to the effectiveness of the city's defenses. In Nahman Avigad's excavations in the Jewish Quarter of the Old City, he uncovered parts of the northern defenses, the most vulnerable side of the city and the direction from which conquerors traditionally came. Avigad uncovered two disconnected parts of the northern wall. One small wall segment contained an angle indicating an offset or a tower. The other, larger segment Avigad interpreted as a gate tower.

The northeast corner of the larger segment contains a right angle extending west and south. The western extension ends abruptly after about 40 feet, suggesting to Avigad that the gateway entrance was here. The smaller segment is a massive structure with walls more than 12 feet thick preserved to a height of more than 25 feet. This may be the Middle Gate referred to in Jeremiah 39:3, where Nebuchadnezzar's officers were billeted after they breached the wall.

A 30-foot-square Israelite tower that helped defend the city during the Babylonian siege. It is preserved to a height of 27 feet. The arrowheads pictured on page 104 were found at the base of this tower. Adjacent to it (in the foreground) are the fragmentary remains of a later, 2nd-century B.C.E. tower.

The black ash from the Babylonian destruction of Jerusalem is clearly visible on the floor and at the base of the adjacent wall of this excavated 8th-century house.

Incidentally, this northern city wall seems unconnected to the Broad Wall that Hezekiah built, although, like the Broad Wall, building it required destroying some rather new 8th-century buildings that lay in the path of the wall. The fact that two separate northern defensive wall systems were constructed so soon after one another in the 8th–7th centuries B.C.E. (the Broad Wall was apparently replaced by the tower wall) indicates that the city fathers were aware not only of the vulnerability of the northern side of the city, but also of how perilous the times were.

The ground surface at the base of the gate tower was covered with a thick layer of charred wood, ashes and soot, evidence of the major conflagration that accompanied the Babylonian victory. Among the debris, the excavators found five arrowheads, four iron and one bronze. The bronze arrowhead is of the Scythian type, which was commonly used by foreign mercenaries, probably the Babylonian troops in this case. The iron arrowheads are the kind commonly used by the Israelites. Lying in the ashes, still fresh after nearly 2,500 years, these arrowheads provide mute evidence of the fierce battle that preceded the fall of Jerusalem.

Shiloh describes the Babylonian destruction of Jerusalem as "total."[59] Evidence has been uncovered in a number of excavations, including Shiloh's own

City of David excavations, which uncovered houses on the eastern slope that had been destroyed in a fierce conflagration. The ash and rubble were preserved in some of these buildings up to the height of the first story ceiling. The archaeological evidence is consistent with the biblical text:

> On the seventh day of the fifth month…the chief of the guards, an officer of the king of Babylon…burned the Temple of the Lord, the king's palace, and all the houses of Jerusalem…The entire Chaldean [Babylonian] force that was with the chief of the guard tore down the walls of Jerusalem on every side.
>
> 2 Kings 25:8–10

In one of the burned buildings Shiloh excavated, called the House of the Bullae, Shiloh found the hoard of 51 bullae with seal impressions. We have already mentioned two of the bullae from this hoard with seal impressions of people mentioned in the Bible, one bearing the seal of "Azariah son of Hilkiah" and the other "Gemariah son of Shaphan." The building in which this hoard of bullae was found must have been an administrative center containing files of important documents. Unfortunately, none of the documents themselves survived. Ironically, the same flames that destroyed all of the documents baked the clay bullae, thus assuring their preservation.

The bronze arrowhead above is of a type known as Scythian, typical of the arrowheads used by the Babylonians. The iron arrowhead at right is Israelite. For a picture of the arrowheads in situ, *see page 104.*

VIII

Jerusalem During the Exile and Return

AFTER THE DEVASTATION OF JERUSALEM, THE BABYLONIANS TOOK THE leading Jewish families into exile. Based on this biblical text, it is often thought that only the poor were left in the city: "The remnant of people that was left in the city [following its destruction], the defectors who had gone over to the king of Babylon—and the remnant of the population—were taken into exile...But some of the poorest in the land were left by the chief of the guards, to be vinedressers and field hands" (2 Kings 25:11–12).

Archaeological evidence, however, suggests that not all the wealthy families were deported. Some remained and continued to live reasonably luxurious lives. The archaeological evidence comes from a site called Ketef Hinnom, the Shoulder of Hinnom, southwest of the Old City near where the Hinnom Valley turns east toward the Kidron. In this area, Tel Aviv University archaeologist Gabriel Barkay excavated some typical First Temple period cave tombs, with burial benches and headrests carved out of the rock on three sides of the burial chambers. In one tomb, he found an unusually wide burial bench fitted with six headrests to accommodate six bodies side by side (see pp. 116–117).

As we have seen before, in many First Temple period cave tombs repositories were carved below the benches. These were also found in some of the tombs at Ketef Hinnom. Unfortunately, much of this rock-cut cemetery had been obliterated as a result of later quarrying. All of the caves had been disturbed and they were in an advanced state of ruin, so no one expected to find anything in the bone repositories. But, *mirabile dictu*, the bone repository under the widest burial bench—the

Earrings, rings, beads and other jewelry from a tomb repository in Jerusalem. The tomb was used by a wealthy Jerusalem family during the period of the Babylonian Exile, which shows that some Jewish life continued in the city, despite the deportation described in the Bible.

115

one fitted for six bodies—was found untouched. A layer of rock from the ceiling of the cave had collapsed and hidden the repository from grave robbers. This is in fact the only intact tomb repository ever found in Jerusalem (see photo, p. 118).

When archaeologists opened the repository, they discovered not only the bones of nearly a hundred individuals, but also more than a thousand artifacts, including burial gifts of pottery (more than 260 whole vessels); jewelry (more than a hundred pieces of silver, as well as gold); arrowheads; bone and ivory artifacts; alabaster; beads of various sizes, colors and materials; a piece of pre-blown glass; and a rare early coin.

The time in which the tomb was used can be determined from these finds, particularly the pottery. The evidence reveals that this tomb complex was in continuous use by a wealthy Jerusalem family from about the 7th century B.C.E. right through the destruction of Jerusalem and the Babylonian Exile into the

Typical First Temple period stone burial benches line three sides of a tomb chamber. The chamber itself no longer exists; only the burial benches remain. Each of the three benches has one or more headrests carved in it. The large bench, where the volunteer excavators are lying in mock imitation of the bodies that once rested here, is unusual in that it has six headrests on it. The headrests can be seen in the view at right. Beneath this bench is a repository for bones and grave goods in which the items pictured on page 114 were found.

6th century B.C.E. and on through the Persian period; then, after a gap during the Hellenistic period, the tomb was again used in the 1st century B.C.E. The coin, the earliest ever discovered in the Holy Land, dates to the 6th century B.C.E. and was minted on the Aegean island of Cos.

The pottery falls into three groups: the First Temple period (7th–early 6th centuries B.C.E.); the Babylonian and early Persian periods (6th–5th centuries B.C.E.); and the late Hellenistic period (1st century B.C.E.). Some of the arrowheads were bent, indicating that they had been used in battle. "Could this be the burial place of the fallen in the war with the Babylonians over Jerusalem?" asks excavator Gabriel Barkay.[60]

What this means is that at least some wealthy Jerusalem families continued to live in the city right through the Babylonian destruction and continued, generation after generation, to bury their dead in luxurious family tombs carved into the outlying Jerusalem hills. In the words of Barkay, "It appears that the families whose ancestors originally hewed the caves at the end of the First Temple period are the ones who continued to bury their dead in these caves also after the destruction in 586 B.C.E."[61]

The most astounding finds in the repository were two very small rolls of pure silver. It took three years for specialists at the Israel Museum to open them. The larger of the two is less than four inches long when opened and about an inch wide. Both scrolls were inscribed on the inside—in tiny letters, barely

The repository as the excavators found it, jam-packed with grave goods. Oil lamps, juglets, glass vessels and earrings are visible in the dirt. The small pick, called a patishe *(Hebrew for hammer), is an archaeologist's tool.*

scratched into the silver, probably with an iron point. Each contains, in part and with some variations, the famous priestly blessing from Numbers 6:24–26:

> May the Lord bless you and keep you.
> May the Lord cause his countenance to shine upon and be
>   gracious unto you.
> May the Lord favor you and grant you *shalom* (peace).[62]

These are the oldest biblical quotations in existence. Based on the shape and stance of the letters, experts have dated these amulets to the end of the 7th century B.C.E. They were apparently meant to be worn around the neck with a string through the hole that is formed when they are rolled up.[63] These amulets are about 400 years older than the earliest biblical texts found among the Dead Sea Scrolls. This blessing is the only biblical text to have survived from the First Temple period (although at that time the blessing may not have been incorporated into a text that we would later call the Bible).

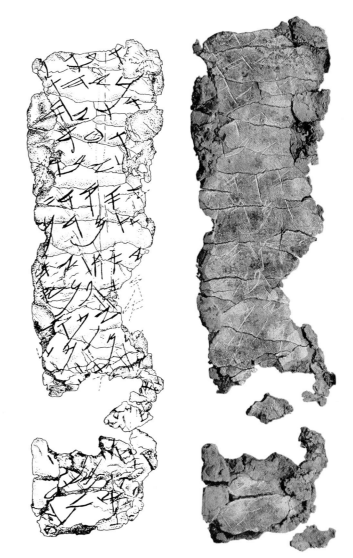

Two pure silver amulets (photos near right and far right) were found rolled up so they could be worn around the neck with a string through the hole. When unrolled, the amulets were found to contain slight variations of the priestly blessing from Numbers. The oldest biblical texts ever discovered, they date to more than 300 years before the earliest of the Dead Sea Scrolls. Pictured here (photo and drawing, far right) is the smaller of the two amulets, about 1.5 inches long. This remarkable image of the unrolled amulet was taken by Professor Bruce Zuckerman, using the latest photographic techniques to show the letters more clearly than ever before.

In 539 B.C.E., the Babylonians met their match—the Persians. The Persians succeeded the Babylonians as the major imperial power in the Near East when Babylon was conquered by Cyrus the Great, the Achemenid ruler of Persia. One leading scholar has described the difference between Persian rulers and the earlier Assyrian and Babylonian rulers in this way:

> In contrast to their Assyrian and Babylonian predecessors, the Achemenid Persians represented themselves to their subject-states as a benevolent power concerned not just with the garnering of taxes but with the maintenance of peace and order throughout the empire. The territories formerly administered by the Assyrians and Babylonians were reorganized into a system of satrapies and provinces; local governments were strengthened; roads and systems of communications were developed; and—most important for the Jews—displaced and exiled peoples were encouraged to return to their ancestral homelands to reestablish local religious and political institutions in order to play supportive roles in this new concept of empire.[64]

The Bible records a decree of Cyrus encouraging the Jews to return to Jerusalem and rebuild their Temple (2 Chronicles 36:23 and Ezra 1:2–3). Cyrus's decree is especially believable because a similar edict permitting subject peoples to resettle in their original homes and rebuild ruined sanctuaries has survived in a cuneiform text known as the Cyrus Cylinder (see photo, p. 120), now in the British Museum.

The Jews appear to have returned in successive waves. The first, soon

The Cyrus Cylinder is a cuneiform text in which the Persian ruler Cyrus permits a foreign people to resettle in its original homeland. The Bible records a similar proclamation by Cyrus allowing the exiled Jews to return from Babylon to the land of Israel in the 6th century B.C.E.

after Cyrus's decree in 539 B.C.E., was led by Sheshbazzar, the son of King Jehoiachin, who had been taken to Babylon as a prisoner in 597 B.C.E. Sheshbazzar *laid the foundations* to rebuild the Temple (Ezra 5:16)—the Second Temple in Jewish tradition. The Temple itself wasn't built until some time later, by Zerubbabel, the last direct scion of the Davidic line mentioned in the Hebrew Bible. Zerubbabel was then governor of the Persian province of Yehud (Judea in Aramaic, the vernacular of the time). Under the inspiration of the prophets Haggai and Zechariah, Zerubbabel completed work on the Temple in 515 B.C.E.

Haggai refers to the splendor of the former Temple (Haggai 2:3), implying that the rebuilt Temple was a far more modest structure, which was appropriate, however, to the relatively impoverished condition of the returnees. Those who remembered the glorious First Temple wept when they beheld the first stages of the Second Temple (Ezra 3:12).

As it was for Solomon's Temple, wood for the Second Temple was brought from Tyre and Sidon—the cedars of Lebanon (Ezra 3:7). Also like Solomon's Temple, not a stone of the Second Temple built by Zerubbabel has survived. Indeed, archaeological evidence from the Persian period in Jerusalem ranges from sparse to nonexistent.

Ezra and Nehemiah returned to Jerusalem in the mid-5th century B.C.E. The precise dates and even the order in which they served are matters of scholarly debate. Nehemiah was governor of Judea under Persian suzerainty, and Ezra was a scribe and proclaimer of the Law. Within three days of his return, Nehemiah

Map of Jerusalem on the Exiles' Return

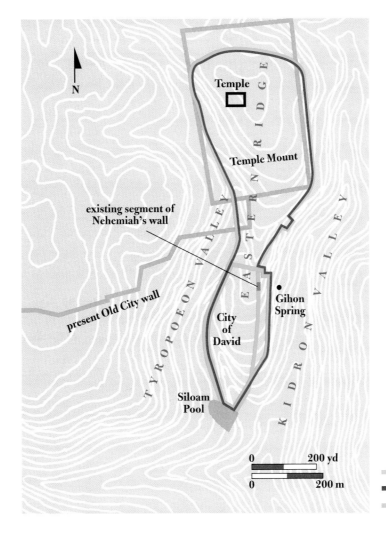

Temple

Temple Mount

EASTERN RIDGE

existing segment of
Nehemiah's wall

present Old City wall

TYROPOEON VALLEY

KIDRON VALLEY

Gihon
Spring

City
of
David

Siloam
Pool

0   200 yd

0   200 m

David's city

Solomon's city

after the exiles return

The exiles from Babylon returned to a Jerusalem which was much smaller than the one they had left; it was confined to the eastern ridge. They no longer needed the precipitous area on the eastern slope of the City of David. The new wall line on the eastern side of the city was at the top of the slope and extended north and south from the Stepped-Stone Structure (above). A piece of the original wall built by the returning exiles can be seen to the right (north) of the Stepped-Stone Structure, just beyond the remains of a later tower.

Archaeologists have recovered little in Jerusalem from the Persian period (6th–4th centuries B.C.E.), when the exiles returned from Babylon. An exception is this coin stamped "Yehud," the name of the Persian satrapy of Judea.

took his famous middle-of-the-night tour of the breached and fallen walls of Jerusalem (Nehemiah 2:11–15). The biblical account is difficult to follow, but at one point the donkey or mule on which Nehemiah was riding was unable to pass, and he had to proceed on foot. The obstacle was probably the tumble of stones from the destroyed terraces on the eastern slope of the City of David.

Nehemiah assigned the task of rebuilding different sections of the city wall, which he had surveyed on his nocturnal circumvallation, to various groups in the community—families, priests, merchants and artisans, such as smiths and perfumers. Remarkably, the final segment of the work was completed in 52 days.

Obviously, in rebuilding the city wall, the old foundations and the remains that still stood were used to maximum advantage—all except on the eastern side of the City of David, where the wall had been so badly destroyed and the tumble on the steep slope was so massive that Nehemiah's donkey could not carry him across. More importantly, because the post-Exilic population was small, there was no need to enlarge the City of David by rebuilding the costly stone terraces.

Instead, on the east side of the City of David, the returnees built a new city wall at the top of the slope. This was easier to build, even though it reduced the size of the city. The new wall was built along the line of the old Stepped-Stone Structure, which may have been the original Jebusite Fortress of Zion that David conquered (see chapter 3). Just north of the Stepped-Stone Structure, Kathleen Kenyon uncovered part of the new wall built by Nehemiah at the top of the eastern slope.

Just as the size of the City of David was reduced by abandoning the eastern slope, so the entire western ridge was also abandoned. The returnees had no need for a large city, and they thus did not resettle the suburb enclosed by Hezekiah's Broad Wall. We know this from archaeological evidence—or rather the lack thereof. In all the modern excavations on the western hill, not a single artifact from the Persian period has been found, with the exception of one coin bearing the inscription "Yehud."[65]

The most reliable population estimates suggest that only about 4,500 people lived in Jerusalem at this time—which was more, however, than the approximately 2,000 inhabitants who lived in the Canaanite or Davidic cities (both con-

Jerusalem's Area and Population Through the Ages

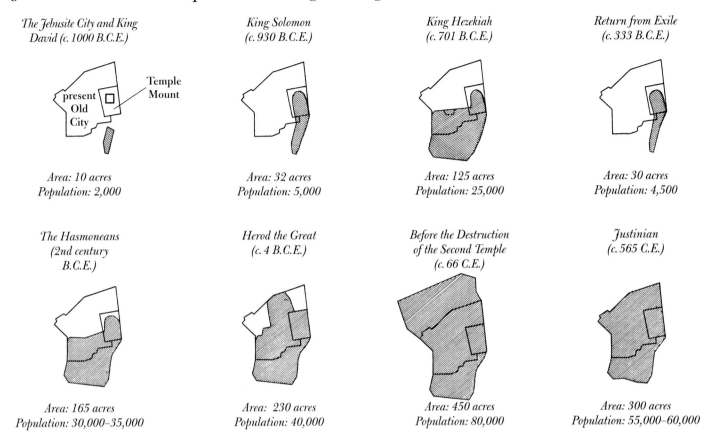

The Jebusite City and King
David (c. 1000 B.C.E.)

Area: 10 acres
Population: 2,000

King Solomon
(c. 930 B.C.E.)

Area: 32 acres
Population: 5,000

King Hezekiah
(c. 701 B.C.E.)

Area: 125 acres
Population: 25,000

Return from Exile
(c. 333 B.C.E.)

Area: 30 acres
Population: 4,500

The Hasmoneans
(2nd century
B.C.E.)

Area: 165 acres
Population: 30,000–35,000

Herod the Great
(c. 4 B.C.E.)

Area: 230 acres
Population: 40,000

Before the Destruction
of the Second Temple
(c. 66 C.E.)

Area: 450 acres
Population: 80,000

Justinian
(c. 565 C.E.)

Area: 300 acres
Population: 55,000–60,000

fined to the City of David). When Solomon expanded the city to include the area of the present Temple Mount, the population had more than doubled, to about 5,000 people. When Hezekiah expanded the city to the western hill in the 8th century B.C.E. to accommodate refugees from the northern kingdom of Israel, which had been destroyed by the Assyrians, the population of Jerusalem grew to about 25,000.

When the exiles returned from Babylonia and Nehemiah rebuilt the walls, however, Jerusalem was once again confined to the eastern hill and the population was a mere 4,500.[66] As Nehemiah remarked after the walls had been rebuilt, "The city was broad and large, [but] the people in it were few" (Nehemiah 7:4).

IX

Hellenistic and Hasmonean Jerusalem

THE PERSIAN PERIOD ENDED IN 332 B.C.E., WHEN ALEXANDER THE GREAT overcame the Persian empire and conquered Judea. Alexander was not simply a geographical imperialist, he was also a cultural and ideological imperialist: Judea soon found itself under the powerful influence of Hellenism.

Upon Alexander's death in 323 B.C.E., his kingdom was divided between his heirs, largely the Ptolemies of Egypt and the Seleucids of Syria, who quickly became bitter rivals. Control of Judea, situated between them, passed back and forth several times in the next 150 years. Egypt and Syria, the two new foci of world power, fought no fewer than five major wars during the 3rd century B.C.E., with Judea in the middle. Garrison troops were posted all over Judea, including Jerusalem.

But almost no archaeological remains from this period have been discovered. In 168 B.C.E., at a time when the country was ruled by the Seleucids, the Syrian king Antiochus IV looted the Temple. What was there to loot? Cyrus the Great had specifically given the Jews returning from Exile "the vessels of the Temple of the Lord that Nebuchadnezzar had carried away from Jerusalem and placed in the house of his gods" (Ezra 1:8). These vessels were probably what Antiochus plundered. (As for the Ark of the Covenant, no mention is made of it after the Babylonian destruction. Presumably it was never recovered.)

When Antiochus looted the Temple, the Jews of Jerusalem rebelled. But Antiochus easily crushed the revolt and erected a new fortress, called the Akra,

Misnamed Solomon's Pools, these second-century B.C.E. reservoirs south of Bethlehem stored water from springs farther south on its way to the Temple Mount. Carried by gravity from the springs to Jerusalem, the water followed a twisting route along the contours of the hills for nearly 45 miles.

near the Temple Mount, where he garrisoned hostile foreign mercenaries.[67] The Akra became a hated symbol of foreign rule. Antiochus proceeded to make matters worse by prohibiting Jewish compliance with the most important Jewish religious laws, including circumcision, religious study and observance of the Sabbath and festivals. He forced Jews to bow down to idols and eat forbidden foods.

When he installed a graven image in the Temple, the Jews again rose in open revolt. The Jewish rebels were led by a certain Mattathias and his five sons. One of the sons, Judas, nicknamed Maccabeus (the Hammer), initially led the Jewish forces. In 164 B.C.E., the Jews captured the Temple and cleansed it of pagan impurities. The event is still celebrated in the festival of Hanukkah.

The Maccabees, as Judas and his four brothers became known, were unable to hold the area, however, especially because of the Seleucid troops in the hated Akra. Intrigue, revolt, suppression and battles ensued for the next quarter century. Finally, in 141 B.C.E., the Maccabees, this time led by Simon, the last of Mattathias's sons, captured the Akra, and the whole of Jerusalem came under Jewish control. An independent Jewish government once again ruled in Jerusalem—for the first time in nearly 450 years. The Maccabean era, more commonly known as the Hasmonean period (from the name of an ancestor whose name became a family name), lasted until 63 B.C.E., when the Roman general Pompey conquered Jerusalem.

The Hasmonean period in Jerusalem was, in general, prosperous and expansive. One of the most exciting changes that occurred involved the city's water supply. Under Hasmonean rule, a new source of water supplied the city. The water came from several springs rising in the hills south of Bethlehem. A channel follows the contour of the hills, so gravity would carry the water a distance of more than 45 miles, from the springs to the channel terminus at the Temple Mount (a direct route would be only about 15 miles). The so-called Lower Aqueduct carries the water from storage reservoirs known (incorrectly, of course) as Solomon's Pools.

In two sections, the water was conveyed in tunnels, each about 1,200 feet long. One of these tunnels, just south of Jerusalem, goes under the ridge on which Government House sits. During the British Mandate, this was the High Commissioner's residence. Later it became the United Nations headquarters in Jerusalem. According to (inaccurate) tradition, the site is the Hill of Evil Counsel, where Caiaphas counseled that one man, Jesus, should die to save the entire nation from the Roman authorities (John 11:50). The site is still known by this name.

A portion of the Hasmonean tunnel under the Hill of Evil Counsel can be traversed, and much of the aqueduct is still extant. A large section of the aqueduct can be found below Yemin Moshe, in the Hinnom Valley and along the southern wall of the Old City. Part can also be seen in the Jewish Quarter of the Old City near the steps going down to the Western Wall. Although rebuilt and often repaired, this aqueduct was used continuously until the 19th century.[68]

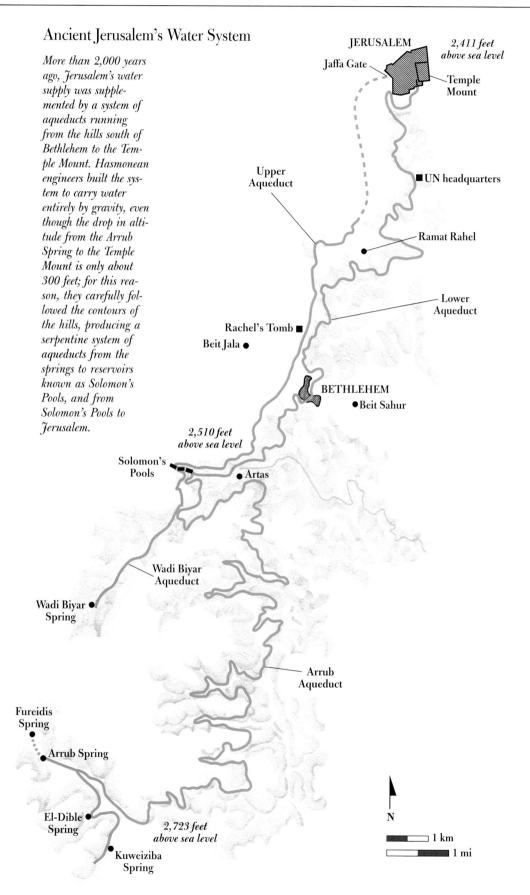

Ancient Jerusalem's Water System

More than 2,000 years ago, Jerusalem's water supply was supplemented by a system of aqueducts running from the hills south of Bethlehem to the Temple Mount. Hasmonean engineers built the system to carry water entirely by gravity, even though the drop in altitude from the Arrub Spring to the Temple Mount is only about 300 feet; for this reason, they carefully followed the contours of the hills, producing a serpentine system of aqueducts from the springs to reservoirs known as Solomon's Pools, and from Solomon's Pools to Jerusalem.

JERUSALEM

2,411 feet above sea level

Jaffa Gate

Temple Mount

■ UN headquarters

Upper Aqueduct

Ramat Rahel

Lower Aqueduct

Rachel's Tomb ■

Beit Jala ●

BETHLEHEM

●Beit Sahur

2,510 feet above sea level

Solomon's Pools

Artas ●

Wadi Biyar Aqueduct

Wadi Biyar ● Spring

Arrub Aqueduct

Fureidis Spring ●

Arrub Spring ●

El-Dible ● Spring

2,723 feet above sea level

Kuweiziba ● Spring

N

1 km

1 mi

Archaeological excavations inside the Citadel, adjacent to Jaffa Gate, revealed walls and buildings from many periods, including the Hasmonean, when the city once again expanded to the western hill.

Hasmonean coins like these were often inscribed in Greek as well as Hebrew, the Greek reflecting a marked Hellenistic influence. The Hebrew inscription (top) is inscribed in Old Hebrew letters, purposefully archaic, which reflect an intense Jewish nationalism.

In the Hasmonean period, the city expanded again to the western hill. The Hasmoneans once more fortified the part of the city on the western hill that had lain empty for more than 400 years. Into the city wall they built a tower immediately adjacent to the old Israelite tower that had defended the city against the Babylonians (see p. 130). The two towers functioned as a single unit in this period. Realizing the wisdom of the old Israelite defense system, the Hasmoneans integrated what remained into their own defenses. Nahman Avigad was able to trace more than 160 feet of the wall to the west of the tower.

All over the western hill, excavators found the Hasmonean stratum directly above the earlier First Temple stratum—with nothing in between. The Hasmonean city extended as far west as the (inaccurately named) Citadel of David, adjacent to the Old City's Jaffa Gate, where extensive Hasmonean remains have also been excavated.

On the eastern ridge, in the City of David, a massive tower was built at the top of the eastern slope to protect the city. This impressive tower is still visible, adjacent to and south of the Stepped-Stone Structure. When Macalister first examined the tower in the early part of this century, he attributed it to King David, which is why it was referred to as David's Tower. When the area was reexcavated in the 1960s by Kathleen Kenyon, however, she securely dated it to the Maccabean period through pottery and coins found beneath the tower.

The Maccabean, or Hasmonean, wall can pretty much be traced all the way around the city. The Hasmoneans often used existing walls and wall lines and repaired sections of wall where necessary—all consistent with numerous statements in 1 Maccabees referring to the rebuilding of the city and the walls. Jonathan Maccabee gave orders "to build the walls and surround Mount Zion with a fortification of squared stones" (1 Maccabees 10:11; see also 1 Maccabees 12:36 and 16:23–24). He also "began to repair and rebuild the city" (1 Maccabees 10:10). Later, his brother Simon Maccabee "hurried on the completion of the walls of Jerusalem until it was fortified on all sides" (1 Maccabees 13:10).

This Hasmonean city wall is referred to by Josephus as the First Wall. It circumscribes the entire city (unlike the additional Second and Third Walls,

The Hasmonean tower (2nd century B.C.E.) on which the man is standing (left center) adjoined the earlier tower behind it, which dates to the period just before the Babylonian destruction of the city. In the Hasmonean period, the city once again expanded to areas abandoned since the Babylonian destruction. For a fuller view of the earlier tower, see page 111.

which defended the city on the north against the Romans in 70 C.E.). In the Hasmonean period, Jerusalem expanded because the population was expanding. At its height, Hasmonean Jerusalem is estimated to have been home to about 35,000 people—up from 4,500 when the Babylonian exiles returned. The population had remained small during the Persian period and later, when the city was often a bone of contention between the Ptolemies and the Seleucids. During the early Hellenistic period (332–141 B.C.E.), Jerusalem was an insignificant backwater. Only when it became the capital of an independent Jewish commonwealth did the city thrive and expand once again.

Jerusalem's population continued to grow. By the time the First Jewish Revolt against Rome broke out in 66 C.E., the number of inhabitants was about 80,000. As the city grew, so did the Hasmonean nation-state. At its height, the Hasmonean state included what is now southern Lebanon and western Jordan, as well as modern Israel (except the Negev).

Although the Hasmonean state is often portrayed as a reactionary bastion against Hellenism established by Jewish nationalists, this is only partly true. The Hasmoneans absorbed many aspects of Hellenistic culture from the Greek world. For one thing, Jerusalemites of this period loved wine from Rhodes; handles from imported Rhodian wine jars have been found all over. Large numbers of coins minted by the Hasmonean kings Alexander Janneus (103–76 B.C.E.) and Mattathias Antigonus (40–37 B.C.E.) were inscribed in Greek as well as in Old Hebrew letters, the kind used before the Babylonian destruction of the Temple.

Hellenistic influence is clearly reflected in some of the most magnificent Jerusalem tombs, which date to the Hasmonean period. From the southeastern corner of the Temple Mount, a road (now blocked) leads down into the Kidron Valley. On the eastern slope near the valley floor are three magnificent rock-cut monuments, at least one of which dates to the Hasmonean period (see photo, pp. 132–133). This monument is a square, freestanding stone structure with a pyramidal roof cut from the surrounding rock and an adjoining tomb. The tomb has two entrances, one from the pyramid-roofed structure and the other from the slope facing the valley; it includes several tomb chambers. The pyramid-roofed structure is known popularly as Zechariah's Tomb (approximately 30 people in the Bible bear this name, including a king and one of the so-called minor prophets).

Fine wines imported in jars like this from the island of Rhodes satisfied the most discriminating palate in Hasmonean Jerusalem.

This Hasmonean tower was built just south of the Stepped Stone Structure (lower right), another indication of the strength and confidence of the city after the Maccabees freed from foreign rule.

Monumental Tombs

Elegant Hasmonean tombs overlook the Kidron Valley. The pyramid-topped tomb carved out of the bedrock is popularly but mistakenly known as Zechariah's Tomb. The tomb on the left, entered between two columns, is identified by an inscription as belonging to a family of priests, the sons of Hezir. The Hebrew inscription from the Bene Hezir tomb is pictured at the bottom of the drawing below. As the drawing shows, the Bene Hezir tomb was also carved into the rock slope.

Plan of Jason's Tomb

Adjacent to Zechariah's Tomb is the tomb of a family of priests named Bene Hezir (sons of Hezir), as we learn from a Hebrew inscription carved on the architrave above two Doric columns in front of the tomb. Incidentally, the Bible mentions Hezir as an Aaronid priest in the days of King David (1 Chronicles 24:1,15).

Another magnificent tomb from the Hasmonean period is the famous tomb of Jason, located west of the Old City right in the middle of Rehavia, one of the most fashionable modern residential neighborhoods. Jason's Tomb definitely fits the period architecturally. Two courtyards precede the structure, which consists of a portico topped by a pyramid and a burial chamber with loculi. The portico is supported by a single column, however, instead of the usual two, the only one like it in all Israel.

Charcoal drawings of ships cover part of the walls of the portico, doubtless reflecting a family connection with the sea. An Aramaic inscription identifies the tomb as belonging to the priestly family of Jason. Inside the tomb chamber are eight body-size horizontal niches in the wall called *kochim* (singular, *koch*) or loculi (singular, loculus), for as many bodies. *Kochim*, as we shall see again and again, are typical of Second Temple period tombs.

Jason's Tomb (left)—the name appears in one of the inscriptions inside the tomb—sits in a now-fashionable residential section of Jerusalem. Three courtyards precede the unique single-columned portico with a pyramidal roof. This photograph was taken from the middle courtyard looking into the inner courtyard. The burial chamber, entered from the portico, contains eight burial niches in the walls. Behind the portico is a separate chamber where bones were collected to make room for newer burials. A number of menorot— *seven-branched candelabra—were scratched into the wall, as were three ships, one of which appears at right.*

Internal strife was the immediate cause of the demise of the Hasmonean kingdom. In 76 B.C.E., the last great Hasmonean king, Alexander Janneus, died; he was succeeded by his widow, Salome Alexandra, who died in 67 B.C.E. Their two sons, Hyrcanus II and Aristobulus II, fought each other for succession to the throne. Both of them turned to the Roman legate in Syria for support, which provided the occasion for Roman intervention. In 63 B.C.E., the Roman general Pompey, representing the new world power, laid siege to Jerusalem and conquered it. At a single stroke the Hasmonean empire was dismantled and reduced to Judea and parts of Galilee. Even these areas, however, although they were not officially incorporated into the Roman Empire, came under *de facto* Roman rule.

In 40 B.C.E., the Parthians from Persia invaded Syria and threatened Roman domination of Judea. At the time, Hyrcanus II, under Roman tutelage, was ethnarch (literally, ruler of the nation) and Antipater was procurator (literally, caretaker). Antipater was of Idumean, not Judean, stock. The Idumeans, who occupied an area south of Judea, had been converted to Judaism when the Hasmoneans incorporated Idumea into their empire.

When Antipater was killed, his son Herod succeeded him. Herod quickly fled to Rome and persuaded the Roman Senate that only he could assure Roman rule in Judea in the face of the Parthian threat. With Roman support, Herod returned to Judea and, after some severe fighting, conquered Jerusalem in 37 B.C.E. Thus began the age that still bears his name, the Herodian period.

X

Herodian Jerusalem

EROD, KNOWN TO HISTORY AS HEROD THE GREAT, REMAINED THE undisputed leader of Judea for more than 30 years (37–4 B.C.E.) One of the great builders of all time, Herod completely changed the face of Jerusalem. Within a single generation, Jerusalem became one of the most beautiful capitals in the world. But Herod himself was hated. "A tyrant, a madman, a murderer, a builder of great cities and fortresses, a wily politician, a successful king, a Jew, a half-Jew, a gentile—Herod was all these and more," according to one recent commentator.[69] He married Mariamme, the daughter of a late Hasmonean king—and proceeded to execute his wife's relations, the surviving members of the Hasmonean aristocracy. Then he murdered his Hasmonean wife as well. At the end of his reign, he even executed his two sons by his Hasmonean wife. But Herod did not play favorites when it came to executions. He also executed various other wives, sons and close relations.

On the other hand, Herod was a builder *nonpareil*. Many of the most popular tourist sites in Israel today are among his construction projects—Samaria, which he renamed Sebaste in honor of the Roman emperor Augustus (Greek, Sebastos); the mountain fortresses of Masada and Herodium; Caesarea, with its remarkable man-made harbor; and many more.

Herod's crowning architectural achievement, however, was in Jerusalem. In addition to building his own magnificent palace (only the foundations have been found, south of Jaffa Gate), he doubled the size of the Temple Mount, in effect burying the old Temple Mount. And he completely rebuilt the Temple itself,

Masada, one of Herod the Great's mountain fortresses, was built to protect himself from his Jewish subjects as much as from foreign enemies.

Herod doubled the size of the Temple Mount, extending it on the north, south and west, but not on the east (at the bottom of the picture) because of the steep drop down to the Kidron Valley. He also dismantled and then rebuilt the modest Second Temple constructed by Zerubbabel. The Temple Mount today is essentially the Herodian Temple Mount, although its upper walls and gates have been repeatedly repaired and rebuilt.

which, in Jewish tradition, remained the Second Temple. Some scholars call Herod's Temple the third temple, counting Solomon's as the first and Zerubbabel's as the second. Generally, however, the rebuilt Second Temple is called Herod's Temple to distinguish it from the much more modest Second Temple built by Zerubbabel when the exiles returned from Babylonia.

Herod's building program in Jerusalem had several purposes: to win support from his restive Jewish subjects, to create a capital worthy of the dignity and grandeur of his expanding kingdom, to immortalize his name and to satisfy his megalomania. Josephus tells a story that Herod, knowing that the Jews would rejoice when he died, ordered the most distinguished elders of the country to be killed upon news of his death. In that way, he assured that his death would be an occasion for mourning.

Like all Roman vassal kings, Herod was given a free hand in ruling the country as long as he maintained stability and peace. His brutality and his violations of Jewish law went unnoticed in Rome. Indeed, the golden eagle he placed over the entrance to the Temple probably won him Roman plaudits. Nevertheless, he did respect many Jewish sensitivities: Only priests worked on the construction of the sacred Temple precincts. The coins he minted had no images, and he did not build pagan temples or pagan cities in Jewish areas of the country.

Although none of the structures Herod built on the Temple Mount has survived, we can learn a great deal just from the retaining wall (the Temple

The seven lowest courses of the western wall of the Temple Mount at the prayer plaza are Herodian. Above these original stones are later construction and repairs. The Herodian masonry, with its carefully cut even margins and flat central boss, is easily distinguishable from the smaller, cruder masonry above.

Machpelah, the traditional burial site of the biblical patriarchs and matriarchs in Hebron, is enclosed by Herodian walls much like those that once enclosed Herod's Temple Mount in Jerusalem. At Machpelah, however, these walls have survived to their full height. Note that about halfway up the smooth surface changes with the introduction of slightly raised vertical pilasters, or engaged pillars. This was also the case at the Temple Mount. We know this because in the 19th century fragments of the Jerusalem enclosure wall with the remains of pilasters could still be seen. Several drawings of these fragments survive. One, by British Lieutenant Claude Conder, is reproduced here. At the bottom of the drawing are two flat ashlars that slant in at the top. This marks the divide between the flat wall below and the wall with pilasters above. The remains of a pilaster (two ashlars wide) adjoin the slanted stones on the right. A small fragment of the pilastered western wall in Jerusalem still survives in a private Arab home built adjacent to the Temple Mount.

140

Mount enclosure wall) and some surviving structures beneath it. The retaining wall enclosed an area approximately the size of 24 football fields. Herod's Temple Mount was the largest site of its kind in the ancient world, about twice as large as the monumental Forum Romanum built by Trajan. Herod extended the old Temple Mount to the north, south and west. So at their base, all three of these walls are Herodian. He could not extend the eastern border because it stood on the edge of the steep western slope of the Kidron Valley. However, he had to extend the eastern wall north and south to accommodate the new north and south walls. We have already examined the Straight Joint on the eastern wall, which marks the beginning of Herod's southward extension (see photos, p. 64).

The Herodian masonry in the Temple Mount enclosure wall—and other similar Herodian masonry—is easy to recognize. Each ashlar, or shaped and worked stone, is characterized by a depressed, flat, finely cut margin on each side. In the center is a smooth, flat boss raised less than half an inch. The boss is framed with an even smoother edging. Each ashlar is carefully cut and fitted to its neighbor without a knife blade of space between them. No mortar was used and none was needed.

Some of the ashlars are enormous. The largest can be seen in a tunnel that runs along the western Temple Mount enclosure wall north of the prayer plaza. It is 45 feet long and weighs 570 tons.

The number of Herodian courses that have survived in the enclosure wall varies from place to place. At the Western Wall, as the prayer plaza is called, the seven lowest courses are Herodian. They are easily distinguishable from the later masonry above. Below the prayer-plaza level are another 19 Herodian courses going down a staggering 68 feet. In the 1860s, Charles Warren dug some shafts adjacent to the Western Wall down to bedrock. Some of these shafts are now lit up in the roofed area north of the prayer plaza, where men pray and where Torah scrolls and prayer books are stored. Deep down, at the bottom of the lit shaft, coins thrown by tourists sparkle.

Judging solely by the exposed masonry, we would imagine that the face of the Herodian Temple Mount enclosure wall was flat. Actually, it was not. About halfway up, the wall was indented slightly; the rest of the way, the flat wall alternated with slightly protruding rectangular pilasters, or engaged pillars. We know this from a few telltale remains that were drawn in the 19th century by Count Melchior de Vogüé and Claude Conder, both early explorers of Jerusalem. In addition, a bit of the indent and part of a pilaster is still extant in a private home adjacent to the Western Wall. (It is almost impossible to get permission to see this, however.) Finally, fragments of the pilasters have been found in recent excavations.

Fortunately, we don't have to imagine what this walled enclosure with the pilasters halfway up looked like when it stood to its full height. An almost

identical, though smaller, Herodian enclosure has survived—in Hebron, around the traditional burial site of the patriarchs Abraham, Isaac and Jacob and the matriarchs Sarah, Rebecca and Leah. The Machpelah enclosure is the only intact Herodian structure standing today. There, as on the Temple Mount, the pilasters begin about halfway up the wall.

At the base of the southern wall of Herod's Temple Mount is a broad monumental staircase consisting of 30 steps, excavated in the late 1960s and 1970s by Hebrew University professor Benjamin Mazar. This staircase led to the major entrances to the Temple Mount itself, where thousands of Jews flocked on the three annual pilgrimage festivals—Pesach (Passover), Shavuot (Weeks, or Pentecost) and Sukkot (Tabernacles). Among those who walked up these stairs in about 30 C.E. was Jesus of Nazareth.

The risers on the steps are quite low, between 7 and 10 inches, and the stair treads vary between 12 and 35 inches, requiring one to walk with a slow, measured gait, as if participating in a processional.

Two gateways on the southern wall provided access to the Temple Mount itself, one known as the Double Gate (with two doorways) and the other known as the Triple Gate (with three doorways). Together they are known as the Huldah Gates, in memory of the prophetess who proclaimed the authority of the Scroll of the Law found in the Temple during King Josiah's repair work in the 7th century B.C.E.

Three arches mark the location of the Triple Gate, but these are not original. The only Herodian stone in these openings is a piece of the original doorjamb, sitting on the floor at the bottom of the left side of the left-hand arch (see photos, pp. 146–147).

The original Double Gate is even more difficult to see, but it is there if you look carefully (see illustrations, pp. 144–145). The Double Gate is on the wall to the left (west) of the Triple Gate, but it is substantially concealed by a perpendicular wall, part of a Crusader addition, that juts out at a right angle from the southern wall of the Temple Mount. Half of the right-hand entry of the Double Gate, which extends to the right of this Crusader addition, is the only part of the Double Gate still visible on the outside. The left-hand doorway is totally obscured by the Crusader structure.

Over the visible right-hand entry is an ornate, decorative half arch added in the Omayyad period (661–750 C.E.). But the original Herodian gate is visible behind this later appliqué. Just above the applied Omayyad arch are large, trapezoidal stones that form the Herodian relieving arch* above the original lintel of the Herodian gateway. Just above this relieving arch is another piece of applied Omayyad decoration.

*This arch "relieves" the pressure on the lintel from the stones above by transferring the force of this weight down the jambs. Otherwise the weight of the wall above would break the lintel.

The Double Gate

Reconstruction Drawing
(from the outside facing north)

L. RITMEYER

Plan

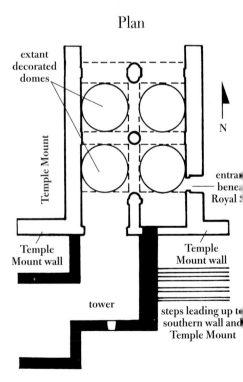

extant decorated domes

Temple Mount

N

entra
bene:
Royal

Temple Mount wall

Temple Mount wall

tower

steps leading up t
southern wall and
Temple Mount

The original Herodian ashlars of the Double Gate are still visible if you look carefully. In the photo above, they can be seen between the decorative Omayyad appliqués consisting of a half arch perpendicular to a Crusader wall (at left) and a short, applied decorative strip above this half arch. Between the two and immediately above the appliquéd half arch is the original Herodian lintel. Just above the lintel are the cleanly cut, smooth, trapezoidal stones that formed a relieving arch (see drawing, top right) sending the weight of the wall above the doorway down the doorjambs instead of onto the unsupported lintel. The reconstruction drawing shows a view into the Double Gate. Inside its simple exterior were elaborately carved columns and domes, some of which have survived intact (see drawings and photo, opposite). The exquisite domes are covered with intricate geometric and floral designs. The photo at opposite bottom shows the view through the Double Gate from the Temple Mount to the southern wall.

Extant Southern Dome
(visible in drawing at left)

Extant Northern Dome
(visible in photo below)

Inside the
Double Gate
(facing south)

145

Remarkably, some internal parts of the Herodian Double Gate have survived intact. It is not easy to get permission from the Moslem authorities to visit this area, but it is well worth a try. Although the outside of the Double Gate was quite plain, inside the gate elaborately carved columns and domes adorned the passageway to the Temple Mount, a preview of the splendor of the Temple itself.

The first four domes—two pairs—and the supporting side walls and columns stand today in their original form. Elaborate carvings of geometric designs, vines and stylized flowers form a complex rosette covering every inch of the impressive domes.

Inside the Double Gate and the Triple Gate were tunnel ramps leading up to the surface of the Temple Mount.

Just east of the Triple Gate, the bedrock dips down, sloping into the Kidron Valley; this can be seen outside the gate. The same thing happens under the southeastern part of Herod's southern Temple Mount extension. Instead of filling in this area to support the southern extension of his platform, Herod built a series of vaults supported by columns. The Crusaders used this vaulted substructure area to stable their horses and, supposing that the structure was Solomonic and that King Solomon, too, had stabled his horses here, they dubbed the place Solomon's Stables, an incorrect attribution that has stuck (see photo, p. 63). If you can get permission from the Moslem authorities to visit Solomon's Stables, by all means do so.

There were other entrances to the Temple Mount on the western wall. The southernmost of these is marked by the spring of a protruding arch near the southern corner of the western wall. This is called Robinson's Arch, after the American orientalist Edward Robinson, who first called attention to it. When Robinson noticed it in the 1830s, he was able to walk up to it at ground level and examine it with his hands. And so it remained until the 1960s, when Benjamin Mazar excavated the area adjacent to the western wall.

Three arches now mark the Triple Gate, but they are not original. The only original bit of masonry in these three doorways that once led up to the Temple Mount is the bottom piece of the left-hand jamb of the left-hand arch. This original part of the jamb can be seen in the close-up of the left-hand doorway, pictured at right.

Herodian Temple Mount

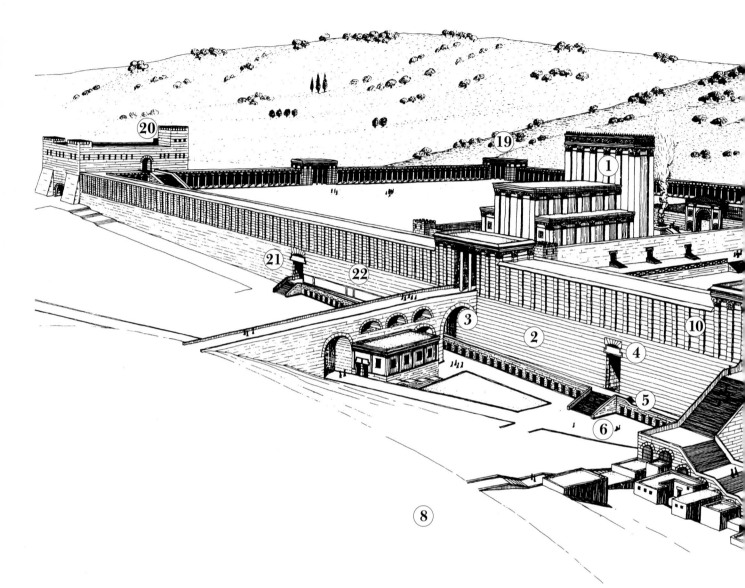

1. The Second Temple
2. Western Wall
3. Wilson's Arch
4. Barclay's Gate
5. Small shops
6. Main N–S street
7. Robinson's Arch
8. Upper City
9. Royal Stoa
10. Pilasters
11. Double Gate
12. Triple Gate
13. Stairway
14. Plaza
15. Ritual bathhouse
16. Council house
17. Row of windows
18. Stairway
19. Herodian tower
20. Antonia Fortress
21. Warren's Gate
22. Largest ashlars

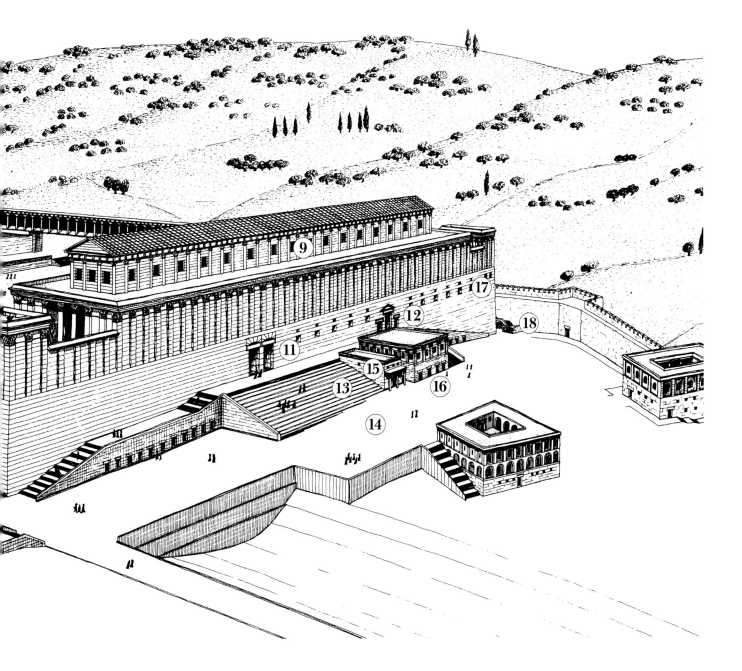

The Royal Stoa

On the southern end of his enlarged Temple Mount, Herod built a
magnificent stoa (right)—the largest structure on the giant platform.
Among other functions, it housed the Sanhedrin, Judaism's supreme
judicial body. Found in the excavations at the base of the southern
Temple Mount wall were fragments (opposite), possibly from the Royal
Stoa, which was destroyed by the Romans along with the rest of the
city in 70 C.E. Remains of a monumental column that originally
stood over 30 feet high (photo, below center, and reconstruction drawing, below left) were found in the Upper City. Whether this too came
from the Royal Stoa is not known. If so, it probably adorned the stoa's
Ionic-style upper story. Corinthian capitals
decorate the Royal Stoa in the artist's reconstruction drawing, at right, in accordance
with Josephus' description.

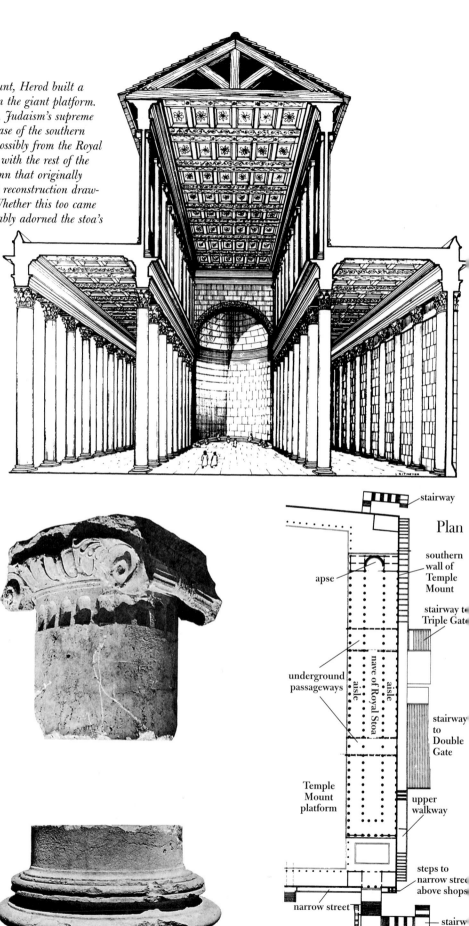

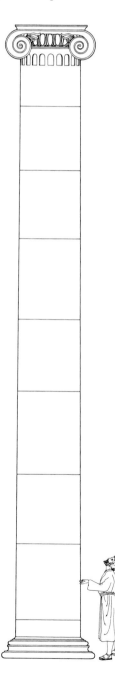

Plan

- stairway
- apse
- southern wall of Temple Mount
- stairway to Triple Gate
- underground passageways
- nave of Royal Stoa
- aisle
- aisle
- stairway to Double Gate
- Temple Mount platform
- upper walkway
- steps to narrow street above shops
- narrow street
- stairway supported by Robinson's Arch

150

These stone fragments and many others like them were recovered in excavations at the foot of the southern wall of the Herodian Temple Mount. They probably fell from the Royal Stoa during the Roman destruction of 70 C.E. The fine quality and intricate design confirms Josephus's extravagant praise of the stoa's dazzling beauty.

Until Mazar's excavation, it was supposed that Robinson's Arch had supported a bridge across the Tyropoeon Valley (or Central Valley) to the Upper City (as it was called in the Herodian period) on the western hill. A series of piers was thought to have supported similar arches that, in turn, supported the bridge. When Mazar excavated the area, he found the pier on the other side that supported the arch whose spring is called Robinson's Arch, but he found no additional piers to the west. Instead, he found sets of piers of gradually decreasing size to the south. To staff architect Brian Lalor and archaeologist Menahem Magen this indicated that Robinson's Arch had supported, not a bridge, but a grand staircase descending south toward the Central Valley (see pp. 154–155). This reconstruction has now been universally accepted.

Under Robinson's Arch, a street ran along the Temple Mount, together with a series of shops that served the needs of pilgrims on their way to the Temple. Among the excavation finds were weights, pottery, coins—and a fragment of a stone vessel that may have been offered for sale in one of the shops. The fragment is inscribed with the Hebrew word *korban*, which means sacrifice. Two crudely drawn birds appear on the vessel (see photo, p. 156). Birds were the traditional offering on the birth of a child. This vessel was probably offered for sale to, or was perhaps purchased by, a family wishing to make a sacrifice in gratitude for the birth of a child.

Although Robinson's Arch did not support a bridge, another arch, known as Wilson's Arch (after the British engineer who studied the area in the 19th century), did support a bridge across the valley to the Upper City as early as the Hasmonean period. Wilson's Arch can still be seen north of the Western Wall prayer plaza in the underground area (see painting, p. 158). Although Wilson's Arch is a complete arch today (not just the spring of an arch, like Robinson's Arch), it was probably reconstructed during the early Arab period. Originally the arch rose nearly 75 feet above the bedrock of the Tyropoeon Valley. Today much of the valley has been filled in, but the arch is still an impressive sight.

On top of his southern addition to the Temple Mount, Herod built the magnificent Royal Stoa, an immense columnar hall, which extended across the entire southern end of the great platform. Built in the style of a Roman basilica, the Royal Stoa was the largest structure on the Herodian Temple Mount. Two rows of 40 huge columns divided the stoa lengthwise into a central hall and two side halls. On the far side of the northern hall, a third row of 40 columns led to an open courtyard from which one could proceed to the Temple itself. At the eastern end of the Royal Stoa was an apse, where the Sanhedrin (the supreme Jewish legislative, religious and judicial authority) met. Josephus effusively praises the Royal Stoa as a "structure more worthy of description than any other under the sun."[70]

Fragments elaborately ornamented with geometric designs found in the rubble at the foot of the southern wall probably fell from the Royal Stoa when it

was destroyed by the Romans. In addition, Mazar found several fragments of a capital of the Ionic order. In excavations in the Upper City, Nahman Avigad also found monumental capitals, bases and column drums. The size and dimensions indicate that the columns originally stood more than 30 feet high. These were also Ionic capitals. At the top of the columns, just below the capitals, were unusual niches; similar niches were found on column fragments excavated by Mazar. It is tempting to suggest that all of these fragments came from the Royal Stoa. But how did the fragments found in the Upper City get there from across the valley?

One thing is clear from these fragments. Their monumental proportions and excellent workmanship and design would have met the highest international standards of the day, despite the fact that they were made in the provinces.

Buried in the debris at the southwestern corner of the Temple Mount was a beautifully inscribed large, smooth stone with a niche in it in which a man might have stood. The stone had apparently been hurled from the pinnacle of the southwest corner of the Temple Mount when the Romans destroyed the area

Robinson's Arch, actually part of the spring of an arch, jutted from the western wall of the Temple Mount at ground level until recent excavations. Before the excavations, it was supposed that this arch was the first of several that supported a bridge leading from the Temple Mount across the valley to the Upper City on the western ridge. Now we know that, instead, the arch supported a monumental staircase leading down to the valley.

153

in 70 C.E. Unfortunately, the end of the inscription has broken off (see photo, p. 157). What survives, elegantly carved in the stone, are Hebrew letters that read: "To the place of trumpeting to [or 'for']…" This stone probably had something to do with the place where the priests announced the beginning and end of the Sabbath from the top of the southwestern corner of the Temple Mount with a trumpet blast. Josephus tells us that just such a spot existed:

> Above the roof of the priests' chambers…it was the custom for one of the priests to stand and to give notice, by sound of trumpet, in the afternoon of the approach, and on the following evening of the close, of every seventh day, announcing to the people the respective hours for ceasing work and for resuming their labors.[71]

The southwestern corner of the Temple Mount was the Times Square of Herodian Jerusalem. Here traffic moving north from the old City of David (now called the Lower City) converged with traffic moving west from the plaza at the foot of the broad staircase on the southern wall and with traffic moving south along a beautifully paved, 40-foot-wide, north–south thoroughfare adjacent to the western wall. In addition to this was the traffic that came down the monumental staircase from the Royal Stoa and the Temple itself.

The central monument of the Temple Mount was, of course, the Temple. Josephus's comment is apt: "To approaching strangers [the Temple] appeared from a distance like a snow-clad mountain; for all that was not overlaid with gold was of purest white."[72] According to the Talmud, "He who has not seen the Temple [of Herod] in its full construction has never seen a glorious building in his life."[73]

The southwestern corner of the Temple Mount after excavation. Robinson's Arch—named for the 19th-century American orientalist who first called attention to it—can be seen protruding from the western wall beneath the large window. In the foreground of the picture are the rectangular lintels of shops that lined the street in the Herodian period. The excavators of the southwestern corner of the Temple Mount discovered piers for successively smaller arches leading to the south, rather than piers of the same size to the west. They concluded that Robinson's Arch was a supporting structure for a monumental stairway and not a bridge to the Upper City as was previously believed. The drawing at left shows the parts the archaeologists actually found in blue.

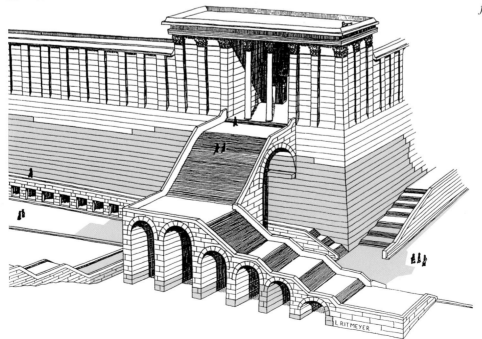

L. RITMEYER

This stone vessel was probably offered for sale in one of the shops that lined the Herodian Temple Mount. Engraved with two crudely drawn birds (the customary offering on the birth of a child) and the Hebrew word kor-ban, or sacrifice, the vessel may have been purchased by a family wishing to make a sacrifice in gratitude for the birth of a child.

Herod did not begin construction of the Temple until the 18th year of his reign. He completed all the preparations necessary for the new building before demolishing the existing structure, thus assuring his restive subjects of the continuity they demanded. With thousands of workmen, Herod completed the new Temple building in only 18 months. Completion of the entire complex, however, took much longer. According to the Gospel of John, it took 46 years, which would mean the complex was finished in 27/28 C.E., long after Herod's death in 4 B.C.E. Josephus reports that the project was not completed until shortly before the First Jewish Revolt broke out in 66 C.E. The Temple was destroyed four years later by Roman legions under Titus.

Three somewhat different descriptions of Herod's Temple have survived. Josephus left two descriptions, one in each of his two major works—*The Jewish War*, which describes the first Jewish Revolt against Rome (in which, incidentally, he was a participant), and *The Antiquities of the Jews*, a history of the Jewish people from the beginning to Josephus's own time. The third

לבית התקיעה להכ׳ז

description of the Temple is in tractate *Middot* in the Mishnah, the earliest codification of Rabbinic law (about 200 C.E.) and the core of the Talmud. The three descriptions vary in the details but are in general agreement, so we can reconstruct with some confidence the Temple that Jesus knew and that the Romans destroyed.

Like Solomon's tripartite Temple, the Herodian Temple consisted of a portico, a main sanctuary and the Holy of Holies (see plan, p. 160). The portico was wider than the other two rooms. An upper chamber extended over the main sanctuary and the Holy of Holies. Again like Solomon's Temple, the facade pointed east toward the rising sun. The entire building was made of marble, and much of it, including the facade, was plated with gold, so it fairly sparkled. It was said that at sunrise, the facade radiated with so fierce a flash that people had to avert their eyes to keep from being blinded. Enclosing the building on three sides up to the ceiling of the main sanctuary and the Holy of Holies was a series of cells—small, windowless rooms—arranged in three stories.

Columns stood in the portico on either side of the entrance to the main sanctuary. The entryway to the main hall had a set of double gold-covered doors. In front of these doors hung a Babylonian tapestry portraying a panorama of the heavens. The tapestry was visible even when the doors were closed. Golden vines decorated the entrance; in the Bible, Israel is sometimes compared to a vine (see, for example, Jeremiah 2:21; Ezekiel 17:5–8; Psalm 80:9–12). Donations and votive offerings of gold were often hung on the vines.

Among the items in the main sanctuary was a seven-branched candelabra called a menorah. Within 300 yards of where this menorah once stood, in the

This inscribed stone fell from the top of the Temple Mount during the Roman destruction of the city in 70 C.E. In beautifully carved Hebrew letters, it reads, "To the place of the trumpeting to [or 'for']...." It apparently designated the place, as shown in the reconstruction drawing (above), from which the priest announced the beginning and end of the sabbath with the blast of a trumpet.

Wilson's Arch (foreground), unlike Robinson's Arch, is complete, though probably rebuilt in the Arab period. It is a monumental arch that supported a bridge across the valley to the Upper City, where Jerusalem's wealthy and priestly families lived. William Simpson painted this picture of it for the Illustrated London News, *which covered the work of the Palestine Exploration Fund in the 1860s.*

Jewish Quarter of the Old City, Nahman Avigad's excavators discovered a depiction of a menorah scratched into the white plaster of a wall dated to the Herodian period (see photo, p. 161). Whoever carved this menorah into the plaster did so when the Temple menorah still stood inside the Temple; he (or she) almost certainly knew the original. It is tantalizing to speculate about how closely the menorah graffito may resemble the exemplar so near at hand.

If you look closely at the two fragments on which the menorah is incised, you will see the outlines of two other artifacts. Professor Bezalel Narkiss of the Hebrew University Center for Jewish Art suggests that the upper one depicts the Temple altar and the lower one the shewbread table. Only part of the drawings of these two accessories has survived on the graffito; the rest must be reconstructed.

Two curtains embroidered with lions and eagles separated the sanctuary from the Holy of Holies, which, in Herod's Temple, was empty and devoid of furnishings. According to *Middot*, inside was a rock, apparently flat and three fingers high, on which the High Priest burned incense on the Day of Atonement

(Yom Kippur). He was the only one permitted to enter the Holy of Holies and even he could do so only once a year, on the holiest day.

By the time of Herod, however, the Temple was not the only Jewish religious institution in Jerusalem. We sometimes forget that the synagogue overlapped in time with the Temple. According to the Talmud, there were 394 synagogues in Jerusalem before the Romans destroyed the Temple in 70 C.E. One of these synagogues was on the Temple Mount itself. If the number seems exaggerated, consider that today there are more than 6,000 synagogues in Jerusalem. Then, as now, most of them were quite small.

Not a single one of the Jerusalem synagogues from the Herodian period has been found. But there is archaeological evidence of the existence of at least one. In 1913, Raymond Weill was excavating a cistern in the City of David when he found a limestone plaque that someone had thrown into the cistern nearly 2,000 years before (see photo, p. 162). The plaque contained an extraordinary inscription revealing that it was a dedicatory plaque from an ancient synagogue.[74] Beautifully chiseled in Greek, the inscription reads as follows:

> Theodotus, son of Vettenos, priest and archisynagogus, son of an archisynagogus, grandson of an archisynagogus, built this synagogue for the reading of the Law and for the teaching of the Commandments, and he has built the hostel and the chambers and the water-fittings for the accommodation of those who, coming from abroad, have need of them. The foundations of the synagogue were laid by his fathers and by the Elders and by Simonides.

The Theodotus inscription, as it is called, has been securely dated to the Herodian period. Although it was not discovered in a dated archaeological stratum, none of the pottery in the cistern in which it was found dated from later than the Herodian period. The rim on the plaque also confirms a Herodian date. And besides, as a matter of history, it was highly unlikely that a synagogue would have been built in Jerusalem after the Romans destroyed the city in 70 C.E.[75]

The inscription clearly indicates that in the Herodian period the synagogue was already a highly developed institution. Here the Law was read and the commandments of the Lord were taught; thus even at this early period, education was a primary function of the synagogue. Attached to this synagogue was a kind of hostel where travelers and strangers could spend the night and take their meals. The hostel even boasted fine plumbing facilities.

The synagogue was led by someone called an *archisynagogus*, a position that appears to have been hereditary. But the synagogue was apparently governed by a kind of board of directors, referred to as the "Elders," who made the decision to build the synagogue and therefore had the honor, together with a dignitary named Simonides, of laying the foundation stone.

Herod's Temple

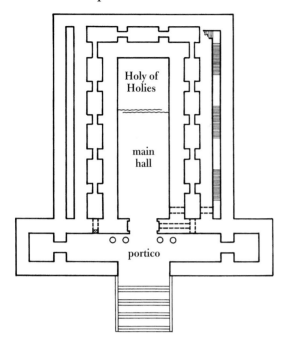

Holy of Holies

main hall

portico

Herod's Temple, although a grander structure than the one it replaced, retained the tripartite plan of Solomon's Temple: a portico, a long hall and a small shrine in the back, which, however, was now empty, except for the Even ha-Shetiah, the Foundation Stone, where the holy Ark once rested. The model of the Temple (photo, top), at the Holy Land Hotel in Jerusalem, shows an elaborate additional gateway with semicircular steps in front of the Temple. The cutaway reconstruction drawing shows the upper chamber extending over the main sanctuary and the Holy of Holies and the three stories of windowless rooms wrapped around the building.

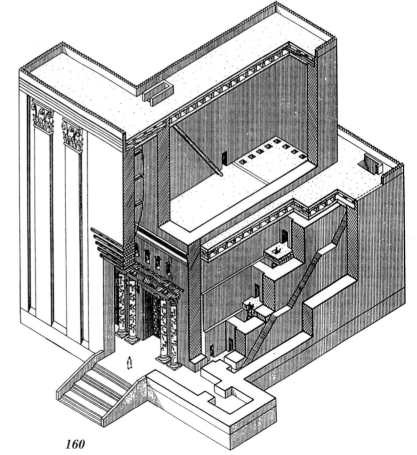

The inscription is written in Greek, rather than Hebrew or Aramaic, indicating just how Hellenized some Jerusalem Jews were at this time. It has been suggested that the use of Greek may indicate that this was the Synagogue of the Freedmen referred to in the New Testament (Acts 6:9).

We turn now to a wealthy residential area of the city. The bridge supported by Wilson's Arch led west, across the Tyropoeon Valley, directly from the Temple Mount to the western hill, the area then known as the Upper City, where the high and mighty lived. Here were the homes of wealthy merchants and powerful priestly families.

A painful paradox allows us to describe, in vivid detail, this sumptuous residential area, which had lain buried since it was destroyed in 70 C.E., covered by later structures and beyond the reach of explorers or archaeologists. When Israel's War of Independence came to an end in 1949, the Old City of Jerusalem remained in Jordanian hands. From 1948 to 1967, the area was largely inaccessible to Jews. During that time, the Jewish Quarter deteriorated, synagogues and

altar

shewbread
table

These two adjoining plaster fragments with a menorah (seven-branched candelabra) etched into them were found a few hundred feet from the Temple Mount. Dating to when the Temple still stood, this depiction provides our most reliable evidence of what the Temple menorah looked like. Also incised on the plaster fragments are parts of what scholars have reconstructed as the Temple altar (upper right) and the shewbread table (lower right). That these two items are Temple furnishings suggests that the artist intended to depict the Temple menorah as well.

The famous Theodotus inscription is engraved on a dedicatory plaque from a Jerusalem synagogue that functioned before the destruction of the Temple. Because the inscription is written in Greek, some scholars have suggested that it may have come from the Synagogue of the Freedmen, referred to in Acts 6:9.

yeshivot (religious schools) were destroyed, and other public buildings, including hospitals, were razed. When the Old City once again came under Jewish rule in 1967, after the Six-Day War, Israeli authorities proceeded to rebuild the ancient Jewish Quarter. Here was the painful paradox: Jordanian destruction had made the area available for excavation for the first time.

The excavation was not pursued according to a pre-established overall plan. It began because archaeologists wanted to get in before the contractors. Whenever construction workers in Israel come upon ancient remains, the law requires that the Antiquities Authority be notified, and construction is stopped until the ancient remains are investigated and sometimes excavated. Unfortunately, contractors sometimes ignore the law and destroy ancient remains to avoid delaying their work. Fortunately, this did not happen during reconstruction of the Jewish Quarter of the Old City.

To direct the excavations, the authorities turned to a distinguished archaeologist who was nearing retirement and was about to go on a sabbatical. At the age of 62, Nahman Avigad accepted the assignment, believing that it would last only a short time. In fact, it lasted 14 years, during which he dug almost continuously—and as meticulously as any archaeologist digging in Israel. Another

A mosaic carpet with interlocking swastikas decorates this room in a wealthy Jerusalem home at the turn of the era. The room is furnished with original tables and pottery found in the excavation.

These richly painted plaster fragments (above) fell from rooms in the lavish residence dubbed "the Mansion." The fragments on the left were painted to resemble marble. On the right are stylized vines and grapes. Some of the frescoes were found intact, like the one shown in the excavation photo at left. None of the decorations contained human or animal figures; the Second Commandment's prohibition against images was interpreted very strictly at this time.

A reconstruction of the luxurious Herodian residence in the Upper City dubbed by the excavators "the Mansion." Note that it had two mikva'ot (singular, mikveh), or ritual baths, indicating that the inhabitants were observant Jews. The lower left photo on p. 163 shows part of the fresco room during excavation.

The vaulted entrance to the larger mikveh in "the Mansion" reveals itself during excavation (above). The geometric mosaic on the floor in front of the entrance can be seen in the photo and in the reconstruction. In the photo, watching at right, is excavation director Nahman Avigad.

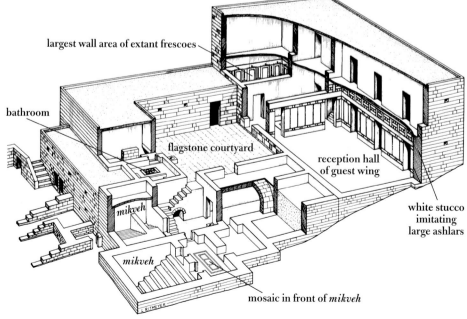

largest wall area of extant frescoes

bathroom

flagstone courtyard

reception hall of guest wing

mikveh

mikveh

white stucco imitating large ashlars

mosaic in front of *mikveh*

L. RITMEYER

An elegant stone table supported by a single leg in the form of a column with base, shaft and capital. The table top was found broken in dozens of pieces, but was restored by carefully gluing the pieces together. The table holds fine, probably imported tableware called eastern terra sigillata *ware, characterized by its high burnish and reddish color.*

distinguished scholar, Frank Moore Cross of Harvard, has described Avigad's investigations:

> The work was undertaken under the most difficult restrictions. He could dig only in small plots where the destruction had opened "holes" among the monuments of the Jewish Quarter, and was forced to fight constantly against the pressures of those intent on keeping time schedules in reconstructing the Quarter for modern habitation.[76]

In the end, Avigad became known as the "High Priest of the Jewish Quarter."

His excavations were especially successful in uncovering remains of the Herodian period. In a spectacular location overlooking the Temple Mount, Avigad

This distinctive pottery is known as "Jerusalem pottery," or "Jerusalem ware." Locally made and found only in Jerusalem, it is very thin and therefore extremely fragile. The red, black and brown decoration consists mostly of floral designs. The advanced state of craftsmanship at this time can also be seen in the workmanship on the surviving fragment of a marble banquet tray shown at right.

This limestone sundial was excavated in "the Mansion." Incised lines divide the concave dial into 12 segments. A horizontal rod attached to the top would have cast its shadow on the dial. Elaborate rosettes decorate the side.

uncovered six palatial Herodian period homes built on terraces extending down the slope of the western hill. Some had two and even more stories. These fine homes were characterized by reception halls, internal peristyle courtyards, finely crafted masonry to which plaster had been applied, frescoes of architectural and floral designs, and elegant mosaic floors. Elaborate water systems with large plastered cisterns assured adequate supplies of water even in the dry summer months. The bathrooms had spacious plastered bathtubs and special basins, probably for washing feet.

Of particular interest were a large number of *mikva'ot* (singular, *mikveh*), or ritual baths, where the inhabitants purified themselves. One house had two large *mikva'ot*, each with doorways located side by side—one for entering before purification and the other for exiting after purification. Other *mikva'ot* had steps separated down the middle by a low wall; the two sides of the steps served the same purpose—to separate the impure from the pure.

The furnishings of these homes were as elegant as the structures—stone jars two feet tall, goblets, cups with lids, limestone sundials, expensive rectangular stone tables that fit against the wall (the wall edge was undecorated), low, round, three-legged tables, large bronze keys, inkwells, perfume bottles, fine marble banquet trays and beautifully painted, thin tableware decorated with distinctive red,

brown and black floral designs, now known as "Jerusalem pottery," or "Jerusalem ware." Among the graceful glassware was an unusually exquisite piece, unfortunately badly damaged, signed in Greek by the famous 1st-century glassmaker Ennion. Only two other signed examples of his work exist.

Archaeologists were able to identify the occupants of one house as the Kathros family. The House of Kathros was a priestly family that abused its position through nepotism and oppression to further its own interests. The Talmud records a folk song with a refrain that includes the line "Woe is me because of the House of Kathros."[77] In the house, which excavators dubbed the "Burnt House," they found a weight inscribed "[Belonging t]o Bar Kathros." Although the name Kathros is Greek, the inscription is in Hebrew letters, the square Aramaic form still used today, which the Jewish exiles brought back from Babylonia. "Bar," meaning son in Aramaic (the vernacular of the period), indicates that "Kathros" refers to the family rather than to a particular individual.

Herodian tombs in and around Jerusalem are as elegant as the residences. We have already looked at some imposing Hasmonean tombs. The Herodian tombs are similar, and together they are referred to as Second Temple tombs. Outstanding examples are Absalom's Tomb (which has nothing to do with King David's rebellious son Absalom) in the Kidron Valley and the Tomb of the Kings (which likewise was erroneously identified—as the tomb of the kings of Judah) north of the Old City near the American Colony Hotel.

Two characteristic features identify Second Temple tombs. One we have already described—*kochim* (loculi), burial niches carved into the rock walls of burial-cave chambers. *Kochim* are cut lengthwise into the rock to a depth of about six feet; the niches are about a foot and a half high and the same in width. The other characteristic feature, arcosolia (singular, arcosolium), are cut width-wise, forming a kind of shelf, or recess, about six feet wide and about a foot and a half deep; the top is arched, hence the name (see photo, p. 171).

Another distinctive characteristic of late Second Temple period burials around Jerusalem is the use of ossuaries, limestone bone boxes into which the bones of the deceased were placed about a year after the initial burial (see photo, p. 170). Thousands of these ossuaries have been found in the Jerusalem area. Some are beautifully carved, never with human figures, but often with architectural elements (such as columns), elaborate rosettes or floral patterns. Some are inscribed—in Hebrew, Aramaic and Greek. Some were placed in *kochim*; some were simply stacked one on top of the other in burial chambers.

The elegant, at times decadent, Herodian lifestyle we have just described ended abruptly with the Great Jewish Revolt that began in 66 C.E. and culminated in 70 C.E. with the destruction of Jerusalem and the burning of the Temple. So powerful was the Herodian influence that even though Herod died

This impressive tomb in the Kidron Valley, known as Absalom's Tomb, actually has nothing to do with David's rebellious son Absalom. It acquired this moniker before scholars could accurately date it; the identification is based on the biblical passage that says that in his lifetime Absalom erected a memorial monument to himself (otherwise, as he knew, no one would memorialize him). According to the Bible, the monument was known as Yad Avshalom (Absalom's Memorial), which stands "to this day" (2 Samuel 18:18). In fact, the structure dates to the Herodian period.

This stone weight is inscribed in Aramaic: "[Belonging t]o Bar Kathros." Found in a building the excavators called the Burnt House because of its condition, it probably belonged to the priestly Kathros family, referred to in the Talmud.

In the late Second Temple period in the Jerusalem area, bones of the deceased were often collected about a year after initial burial and reburied in stone boxes called ossuaies. Thousands of ossuaries like these have been found in and around Jerusalem.

in 4 B.C.E., the years through 70 C.E. are included in the Herodian period. The distinctive material culture of his reign did not die with him.

Politically, however, matters changed dramatically after Herod's death. The brutality with which he had ruled could no longer keep the populace in check. As he lay on his deathbed, the eagle he had erected over the entrance to the Temple was hacked to pieces. Upon his death, riots broke out in Jerusalem as well as in other parts of Judea, Galilee and even Transjordan, reflecting the sharp social differences created by Herod's high taxes and extravagant spending.

Herod had been a vassal king of Rome. When he died, his kingdom was divided among his three sons, who also ruled by Roman leave. Archelaus, who took over Judea, was soon deposed, however; Judea (and adjoining territories) was ruled thereafter by Roman prefects residing in Caesarea, a mixed Jewish-pagan city on the Mediterranean coast.

Pontius Pilate served as Roman prefect from 26 to 36 C.E. By all accounts, he was a harsh ruler. According to the Gospels, he massacred a group of Galileans (Luke 13:1) and brutally suppressed a rebellion (Mark 15:7), quite aside from crucifying Jesus in about 30 C.E.

For a brief three-year period, beginning in 41 C.E., the Roman emperor appointed Herod's grandson Agrippa I as king over a large area that included Judea. Upon Agrippa's death in 44 C.E., however, the country reverted to direct Roman rule, governed by Roman dictators now called procurators.

After Agrippa's brief reign, a series of incompetent, insensitive and often corrupt Roman procurators finally brought the Jews to open rebellion in 66 C.E. The Roman general Vespasian, assigned to suppress the rebellion, soon captured Galilee and the Golan, but he was recalled to Rome upon the assassination of Nero in 68 C.E. and was proclaimed emperor a year later. He sent his son Titus to complete the suppression of the Jewish revolt. In the spring of 70 C.E., Titus laid siege to Jerusalem.

The fighting that raged over the city's fate was fierce. The major rallying point of the revolutionaries was the Temple, which thus became the major target of the Romans. Titus approached the city, as did most conquerors, from the north. Methodically, he advanced toward his goal, breaching in turn each of the three protective northern walls.

Second Temple period tombs are characterized by kochim, *or* loculi *(long, narrow niches in the wall), and* arcosolia. *The latter are so named because of the arch over the broad burial shelf carved into the wall, as shown in the arcosolium in this picture.* Kochim *are shown on p. 204.*

*Jerusalem's
Three Walls*

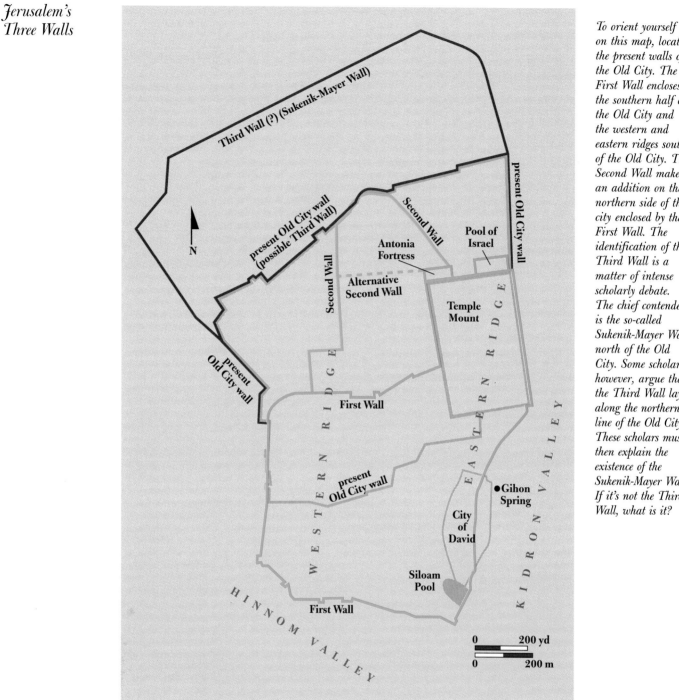

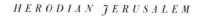

To orient yourself
on this map, locate
the present walls of
the Old City. The
First Wall encloses
the southern half of
the Old City and
the western and
eastern ridges south
of the Old City. The
Second Wall makes
an addition on the
northern side of the
city enclosed by the
First Wall. The
identification of the
Third Wall is a
matter of intense
scholarly debate.
The chief contender
is the so-called
Sukenik-Mayer Wall
north of the Old
City. Some scholars,
however, argue that
the Third Wall lay
along the northern
line of the Old City.
These scholars must
then explain the
existence of the
Sukenik-Mayer Wall.
If it's not the Third
Wall, what is it?

We have already described the First Wall, which circumvallated both the western and eastern ridges. This wall was completed by the Hasmoneans and incorporated much of the earlier Israelite wall. Of the Second Wall, nothing has been found.

The location of the Third Wall is a matter of intense scholarly disagreement.[78] At various times, explorers and archaeologists have identified fragments of a wall about 1,500 feet north of the Old City as the Third Wall. This wall is sometimes

called the Sukenik-Mayer Wall, after two Israeli scholars who studied and exca-vated parts of it in the 1920s and 1930s. Approximately 2,500 feet of this wall have been found. One segment can be seen in front of the American consulate in East Jerusalem.

Most scholars have identified this as the Third Wall, as described by Jose-phus. But a number of other scholars have identified the northern wall of the Old City as the line of the Third Wall. If that was the line of the Third Wall, then what was the wall 1,500 feet further north? Various answers to this question have been given.

Kathleen Kenyon suggested that the wall was built by Titus to prevent the Jews from getting out of the starving city. But this explanation has been largely discredited by an Israeli team, led by Ehud Netzer and Sara Ben-Arieh, who have clearly shown that the wall had towers on the north face, indicating that the wall faced north to meet an expected enemy.

Pierre Benoit of the École Biblique suggested that it was an additional bar-rier wall (a kind of fourth wall) put up by the Jewish rebels (evidenced by patches of rough, irregular, and therefore rushed, construction). This idea has

Fragment of a wall about 1,500 feet north of the Old City. Most scholars believe it is the Third Wall identified by the Jewish historian Josephus that defended the city from the Romans on the vulnerable northern approach to the city.

been supported by another scholar, Emmett Hamrick, who argues that this wall was intended to keep Roman catapult stones (which had a range of about 1,250 feet) from reaching the city proper. To most scholars, this argument is unconvincing. Why didn't Josephus mention it in his detailed account of the revolt? But the debate among scholars continues unabated.[79]

There are also problems with the identification of the Sukenik-Mayer Wall as the Third Wall. For example, according to Josephus, the Third Wall enclosed a northern suburb, which the Romans ultimately burned. But no one has found any evidence of burning, or even of houses from this period, in the area between the supposed Third Wall and the northern wall of the Old City. In short, the location of the Third Wall remains a puzzle.

There is no reason, however, to doubt Josephus's vivid description of the Romans' horrible destruction of the city. They captured the Temple on the Ninth of Av (August 28, 70 C.E.; the Babylonians destroyed the First Temple on the same date, the Ninth of Av), but the Upper City stubbornly held out for another month. On the seventh of Elul, the Romans attacked the Upper City in full fury:

> Pouring into the alleys, swords in hand [the Romans] massacred indiscriminately all whom they met, and burnt the houses with all who had taken refuge within. Often in the course of their raids, on entering the houses for loot, they would find whole families dead and the rooms filled with the victims of the famine…Running everyone through who fell in their way, they choked the alleys with corpses and deluged the whole city with blood…Toward evening they ceased slaughtering, but when night fell the fire gained the mastery, and the dawn of the eighth day of the month of [Elul] broke upon Jerusalem in flames.[80]

Josephus's description is confirmed by the archaeological record. Evidence of the fiery destruction was found all over. We will look only at one house where the destruction was particularly dramatic. This house, the house of the Kathros family, referred to by the excavators as the "Burnt House," was thoroughly consumed by the flames. Even the stones of the walls turned multicolored from the intense heat of the fire. The debris that filled the rooms was a mixture of ash, soot and huge quantities of charred wood. The archaeologists' faces turned black as they excavated it.

The coins and the pottery confirm the date of the destruction. The latest coins were dated to the fourth year of the revolt—69 C.E. There is no doubt that this fire occured during the Roman destruction of the city in 70 C.E. Excavator Nahman Avigad describes the effect on Jerusalemites who thronged to the site when they heard of the discovery—the first clear archaeological evidence of the burning of the city:

This spear is shown where it was found in the corner of a room in a palatial residence that was destroyed by the Romans in 70 C.E. Apparently placed there by the owner for a final defense of his home, it was never used.

As the Romans poured into Jerusalem's streets and set the city afire, a young Jewish woman of about 20 fled from her kitchen and fell. Her hand grasped a step as the flames consumed her. Nearly 2,000 years later, archaeologists found the delicate bones of her arm and hand reaching for the safety that never came.

Something amazing occurred in the hearts of all who witnessed the progress of excavations here. The burning of the Temple and the destruction of Jerusalem—fateful events in the history of the Jewish People—suddenly took on a new and horrible significance. Persons who had previously regarded this catastrophe as stirring but abstract and remote, having occurred two millennia ago, were so visibly moved by the sight that they occasionally would beg permission to take a fistful of soil or a bit of charred wood "in memory of the destruction." Others volunteered to take part in uncovering the remains, regarding such labor as sacred.[81]

As the excavators removed ash and debris from the house—from the kitchen, near the steps and beside the oven—they slowly uncovered the skeletal remains of the lower arm and hand of a young woman, about 20 years old. The fingers appeared to be trying to grasp the step as she fell, in a final attempt to escape the flames. Avigad described the scene: "This tangible evidence, surprising in its freshness and shocking in its realism, gave us the feeling that it had all happened only yesterday."[82]

In another room, archaeologists found a spear propped against a wall, where the owner could grab it in an instant to defend himself against invading Romans. But the house burned so quickly that the spear was never touched; it was simply buried in the fiery debris.

XI

The Jerusalem of Jesus

L ET'S RETRACE OUR STEPS A BIT, BACK IN TIME TO ABOUT 30 C.E., WHEN A wise preacher from Galilee entered Jerusalem. We already know a great deal about what the city was like at that time. But a few places in Jerusalem are especially associated with his ministry and crucifixion.

One archaeological find is not related to a place, however, but to an event. Archaeologists have recovered the bones of a Jewish man who was crucified in Jerusalem in the 1st century C.E. An iron nail, more than seven inches long, is still embedded in his heel bone. The bones were found in an ossuary at a site known as Givat ha-Mivtar, north of the Old City. Based on a study of the bones, paleo-osteologists have concluded that the victim was in his mid- to late twenties. Because he was buried in this affluent cemetery, he probably came from a good family; it is doubtful that he was a common thief. Excavator Vassilios Tzaferis, of the Israel Antiquities Authority, thinks the victim was probably guilty of a political crime. One member of the victim's family, whose bones were found in another ossuary, is identified by an inscription as "Simon, builder of the Temple." Apparently, the family was politically active in this turbulent period. We also know the name of the crucified man, which was scratched on the side of his ossuary: "Yehohanan, son of Hagakol." The rest is speculation.

Jesus of Nazareth, who would also be crucified, approached the city for the last time from Bethphage and Bethany. He came down the Mount of Olives, crossed the Kidron Valley and entered the city from the east. As he descended the Mount of Olives, a multitude of his followers rejoiced. Crowds went before

A large iron nail pierces the heel bone of a Jewish man in his mid- to late twenties who was crucified in Jerusalem in the 1st century C.E. The nail apparently hit a knot in the cross and curled backward. That the victim's bones were found in an ossuary suggests he was not a common thief; the excavator believes he was probably guilty of a political crime.

Jerusalem from the Mount of Olives, with a view of the eastern wall of the Old City. Jesus entered the city for the last time from this direction. The Golden Gate appears slightly to the right of center.

and after him, shouting, "Hosanna to the Son of David. Blessed is he who comes in the name of the Lord" (Matthew 21:1–9; Mark 11:1–10; Luke 19:28–38).[83]

Jesus probably entered Jerusalem through an eastern gate. Because he went directly to the Temple, he probably used the gate that led directly there. Today that is the double-arched Golden Gate, which was blocked sometime after the Moslems expelled the Crusaders from Jerusalem (see photo, p. 182). According to one unconfirmed story, the Golden Gate was closed to keep the Messiah, who was expected to come from the east, from entering.

The applied decoration above the Golden Gate is quite similar to the applied decoration above the Double Gate on the southern wall of the Temple Mount (see photo, p. 144); both date to the Omayyad period (7th–8th centuries C.E.). But, as with the Double Gate, there is probably an earlier gateway behind the Golden Gate. Evidence of an earlier gate is extant inside the current gate, but scholars have been unable to agree on the date of the original Golden Gate. It is possible that Jesus entered Jerusalem through this earlier gate.

But that's not the end of the story. One fresh morning in April 1969, James Fleming, a young Bible student from the American Institute of Holy Land

Studies in Jerusalem, was exploring the Golden Gate after a heavy rain the day before. As he kneeled to frame a picture of the gate in the viewfinder of his camera, he felt the ground beneath him suddenly give way. Disoriented, but uninjured, he found himself in an eight-foot hole, knee deep in human bones. He had fallen into a mass grave.

As Fleming acclimated himself to his surroundings, he began to examine the face of the wall beneath the Golden Gate. To his astonishment, directly beneath the arches of the Golden Gate he found five wedge-shaped stones set neatly in a massive arch. Here, beneath the Golden Gate, were the remains of an earlier gate to Jerusalem that had been hitherto unknown. Fleming and the director of the school managed to take a few amateur pictures of the five arched stones (see photo, p. 183), but Moslem religious authorities promptly cemented over the area with uncharacteristic efficiency and enclosed it in a wrought-iron fence. It is unlikely that anyone will ever see this underground gate again. All we have are a few pictures.[84]

Proposed dates for the gate beneath the Golden Gate vary from Solomonic to Herodian. I believe the most likely date is Herodian—when the Temple Mount enclosure on the eastern wall was reconstructed following the line of the earlier

The gate below the Golden Gate was discovered only accidentally in the late 1960s when, after a heavy rain, a young Bible student fell into a hole containing a mass of human bones. Examining the wall directly beneath the Golden Gate, he noticed an arch of five trapezoid-shaped stones—the remains of what appears to be an earlier gate. The similarity of the stones to the Herodian masonry of the original Double Gate on the southern Temple Mount wall suggests that this lower gate is also Herodian. If so, it is probably the gate Jesus rode through on a donkey when he entered Jerusalem.

enclosure wall. One objection to a Herodian date is the plainness of the five arched stones that Fleming saw. They are flat, with no margins, bosses or decorations; and there appears to be no frame of any kind. Would Herod have constructed such a simple gate here, especially in light of the apocalyptic and messianic associations of the eastern gate of the city?*

The argument against a Herodian date becomes stronger when the plain stones of the gate under the Golden Gate are compared to two other Roman period gateways. One is the Roman gate beneath the Damascus Gate (see photos, pp. 221–222); the other is the Ecce Homo arch (see photos, pp. 194–195), which passes through the Sisters of Zion Convent. Both of these feature arches composed of elegant receding arcs. But I think this argument is easily refuted, because both the Ecce Homo arch and the arch of the gate below the Damascus Gate are post-Herodian, actually 2nd century C.E.

More significant, however, is that everyone agrees that the Double Gate, the original stones of which can be seen on the southern wall behind the applied Omayyad decoration (see photo, p. 148), is Herodian. And yet, this Herodian gate, the main entrance to the Temple Mount, is composed of plain ashlars, just like the stones in the arch below the Golden Gate. Indeed, the consensus of a

The Golden Gate, now blocked, in the eastern wall of the Old City, dates to the Omayyad period (7th–8th centuries C.E.), but beneath this gate is an earlier gate through which Jesus may have entered the city.

*The prophet Zechariah delivered an oracle regarding the day of the Lord's coming: "On that day his feet shall stand on the Mount of Olives which lies before Jerusalem on the east...Then the Lord your God will come, and all the holy ones with him" (Zechariah 14:4–5).

The prophet Joel also delivered an oracle on the "Day of the Lord": "And I will give portents in the heavens and on the earth, blood and fire and columns of smoke. The sun shall be turned to darkness, and the moon to blood, before the great and terrible day of the Lord comes (Joel 2:30–31). The oracle goes on: "I will gather all the nations and bring them down to the Valley of Jehosaphat, for there I will sit to judge all the nations" (Joel 3:2). The Valley of Jehosaphat is another name for the Kidron Valley. The Messiah was thus expected to enter through the eastern gate.

This is the Garden of Gethsemane (above), with its gnarled, ancient olive trees (probably not 2,000 years old, however). But the Gospels don't actually speak of a "garden" of Gethsemane; both Matthew and Mark tell of a "place called Gethsemane."

Herodian date for the Double Gate almost certainly confirms that the gate below the Golden Gate is of the same period.[85]

In short, when Jesus entered Jerusalem, he probably entered through the recently discovered gate beneath the Golden Gate.*

Few sites in Jerusalem are as well known as the Garden of Gethsemane, on the lower slope of the Mount of Olives, with its extraordinary olive trees, gnarled and twisted with enormous age. The trouble is that the Gospels never mention a *garden* of Gethsemane.

*Recently, my friend Leen Ritmeyer suggested in personal correspondence that the arch beneath the Golden Gate supported a stairway to the upper gate, much like the arched structure of which Robinson's Arch, was a part and was not a part of the gate itself. Ritmeyer points out that the Golden Gate now sticks out seven feet from the wall. The current gate dates to the Arab period, but within this gate are two pillars from an original gate. The staircase, says Ritmeyer, led up to the gateway of which these pillars were once a part. If that is the appropriate reconstruction, then upon entering the city Jesus probably ascended the stairway supported by the stones of this arch.

The Gethsemane events described in the Gospels probably occurred in this cave (right). Gethsemane means "oil press," and evidence of an ancient olive-pressing plant was discovered inside the cave, the largest on the eastern slope of the Mount of Olives. It is here that Jesus probably spent the night before his arrest and here that Judas betrayed him with a kiss.

The place where the disciples go to pray, where Judas betrays Jesus by identifying him to the authorities with a kiss, and where Jesus is arrested, is identified as a "place called Gethsemane" (Mark 14:32; Matthew 26:36). The Gospel of John does refer to a *kepos* (John 18:1), which can be translated "garden" but really means a cultivated tract of land, rather than a small plot with flowers, shrubs and a few vegetables in a park-like setting. Moreover, John never refers to Gethsemane. The tradition about the Garden of Gethsemane was created by conflating the reference to *kepos* in John with references to Gethsemane in other gospels.

According to a recent archaeological study, the events of Gethsemane took place, not in a garden, but in a spacious cave that can now be reached by a long corridor to the right of the courtyard leading to the traditional Tomb of the Virgin.

Gethsemane means "oil press" (*gat-shemanim*) and probably refers to an olive press located in the cave, where remains of such an installation have been found. Olive presses were often placed in caves because their warmth hastened the extraction of oil. Olives were pressed only in fall and winter, after the harvest. By spring (the Passion occurred in this season, just before Passover), the cave would have been available to pilgrims flocking to Jerusalem for the holy week. The cave would have been an excellent place to spend the night—warm, dry and roomy. "It is extremely improbable," argues archaeologist Joan Taylor, "that Jesus and his disciples would have spent the night out in the open sleeping amid olive trees…[In spring] the nights are cold and the dew is heavy. One simply cannot camp out without shelter at this time of year without getting very cold and damp. The Gospel of John explicitly states that it was cold on the night Jesus was arrested (John 18:18)."[86]

There is no mention of the Garden of Gethsemane before the 12th century. According to Taylor, Jesus was really arrested in the cave, which now takes its place as one of the authentic sites related to Jesus' ministry in Jerusalem.

Another traditional site that appears to be wrongly attributed is known as Akeldama, or the Field of Blood. After Judas betrayed Jesus, he was overcome with remorse. Slightly differing accounts as to what happened next are given in the Gospel of Matthew and in the Acts of the Apostles. In Matthew, Judas attempts to return to the Temple priests the 30 pieces of silver he received as payment for his betrayal; the priests refuse to put the money in their treasury—it is contaminated "blood money"; Judas then throws the money on the floor, and the priests use it to buy a potter's field, where the poor are buried. After this, according to Matthew, Judas hangs himself (Matthew 27:3–8).

In Acts, Judas buys a field with the money. Then, "falling headlong, he burst open in the middle and all his bowels gushed out. This became known to all the residents of Jerusalem, so that the field was called in their language Akeldama, that is, Field of Blood" (Acts 1:18–19).

A tomb at the traditional site of Akeldama, the Field of Blood, where Judas hanged himself in remorse for betraying Jesus.

Several recent studies reject the identification of the traditional site of Akeldama as the Field of Blood. In fact, rather than a burial place for the poor, this site was a burial ground for influential Jews of the late Second Temple period. Some of the most elegant and best-preserved tombs of the time have been found here, including, quite probably, the tomb of the high priest Annas (see photo, p. 188). It is not likely that the poor would have been buried in this prime piece of real estate, in view of the Temple and alongside the nobility of the community.[87] Annas, who served as high priest from 6–15 C.E.,[88] had five sons as well as a son-in-law, all of whom served as high priest at one time or another. Annas's son-in-law was none other than the high priest Caiaphas, who presided at Jesus' trial (Matthew 26:57). Josephus refers to him as "Joseph who was called Caiaphas of the high priesthood,"[89] indicating that Caiaphas was a kind of family nickname (people didn't have family names in those days).

In the winter of 1990, Zvi Greenhut, an archaeologist with the Israel Antiquities Authority, conducted an emergency excavation in the Jerusalem Peace Forest after contractors came upon ancient remains. The site turned out to be an ancient tomb from the late Second Temple period. Among the finds were 12 ossuaries, or bone boxes, two of them with the name "Caiaphas" scratched on them (see photos, pp. 190–191). Indeed, one was even more specific. It read, "Joseph son of Caiaphas," recalling the passage from Josephus in which the high priest who the Gospels say presided at Jesus' trial was "Joseph who was called Caiaphas." The name was scratched in the limestone ossuary with a nail, probably to identify the person whose bones were inside. The letters are in the standard Jewish script of the period.

This is the first time we have found the original Semitic form of the name of this high priest. The name Caiaphas in both Josephus and the New Testament is in Greek.

The interior of one of the most magnificent tombs at the traditional site of Akeldama features a large rosette carved into the stone ceiling. Unfortunately, the tomb is not well maintained. The drawing at right indicates what the tomb chamber originally looked like. Three kochim *(*loculi, *or burial niches) can be seen in the wall at back. Note the false doorway engraved over the middle* koch *(the* koch *highlighted in brown) and the doorway at left. The high priest Annas (6–15 C.E.) was probably buried in this tomb. One of Annas's daughters married a man named Caiaphas, who would also become a high priest. According to the Gospels, Caiaphas presided at the trial of Jesus.*

The ossuary marked "Joseph son of Caiaphas" contained the bones of a 60-year-old man. Thus we may not only have the ossuary of the man who, according to the Gospels, presided at the trial of Jesus, we may even have his bones.[90] Of one thing there is no doubt: This is one of the most beautiful ossuaries discovered in more than 800 Jerusalem tombs (see photo, p. 190). It is surely a fitting ossuary for a high priest.

The Via Dolorosa, the "Way of Tears" (see photo, p. 193), was the route Jesus followed from imprisonment to Calvary, where he was crucified. The Ecce Homo arch crosses the Via Dolorosa at the Second Station of the Cross, in front of the Sisters of Zion Convent in the Old City. In the basement of the convent is a polished stone pavement, which was long thought to be the *lithostrotos*,[91] the stone pavement where Jesus is said to have been judged by Pontius Pilate (see photo, p. 192). The Ecce Homo arch is the place on the route where Pilate proclaimed, "Behold the Man" (John 19:5).

Alas, none of these identifications holds up under careful scrutiny.

Of the Via Dolorosa, little need be said. As Father Jerome Murphy-O'Connor of the École Biblique has respectfully written, "The Via Dolorosa is defined by faith, not by history."[92]

190

Caiaphas Ossuary

אמטסבקטא
קפא בר יהוסף

A masterpiece of the stonecutter's art, this ossuary, or bone box, found in a recently excavated tomb, contained the bones of a 60-year-old man who is probably to be identified as the high priest Caiaphas (18–36 C.E.), referred to in the New Testament. The name Caiaphas was scratched both on the back and on one side of the ossuary.

"Joseph son of Caiaphas" reads the inscription on the side of the ossuary. The same inscription appears on the back of the ossuary (below), although Caiaphas is spelled with an additional letter. In the New Testament he is called simply Caiaphas, but the 1st-century historian Josephus identifies this high priest, who presided at the trial of Jesus, as "Joseph who was called Caiaphas."

This glistening pavement in the basement of the Sisters of Zion Convent was long identified as the lithostrotos *where Pontius Pilate judged Jesus, proclaiming, "Behold the Man" (John 19:5). The dice-game board carved in the pavement (left) was thought to be associated with the dice game Roman soldiers played for Jesus' clothes after his crucifixion (Matthew 27:35; Mark 15:24; Luke 23:34; John 19:24). Archaeologists have now shown, however, that this pavement was not laid until the 2nd century.*

The pavement in the basement of the Sisters of Zion Convent fairly glistens with age, polished by countless footsteps and horses hooves. The pavement is made of large, beautifully cut ancient flagstones, grooved to prevent horses from slipping.

At one point, the board of an ancient dice game called *basilikos* (king) was scratched into the stones, perhaps by bored guards. According to the throw of the dice, players advanced through increasingly larger boxes in a race to the king's tower in the center.

For years, this pavement was shown to visitors as the *lithostrotos* (literally, the stone pavement), referred to in John 19:13. In this passage, Pontius Pilate brings Jesus outside; depending on the translation, either Jesus is seated on the seat of judgment or Pilate is seated on the judge's chair; in either event, Jesus is condemned. The place where this happened is identified as the *lithostrotos*, usually translated either as "The Pavement" or "The Stone Pavement."

The alacrity with which the pavement was identified as the *lithostrotos* in the early part of this century should caution us about making identifications without adequate evidence. Although the dice-game board brings to mind the Roman soldiers who divided the garments of the crucified Jesus by casting lots for them (Matthew 27:35; Mark 15:24; Luke 23:34; John 19:24), this dating was not based on hard evidence.

The identification was first suggested by one of the sisters and was then confirmed by the great French authority on Jerusalem, Father Louis-Hugues Vincent.[93] But it has been definitively disproved by another great French scholar, also of the École Biblique, Father Pierre Benoit.[94] Benoit noted the problems with dating the pavement by the masonry alone; similar pavements uncovered in Jerusalem date from Herodian to Byzantine times.[95] Benoit then proceeded to date the pavement on a basis other than the masonry. He found that the pavement is contemporaneous with the vaults underneath it, which arch over the Struthion Pool, a double pool still extant beneath the Sisters of Zion pave-

Pilgrims carry a cross on the traditional Via Dolorosa, the way of the cross.

ment. According to Josephus,[96] the Struthion Pool was not covered during the Roman siege of Jerusalem in 70 C.E. Therefore, the vaults over the pool and the pavement over the vaults must be later than 70 C.E.

Another important bit of evidence relates to the Ecce Homo arch. Beneath this arch, according to tradition, Pilate displayed the scourged Jesus to the crowd, proclaiming, "Behold the Man [*Ecce Homo*]" (John 19:5). The Ecce Homo arch was originally a triple arch—a large central arch with smaller, lower arches on either side. One of the side arches is still preserved in the Sisters of Zion Convent, as is the beginning of the large central arch. The central arch then proceeds through the outer wall of the convent, emerges over the street traditionally identified as the Via Dolorosa, crosses the street and enters the building on the other side of the street.

In 1966, excavations at the base of one of the piers of the Ecce Homo arch revealed that it rested on bedrock. The pavement that was supposedly the *lithostrotos* was carefully cut to lie adjacent to the pier. In short, the pier does not rest on the pavement, as would have been the case if the pavement were older than the pier. The pavement was therefore later than the pier. In fact, the arch (and piers) has been shown to be Hadrianic (2nd century C.E.).

Hadrian erected more than one of these arches to commemorate his suppression of the Second Jewish Revolt (132–135 C.E.). (See pp. 220–222 in connection with the triumphal arch beneath the Damascus Gate.) The pavement that was supposedly the *lithostrotos* was part of the Hadrianic forum, in the center of which was a triumphal arch. Alas, this arch was erected to commemorate Hadrian's suppression of the Second Jewish Revolt and has nothing to do with Jesus.

In short, neither the pavement known as the *lithostrotos*, nor the arch known as the Ecce Homo arch nor the street called the Via Dolorosa can be dated to the time of Jesus or associated with his crucifixion.

Yet, not quite so. The Sisters of Zion no longer tell visitors that the pavement in the basement is the *lithostrotos*. They now describe it as a Roman plaza from a hundred years after Jesus' crucifixion. The sisters say they welcome the historical approach to the archaeological remains with which they live. But Sister Brigitte Martin-Chave adds: "Through pilgrimage, the convent acquired a sanctity that history may not have bestowed

This painting of the Ecce Homo arch (upper left) was made before the construction of the building that now serves as the convent of the Sisters of Zion. Today only half of the large arch can be seen on the outside of this building (right). Originally, this high arch was flanked on either side by lower, smaller arches. One of the smaller arches is now in the basement of the convent, as shown in the photo at lower left Once thought to mark the spot where Pilate declared "Behold the Man," this triple-arched monument has now been shown to have been constructed by Hadrian after he suppressed the Second Jewish Revolt (135 C.E.). The pavement, once thought to be the lithostrotos *referred to in the New Testament, was part of the Roman forum, of which the three-arched monument was the central focus.*

upon it. This site has been made holy by the prayers that have been offered here over the years."[97]

The most heated debate among archaeologists and religious groups has been over the site of Jesus' burial. At one time, the matter devolved into a sectarian dispute. Tempers became heated as pilgrims were shown competing sites where Jesus was supposedly buried. Catholics defended the Church of the Holy Sepulchre (see photo, p. 209). Protestants flocked to the serenity of the Garden Tomb, outside the walls of the Old City (see photo, p. 198).

The Garden Tomb was not proposed as the tomb of Jesus until the 19th century. Nevertheless, it has several apparent advantages over the Church of the Holy Sepulchre. First, the Garden Tomb is outside the Old City walls; as we know, burials were not permitted in the city at the time of Jesus' crucifixion. Second, it is located in a garden; as the Gospel of John tells us, "At the place where he had been crucified there was a garden, and in the garden a new tomb, not yet used for burial; there…they laid Jesus" (John 19:41–42). Finally, the tranquillity of the site contrasts sharply with the hustle and bustle of the Church of the Holy Sepulchre.

The Garden Tomb was discovered in 1867. At the time, it was just one of many burial caves in and around Jerusalem. It was General "Chinese" Gordon who gave the tomb its cachet as the burial place of Jesus. Charles George Gordon was the best known and best loved British military hero of his time. Before coming to Jerusalem, he had fought in the Crimean War as well as in Egypt; he had successfully suppressed the Taiping Rebellion in China, for which he received his famous sobriquet. Somewhat of a mystic and subject to spiritual hallucinations, Gordon came to Jerusalem in 1883 and stayed less than a year. In January 1884, he was dispatched to Khartoum where he was killed in an attempt to dislodge the Mahdi.

During his short stay in Jerusalem, Gordon identified Golgotha (which means "skull" in Aramaic), where Jesus was crucified, with a scarp near the cave that was to become the Garden Tomb. When the light is right, it is easy to imagine a skull in the face of the scarp, with two small, shallow caves as eyes. Indeed, Gordon imagined the topography of Jerusalem in the shape of an entire human skeleton. The skull (Golgotha) lay north of the Old City at this mysterious scarp, the pelvis lay on the Temple Mount, the leg bones extended south on the eastern ridge, and the foot bones rested at the Pool of Siloam, in the City of David. Although these wild speculations were published only after Gordon's death in the Sudan, they attained extraordinary notoriety and authority, chiefly

General Charles George "Chinese" Gordon, a British military hero and mystic, inspired the identification of the Garden Tomb as the site of Jesus' burial.

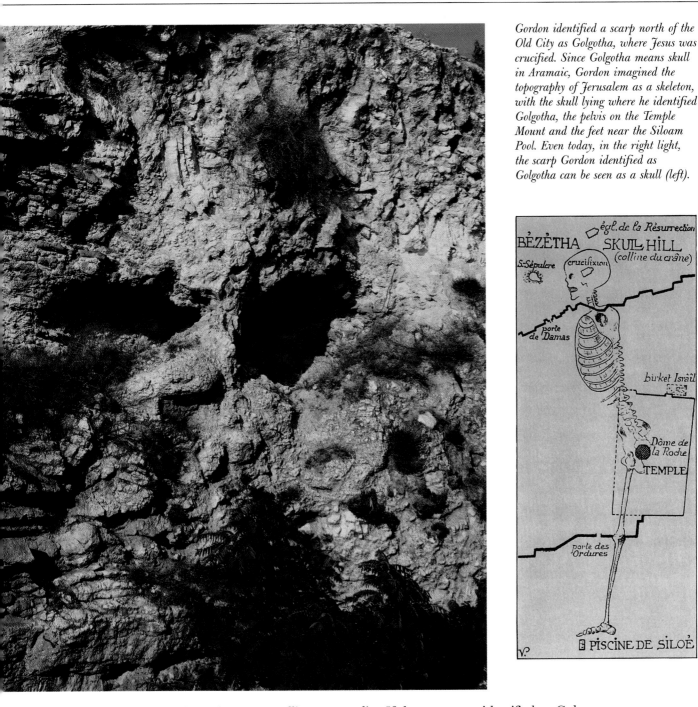

Gordon identified a scarp north of the Old City as Golgotha, where Jesus was crucified. Since Golgotha means skull in Aramaic, Gordon imagined the topography of Jerusalem as a skeleton, with the skull lying where he identified Golgotha, the pelvis on the Temple Mount and the feet near the Siloam Pool. Even today, in the right light, the scarp Gordon identified as Golgotha can be seen as a skull (left).

because of Gordon's compelling personality. If the scarp was identified as Golgotha, then the Garden Tomb had to be where Jesus was buried.

Actually, the Garden Tomb was known as Gordon's Tomb in those days. In 1894, the site was acquired by an influential group of Englishmen, including the Archbishop of Canterbury, under the name the Garden Tomb Association. This is how the burial cave came to be known as the Garden Tomb; and the adjacent area was landscaped appropriately to fit the description in the Gospel of John.

The Garden Tomb also served political purposes. It was the Protestant answer

The Garden Tomb was for generations the Protestants' candidate for the true tomb of Jesus. Lately, Israeli archaeologists have shown that this tomb, cut into the rock, was used hundreds of years before Jesus' time and again hundreds of years later, but not at the time of Jesus.

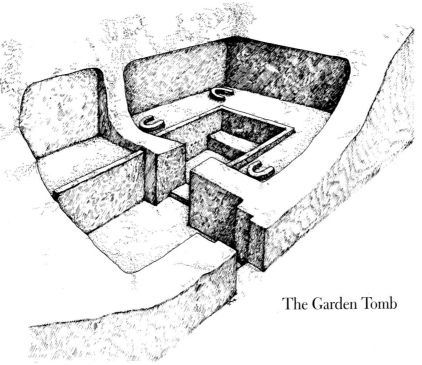

The Garden Tomb

The burial chamber of the Garden Tomb initially held three burial benches on the three uninterrupted walls. Burial benches like these are typical of the First Temple period (10th–6th centuries B.C.E.). In the Byzantine period (4th–7th centuries C.E.) these benches were carved out to form sarcophagi-like receptacles for later burials. The drawing shows the tomb chamber as it would have appeared in the First Temple period.

to the Catholic-championed site of the Church of the Holy Sepulchre as the burial place of Jesus. Four or five different Christian denominations had been vying and fighting over every inch of the Church of the Holy Sepulchre, but none of them was Protestant. The location of the church within the Old City, with buildings crowding around it, clearly showed that it could not have been the tomb of Jesus; Jewish law required that burial be outside the city walls.

Most of the published articles for and against the two contenders for the burial site, although masquerading as scholarship, were thinly disguised polemics. Father Vincent, for example, called the Garden Tomb claim a myth. Protestant scholars were equally dismissive and hyperbolic.

In 1974, Israeli archaeologist Gabriel Barkay decided to restudy the Garden Tomb. By that time, a great deal more was known than in the 1880s about First Temple and Second Temple tombs in Jerusalem, including their distinctive styles. Barkay found that the Garden Tomb was hewn in the First Temple period, in the 8th or 7th century B.C.E. If this was true, the tomb was immediately disqualified as Jesus' tomb because the Gospel of John specifically states that Jesus was buried in "a new tomb, not yet used for burial" (John 19:41).

Barkay based his conclusion on several factors. As a series of discoveries had shown, this area was a cemetery in the First Temple period. And the Garden Tomb was right in the middle of this cemetery. Indeed, it lies just a few feet south of the magnificent First Temple tombs on the grounds of the École Biblique and was, no doubt, originally part of that tomb complex. By contrast, not a single Second Temple tomb has been found in this area.

Moreover, the Garden Tomb bears all of the characteristics in style and layout of a First Temple tomb. For example, burial benches were cut along the cave walls on three sides, all except the entrance wall. These typical First Temple period burial benches, Barkay observed, were later hollowed out to form sarcophagi in the rock, a common practice in the Byzantine period (4th–7th centuries C.E.). But we know these tombs are not Byzantine because Byzantine cave tombs have vaulted ceilings, never flat ceilings like the Garden Tomb. A Second Temple period tomb, on the other hand, would have long burial niches (*kochim,* or loculi) cut into the rock walls for the bodies, instead of burial benches along the walls. Thus, it is clear that the Garden Tomb was first used in the 8th–7th century B.C.E. and that it was reused in the Byzantine period when the burial benches were converted into sarcophagi.

Finally, Barkay was able to locate some pottery that had very probably been found in the Garden Tomb, as well as pictures of other pottery from the tomb, which was lost. All of the pottery dates to the 7th century B.C.E., thereby confirming his observations based on the tomb itself.

In short, although the Garden Tomb was used both in the First Temple period and the Byzantine period, there is no indication whatever that it was used in the

Buildings in the Old City crowd around the Church of the Holy Sepulchre (with its two prominent domes), which would seem to discredit it as the site of Jesus' burial. A 1st-century criminal would never have been buried inside the city. But was this site within the city at the time of Jesus' crucifixion?

late Second Temple period, the time of Jesus' burial. Although more than one hundred thousand visitors a year still enjoy the calm serenity and the peaceful gardens of the site, guides no longer identify it as the tomb of Jesus.

But what about the Church of the Holy Sepulchre? Does it have any better claim of being the burial place of Jesus? The answer, surprisingly, is yes. The same circumstance that arouses our suspicion—that the church lies within the city walls—in the end supports the identification.

The Church of the Holy Sepulchre, as it now stands, is one of the most complicated, yet fascinating, structures in existence. Beginning in the 1960s, the religious communities responsible for its care embarked on a reconstruction project that also involved conducting archaeological excavations, from which a great deal has been learned. Combined with several ancient literary references and other nearby excavations, this new information enables us to reach some reasonably firm conclusions.

A Crusader period facade provides the modern entrance to the Church of the Holy Sepulchre.

The excavations disclosed that beneath the church is a rather extensive stone quarry, more than 40 feet deep in some areas, used from the First Temple period until the 1st century B.C.E. In some places the stonecutters left partially cut ashlars still attached to the bedrock. Elsewhere, the lines of their cuttings are observable. The pottery in the fill goes back as far as the 7th century B.C.E.[98]

According to Father Virgilio Corbo, who, before his recent death, was professor of archaeology at the Studium Biblicum Franciscanum, in the 1st century B.C.E. the quarry under the Church of the Holy Sepulchre was filled in with reddish-brown soil, and the area became an orchard or garden, where cereals, fig trees, carob trees and olive trees grew.

At the same time, the area was used as a cemetery. Four characteristic Second Temple rock-cut tombs have been found beneath the church compound. Three are traditional *kochim*, or loculi, long, narrow rock-hewn recesses in a burial cave (see photo, p. 204). The fourth is an arcosolium, a shelf carved *into* the rock parallel to the rock face, with the top side carved into an arch over the niche.

So, as a first step, there appears to have been an appropriately dated cemetery here at the time of Jesus' crucifixion—and even a garden or orchard, conforming with the description in the Gospel of John, "in the garden there was a new tomb in which no one had ever been laid" (John 19:41).

Of course the question that immediately arises is what was a cemetery doing inside the city? The answer is that this area was very probably not inside the city until the 40s of the Common Era, a few years after Jesus' burial. Clearly, the area is outside the city enclosed by the First Wall, as described by Josephus and confirmed by archaeology. The Third Wall was not constructed until the 40s, a decade after Jesus' crucifixion. The question is whether the site was within the Second Wall.

We know very little about the Second Wall (see map, p. 172)—and have found almost nothing archaeologically, despite the fact that it was the northern line of the city at the time of Jesus' crucifixion. One authority has remarked that "the line of the Second Wall and the date of its construction constitute one of the most complex unsolved problems in the study of Jerusalem in the Second Temple period."[99]

A very small excavation by Ute Lux in the nearby Church of the Redeemer is often cited as proof that this area was not within the Second Wall. The proof consists of the discovery of a quarry here, which Lux dated to the 1st century C.E., from which she concluded that the area was not within the Second Wall. Kathleen Kenyon reported similar results in a few small squares she excavated nearby. Second Temple period tombs in the quarry area also suggest that this area was outside the city at the time. But based only on this meager archaeological evidence, the conclusion that the Church of the Holy Sepulchre lay outside the Second Wall seems a bit shaky. And the line thus required of the Second Wall seems a bit strange (see map, p. 172).

A bit of history preserved in ancient literary sources, however, does tend to support identification of the Church of the Holy Sepulchre as the site of Jesus' tomb. In the 2nd century C.E., the Roman emperor Hadrian built a raised platform where the church now stands, on which he constructed a temple to Aphrodite. In 326 C.E., when Empress Helena, the mother of Emperor Constantine, came to Jerusalem looking for relics of Jesus and his life on earth, she naturally inquired about his tomb. The site of the Hadrianic temple was pointed out to her. When she visited the site, the legend continues, she discovered the true cross. The condition of the Aphrodite temple at that time is uncertain; it may already have been destroyed by the reigning Christians.

In any event, the site was razed so that Constantine could build a large, columned rotunda around the site that had been pointed out to his mother as

Jesus' tomb. The rotunda, called the Anastasis (Resurrection), was almost 70 feet in diameter. Despite subsequent calamities, the original wall of this Constantinian rotunda has survived up to a height of more than 30 feet in places inside the church and around Jesus' cenotaph (see photo, p. 209).

In front of the Constantinian rotunda was a rectangular colonnaded garden. On the other side of the garden, Constantine had built a large basilical church with an apse at the back facing the garden. The front faced the main city thorough-fare, the Cardo Maximus (part of which has been archaeologically recovered; see photos, pp. 218–219).

The Constantinian complex commemorating Jesus' tomb is shown on a famous Byzantine mosaic map of Jerusalem found in a 6th-century C.E. church in Madaba, Jordan (see photos, pp. 206–207). The city is drawn as an oval, with west at the bottom and north at the left. Horizontally, crossing the center of the city, is the Cardo Maximus, with a columned portico on either side of the street. Adjacent to the Cardo Maximus, in the middle of the city, is the Constantinian complex of the Holy Sepulchre, precisely as it is described in literary sources. It is upside down as we look at it. Proceeding from the street, we first see four steps leading up to the basilical church. Then we see the facade of the church (lying flat), with three doors (the center one somewhat larger) and a triangular pediment. Next comes the roof of the basilica in red tesserae. Behind that is the golden rotunda dome over the tomb of Christ.[100]

The gold dome has special significance. When the Romans destroyed the Jewish Temple in 70 C.E., they replaced it with statues to pagan gods that probably included a shrine of some kind.[101] After suppressing the Second Jewish Revolt in 135 C.E., Hadrian built a temple to Aphrodite where the Church of the Holy Sepulchre now stands, perhaps to obliterate the memory of Jesus' tomb (the church historian Eusebius tells us, "Godless people [i.e., Hadrian et al.]…had gone to great pains to cover up this divine memorial of immortality [Jesus' tomb] so that it should be forgotten"[102]) and also to shift the focus of the new Roman city from the old Jewish Temple Mount to the new enclosure/platform supporting the Aphrodite temple.[103] Hadrian even imitated the Herodian enclosure of the Temple Mount in his enclosure of the Aphrodite temple, using ashlars from the destroyed Herodian structure and closely mimicking the architecture (a telltale piece of the Hadrianic enclosure wall is extant in the Church of the Holy Sepulchre complex).[104]

At the same time, in order to obliterate any Jewish associations, Hadrian changed the name of the city to Aelia Capitolina. Aelia memorialized his own name, Hadrian Aelius; Capitolina referred to the temple of Jupiter planned for the Temple Mount. For similar reasons, the name of the country was changed from Judea to Syria-Palaestina, or Palestine (derived from "Philistine"). Hadrian also plowed a furrow, called a *pomerium*, around the city, which in Roman tra-

In the 1st century, the site of the Church of the Holy Sepulchre was indeed a cemetery, as evidenced by these two kochim *(loculi, or burial niches) found under the north wall of the church's rotunda.* Kochim *like these are typical features of 1st-century tombs.*

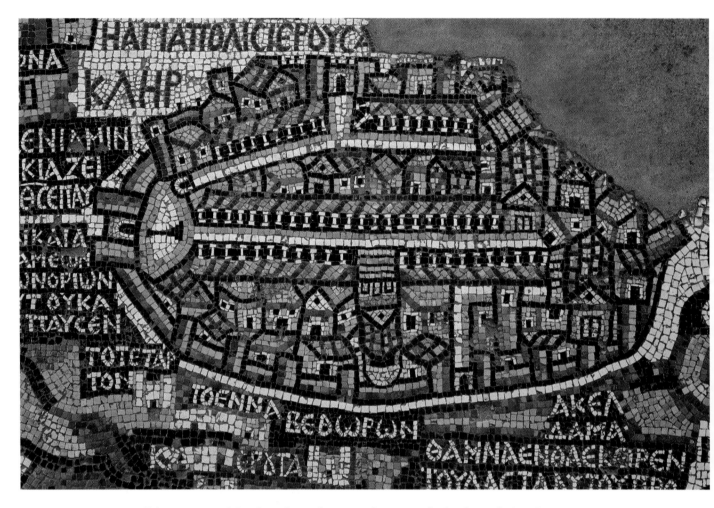

dition was used by founders of a new city to mark the boundaries. Jews were banned from Aelia Capitolina.

When the Christians obtained control of the city in the 4th century, they built over Jesus' tomb the Constantinian shrine with the golden dome pictured on the Madaba map. During the Byzantine period, when Jerusalem was a Christian city, the Temple Mount was treated as a garbage dump to signify the demise of Judaism and the fulfillment of the New Testament prophecy of the Temple's destruction.

But back to Constantine. Like Hadrian before him, Constantine attempted to replace the glory of the Jewish Temple, this time with the glory of the basilica in front of Jesus' tomb, the traditional site of Golgotha. Eusebius tells us that Constantine's basilica (like the Temple) "looked toward the rising sun...[and was] a spectacle of surpassing beauty...[Its interior walls were] overlaid throughout with radiant gold; it made the whole temple, as it were, to glitter with rays of light."[105] Like the Jewish Temple, the basilica construction included cedars of Lebanon. Outside facilities were similar to the ones provided by "our most peaceful Solomon." Eusebius concludes, "How true it is that 'the latter glory of this house exceeds the former.'"[106]

The Church of the Holy Sepulchre

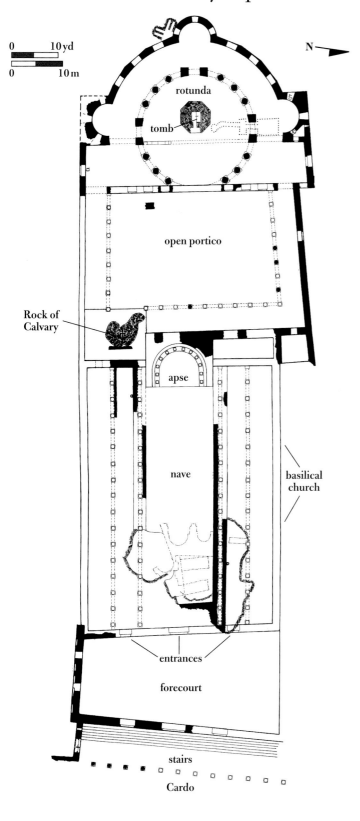

0 ____ 10 yd
0 ____ 10 m

N →

rotunda

tomb

open portico

Rock of Calvary

apse

nave

basilical church

entrances

forecourt

stairs

Cardo

Jerusalem, as pictured in the 6th-century Madaba mosaic map, far left, is oval shaped. East, rather than north, is on top. On the left of Jerusalem is the Damascus Gate. Inside the gate is a forum with a column standing in the center. Running through the center of the city from north to south is the Cardo Maximus, with a colonnaded portico on each side of the street. On the west side of the street, a building interrupts the columned portico—the Church of the Holy Sepulchre, as it existed at that time. Seen upside down on the map and in greater detail above, the church is entered via several steps. Then comes a three-entry facade with a triangular pediment, leading into a basilica with a red roof. Behind the basilica is the golden dome of the rotunda that stood over the tomb. A plan of the church complex as constructed by the Emperor Constantine in the 4th century is shown at left.

Even the Jewish traditions that had become attached to the Temple Mount—that this is where Adam was created and was also the site of Mt. Moriah, where Abraham offered to sacrifice his beloved son Isaac—were transferred to the Constantinian basilica. Eusebius tells us that at the site of Constantine's basilica, "Adam was formed out of the clay; here Abraham offered up Isaac his son, as a sacrifice, in the very place where our Lord Jesus Christ was crucified."[107] In the complex Jewish mythology surrounding the Temple Mount, the Temple was also considered the *omphalos* (navel, or center) of the universe. This tradition, too, became attached to the Constantinian basilica, transferred, as it were, from one Jerusalem hill to another.

In the 7th century, when the Arabs conquered Jerusalem, they wanted to change the focus of the city once again—back to the old Temple Mount, but this time with a Moslem, rather than a Jewish, centerpiece. The Dome of the Rock with its golden dome—exactly the same size as the rotunda dome over Christ's tomb—was built to redirect attention to an even grander structure than the venerated Christian structure.

Excavations south of the Temple Mount recovered a beautifully crafted gold ring, probably intended to depict the rotunda over Jesus' tomb. Apparently dating to the 4th century C.E., the ring testifies to the importance of the shrine from the moment it was built.

This gold ring, excavated south of the Temple Mount, probably represents the rotunda, or Anastasis, that stood over Jesus' tomb in the Byzantine period. The cupola on top sits on large round vaults composed of gold granulation. A wavy line meanders around the finger ring.

The key to the validity of the identification of the site of the Church of the Holy Sepulchre as the authentic tomb of Jesus, however, is the fact that it was identified as such to the Empress Helena in the 4th century, when the identification seemed as unlikely as it does today.[108] In 326 C.E., when she was told that this was where Jesus was buried, the site was covered by Hadrian's Aphrodite temple (or, if the Christians had already destroyed it, the temple's remains). And at the time, the site was already *within* the city walls. If someone wanted to make up a story for Empress Helena, they would have located the tomb outside the walls instead of identifying a site that would be immediately suspect because it was within the walls.

Moreover, there is good reason to believe that knowledge of the location of Jesus' tomb was preserved from about 30 C.E., when he was crucified, to 326 C.E., when Empress Helena visited Jerusalem. The Christian community in Jerusalem was never dispersed during this period. And the succession of bishops was never interrupted, so it would not be surprising if the memory of the loca-

The cenotaph of Jesus, in the Church of the Holy Sepulchre, beneath the reconstructed rotunda originally built by the emperor Constantine in the 4th century.

tion of Jesus' tomb was preserved for those 300 years. Indeed, the Hadrianic enclosure and Aphrodite temple may have preserved the very memory it was designed to obliterate.

The Constantinian rotunda and adjacent basilical church were destroyed by the Fatimid caliph Hakim in 1009. Father Murphy-O'Connor paradoxically laments the fact that it had not been turned into a mosque when the Moslems took control of the city in the 7th century. When the Moslem caliph Omar entered the city in 638, he graciously and considerately refused an invitation to pray in the Church of the Holy Sepulchre, saying, "If I had prayed in the church it would have been lost to you [Christians], for the Believers [Moslems] would have taken it, saying: 'Omar prayed here.'" Ironically, if that had happened, Hakim would not have destroyed the structure later.

The calamitous vicissitudes that befell the church are too numerous and too complex to recount here. Suffice it to say that the present structure is largely Crusader, although some parts, including two columns of the rebuilt rotunda, are from the original Constantinian structure, dating to the 4th century C.E.[109] The cenotaph in the center of the rotunda preserves the site of Jesus' burial.

But, in the end, we are left with a nonhistorical discomfort. Where are the peace and calm of the original rotunda setting? No one has better described the current atmosphere of the church than Father Murphy-O'Connor:

> One looks for numinous light, but it is dark and cramped. One hopes for peace, but the ear is assailed by a cacophony of warring chants. One desires holiness, only to encounter a jealous possessiveness: the six groups of occupants—Latin Catholics, Greek Orthodox, Armenians, Syrians, Copts, Ethiopians—watch one another suspiciously for any infringement of rights. The frailty of humanity is nowhere more apparent than here; it epitomizes the human condition. The empty who come to be filled will leave desolate.[110]

Behind the church's Chapel of St. Helena, in the underground Chapel of St. Vartan, on a wall that once belonged to the substructure of Hadrian's temple, is a drawing, or graffito, of a ship on one of the ashlar blocks. The wall was probably exposed during the Constantinian destruction of Hadrian's temple and was soon filled up again, during construction of the basilical church. But while the wall was exposed, a Christian pilgrim in about 330 C.E. came to the site, smoothed and polished one of the ashlars in the wall and drew the ship—a small Roman merchantman typical of the ships then popular in the Mediterranean (see photo, p. 212). Perhaps the pilgrim, grateful for having survived a storm at sea, painted the ship that brought him safely to the Holy City. Some have suggested that the mast looks broken. Perhaps, by some miracle, the ship arrived safely despite the broken mast.

The Chapel of St. Helena, named after Constantine's mother, who, according to tradition, found the true cross here in 326 C.E. At a still lower level, archaeologists have uncovered what is claimed to be the earliest evidence of Christian pilgrimage—the graffito of a ship inscribed "Lord, we went," shown on page 212.

The pilgrim who painted the ship, in shades of black and ochre with a duck's head on the stern, also left a Latin inscription underneath the ship: *"Domine Ivimus,"* or "Lord, we went." This may allude to Psalm 122:1–2: "I rejoiced when they said to me / Let us go to the house of the Lord." In Latin, the second line of the psalm reads: *"In domum Domini ibimus."* The grateful pilgrim had probably come a great and dangerous distance—from the western part of the empire; if he had come from the east, he would have written in Greek, not Latin. This graffito is the earliest physical evidence of Christian pilgrimage to the Holy City.[111]

But wait. Recently, an entirely different interpretation of the painting and inscription have been put forward, illustrating in a peculiar way the intrigue, as well as the uncertainty, that often characterizes archaeological conclusions. The interpretation given above is that of Magen Broshi, an Israeli archaeologist, with whom almost everyone agreed at the time, in the mid-1970s. In late 1994, however, Shimon Gibson, of the London-based Palestine Exploration Fund, and his colleague Joan Taylor claimed that the painting and inscription had been *altered* and that Broshi had been misled by the alterations. They based their claim on pictures of the stone taken before it had been cleaned by a well-known Franciscan archaeologist and epigraphist, Father Emmanuele Testa.

This painting of a ship with an inscription below was uncovered in excavations in the bowels of the Holy Sepulchre Church. The painting is now the subject of heated scholarly controversy. This photograph was taken after cleaning. Several scholars claim that the cleaning was botched and the ship redrawn with different characteristics. Depending on who is to be believed, the ship may evidence the earliest Christian pilgrimage to the Holy Land, about 330 C.E., or it may be a 1st-century ship that brought Jews to Jerusalem for one of the pilgrim festivals. The inscription, in Latin, reads, "Lord, we went" or, alternatively, "Master [the shipowner], we [the crew] went [as instructed]."

Gibson and Taylor found "substantial differences" between the pre- and post-cleaning pictures of the stone. According to Gibson and Taylor, "[M]any of the original ship details have been either eliminated, enhanced or transformed." According to another observer, "An alarming proportion of detail that was clearly visible at the time of the discovery…seems to have disappeared."

The implication is that Testa botched the job of cleaning the stone and then redrew some of the picture. As Gibson and Taylor note, "Testa has not published a conservation report on the methods and procedures of the cleaning, despite controversy concerning the authenticity of the present drawing," adding, with a fine mock-heroic twist, "We would not like to suggest that Father Testa cleaned the stone badly, but the scholarly community would benefit from a full report." As to who changed the drawing: "It is conceivable that any one of the visitors may have been responsible for the changes made to the original drawing." If Gibson and Taylor say this with the wink of an eye, it doesn't appear on the page. They call for laboratory analysis of the pastes used to draw the suspicious new lines. Testa, meanwhile, has refused to comment.

On the basis of details they see in the pre-cleaning photographs, Gibson and Taylor would date the ship—and therefore the drawing—to the 1st or 2nd century C.E. As for the inscription, "*Domine,*" they say, refers to the captain of the ship, or perhaps to the person who sent them on the journey, not to the Christian God, and the inscription probably means, "Master, we went," that is, we completed the journey you ordered. With the new details they see, Gibson and Taylor say the mast is not broken, but the ship is shown in the harbor with the sail safely furled. The ship and inscription, according to Gibson and Taylor, "may even have a Jewish author, who has come with his companions to Jerusalem" for one of the Jewish pilgrimage festivals.[112]

XII

The Second Jewish Revolt and Aelia Capitolina

WE RETURN NOW TO JERUSALEM AFTER THE ROMAN DESTRUCTION OF 70 C.E. The trauma of that event was enormous. The central religious institution of the Jewish people, which had stood for almost 600 years, was no more. A new tax, the *fiscus Judaicus*, was imposed on all Jews in place of the annual contribution to the Temple. Although Jews were not barred from Jerusalem, the city was reduced to an impoverished village.

The flickering flame of Jewish nationalism was not quite snuffed out, however. As usual, Jews remembered. Seventy years after the *First* Temple was destroyed by the Babylonians, it was rebuilt; God's face would not forever be averted. The hope and expectation of a divine plan enabling the Jews to rebuild the Temple once more fanned the embers of revolt. In 132 C.E., under the military leadership of Bar-Kokhba (whose real name we learn from recently discovered original correspondence was Simeon Bar-Kosiba)[113] (see photo, p. 216) and the religious inspiration of Rabbi Akiva, the Second Jewish Revolt against Rome began. It ended three years later, in 135 C.E., just as the First Jewish Revolt had ended—in defeat. The final battle took place at Bethar, seven miles southwest of Jerusalem.

This time, as we previously noted, the city was plowed around, and a new, Roman city named Aelia Capitolina arose on the ruins. Jews were barred from living in or, on pain of death, even visiting what had been their Holy City. After more than a thousand years, the center of Jewish life shifted from Jerusalem to the Galilee.

"Judaea Capta" reads the inscription on this Roman coin. Judea is seated mourning under a palm tree. A Roman soldier stands triumphantly to the left. Enormous quantities of "Judaea Capta" coins—far more than coins commemorating Roman victories over the Egyptians, Germans, Daciens or tribes of Spain—were struck in gold, silver and bronze to commemorate the Roman victory over the Jews. The "SC" at the bottom of the coin stands for Senatus Consulto—issued by decree of the Roman Senate.

215

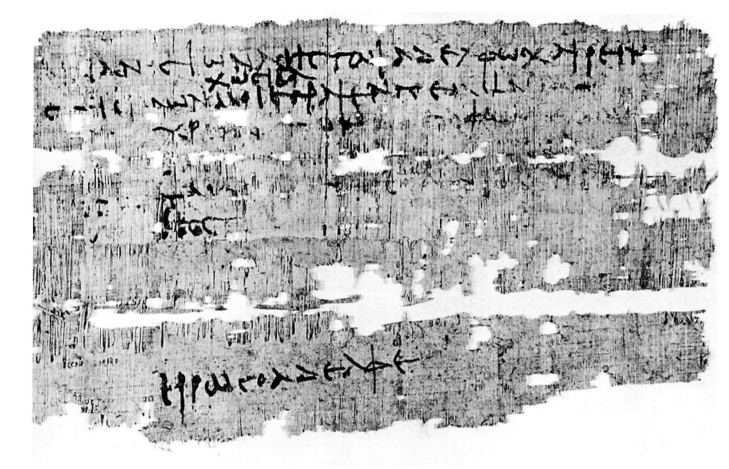

So Hellenized had Judea become by the time of the Second Jewish Revolt (132–135 C.E.) that the military leader of the revolt sometimes wrote his letters in Greek, rather than Aramaic or Hebrew. From these letters, we now know that his name, usually written Bar-Kokhba, was actually Simeon Bar-Kosiba. Pictured here is a Greek letter by Bar-Kokhba or one of his lieutenants.

Almost no archaeological evidence has survived in Jerusalem either from the period immediately after the First Jewish Revolt or from the period of the Second Jewish Revolt. As they did during the First Jewish Revolt, the Jews of the Second Revolt minted coins that have been found in excavations. More than 80 percent of these Second Revolt coins mention Jerusalem, reflecting its continuing importance as the center of Jewish national identity. Most of them depict the Temple that had been destroyed. Jerusalem is written in the Old Hebrew script that was used before the Babylonian destruction of the First Temple, stirring nationalist sentiment by recalling days of glory.

Aelia Capitolina was laid out in typical Roman colonial fashion, generally rectangular in shape and divided into four sections by a major north–south street, known, as in other Roman cities, as the Cardo Maximus, and an east–west street intersecting the Cardo called the Decumanus. The beautiful column-lined Cardo Maximus is clearly depicted on the 6th-century mosaic map of Jerusalem from Madaba (see photo, p. 206).

Part of the Cardo Maximus, now beautifully restored, was discovered in Avigad's excavation in the Jewish Quarter of the Old City (see photos, pp. 218–219). Avigad excavated about a tenth of a mile (nearly 600 feet) of the Cardo. The street itself is nearly 40 feet wide and is paved with well-dressed flagstones. Both sides of the street are lined with columns. The columns are monoliths, made from single stones rather than from column drums. Including base, shaft and capital, the columns stood more than 16 feet high. They supported a roofed pedestrian walkway on either side of the roadway. The west portico ends in a wall. Adjacent to the east portico, however, is an arcade of arches resting on square pillars. The archways form the entrances to shops.

At first, the Jerusalem Cardo looks like a typical Roman cardo, and the excavators initially thought they would have no problem dating it to the Roman period. This was obviously the main street of Roman Jerusalem. But when they lifted parts of the pavement, they found Byzantine pottery (4th–7th century C.E.) underneath it. If Byzantine pottery was found *under* the street, the street could be no earlier than the Byzantine period.

At first, the archaeologists thought perhaps they had excavated a Byzantine renovation of an earlier Roman street. But they could find nothing to support this theory. When they began measuring, they found that the Cardo was built according to the Byzantine foot, approximately 12.5 inches (32 centimeters), instead of the Roman foot, 11.5 inches (29.6 centimeters). Next they noticed the poor workmanship on the capitals of the columns, which was typical of Byzantine architecture and far below the high standards of Roman architecture, even in the provinces.

Apparently Roman Jerusalem, the Jerusalem of Aelia Capitolina, was confined largely to the northern half of the area of the Old City. The part of the Cardo Avigad excavated was in the southern half. During the time the city was known as Aelia Capitolina, the southern half of the city was occupied by the Tenth Roman Legion, "Fretensis," which had been part of the Roman forces that conquered and destroyed the city in 70 C.E. Afterwards, the Tenth Legion was left behind to guard the city. The main part of their camp spread east and south of Jaffa Gate, the current western gate of the Old City, but secondary barracks apparently extended into the eastern slopes of the western hill, beneath the present Jewish Quarter. Roof tiles stamped "Leg[io] X. Fr[etensis]" are common finds in this area (see photo, p. 220).

When the Byzantine Christians took control of Jerusalem in the 4th century, the city expanded southward to include the area once occupied by the Tenth Legion. Apparently, the Roman Cardo (traces of which *have* been found in

A tetra-drachma (top right) from the Second Jewish Revolt (132–135 C.E.) depicts the Temple prior to destruction. Four columns flank the entrance. The Ark of the Covenant may be represented between the columns. The Second Revolt didrachma, both sides of which can be seen at right, is inscribed in Old Hebrew letters, the kind used before the destruction of the First Temple. The bunch of grapes may represent the golden grapes that hung from a vine above the entrance to Herod's Temple.

The Cardo Maximus

The Cardo Maximus during excavation, near right. The street runs from left to right in this picture, as indicated by the spina (a row of stones that serves as a kind of spine, interrupting the rows of perpendicular stones) in the center of the street, near the bottom of the picture. A square pillar at the back of the street supported one side of an arch that provided the entrance to a merchant's shop. Both the spina and the square pillar supporting the arched entryway can be seen more easily in the reconstruction drawing below. The restored Cardo Maximus is shown at far right.

the northern part of the Old City) was extended at that time into the southern half of the city. As we shall see later, Jerusalem flourished in the Byzantine period, so the imitation Roman Cardo, as it were, should not be surprising.

Although the portion of the Cardo Avigad uncovered cannot be ascribed to Aelia Capitolina, we can point with confidence to the northern gateway of the Roman city as an authentic relic. This gateway can be securely dated to the 2nd century C.E.

The most elaborate and beautiful contemporary entry into the Old City is the Damascus Gate, on the northern wall. Directly underneath the Damascus Gate, archaeologists discovered the northern gateway of Aelia Capitolina, consisting of three arched gateways with the largest and highest one in the center.[114] On either side of this three-arched gateway were projecting towers (the easternmost tower has been preserved to a height of more than 35 feet).

The smaller, left-hand (eastern) archway has survived intact and is now fully visible at the site. It includes not only the arch but also engaged pillars on either side. The entryway, once blocked, has recently been cleared, and visitors can again enter the Old City through this Hadrianic gateway (see photo, p. 222).

If you notice what look like Herodian ashlars in the construction of the gateway, congratulate yourself. They are. But they were taken from elsewhere in the destroyed city to become part of this later gateway. We can date the gateway not only by the trim around the arches (which is an uncertain indication) but also by the pottery associated with it and by a badly mutilated inscription above the keystone of the left-hand arch that reads: "…according to the *decurians* [the city council] of Col[onia] Ael[ia] Cap[itolina]."

A roof tile stamped "Leg X. Fr," for Legio X. Fretensis, the Tenth Roman Legion, which was garrisoned in Jerusalem after the suppression of the First Jewish Revolt, in 70 C.E. Similar roof tiles have been found by the thousands in the area.

Below the current Damascus Gate, archaeologists have found part of the city gate built by Hadrian in the 2nd century C.E. as an entryway to Aelia Capitolina. The Hadrianic gateway (as seen in the reconstruction) consisted of a large central archway, flanked on either side by a smaller, lower arch. The lower gate seen in the photograph (also see p. 222) is the smaller Hadrianic arch to the left of the central arch. The remains of the large central arch are buried beneath the current Damascus Gate. The reconstruction drawing shows that a column, also depicted in the Madaba map (p. 206), once stood in the center of the forum inside the Hadrianic city. In Arabic, the Damascus Gate is still known as Bab el-Amud, the Gate of the Column.

When this archway was excavated, it created a new entrance to the Old City of Jerusalem. It was originally the eastern archway of the triple-arched northern gateway constructed in the 2nd century C.E. by the emperor Hadrian. It led to a typical Roman forum immediately inside. We can be sure of the date because of a Latin inscription above the keystone.

Inside the gateway was a large, open plaza, nearly 100 feet of which has been found, at the same level as the gate. The paving stones are magnificent—beautifully polished and huge. The largest measures five by seven feet; none is smaller than four by five feet. The stones are grooved to prevent horses from slipping.

This plaza confirms the accuracy of the Madaba map, which also shows an open plaza inside the northern gateway of the city during the Byzantine period. In the center of the plaza (on the map) is a high column with nothing on it. This column was probably erected by Hadrian and was once topped by a larger-than-life statue of the emperor himself. No doubt the statue was removed by Christians in the Byzantine period, leaving the bare column as it is pictured on the Madaba map.[115]

Unfortunately, despite their high hopes, archaeologists were unable to find any remains of the column. But curiously enough, a memory of the column apparently survives in one of the Arabic names of the Damascus Gate—Bab el-Amud, the Gate of the Column.

In the previous chapter, we discussed other Hadrianic remains—the pavement once thought to be the *lithostrotos* in the Sisters of Zion Convent and the Ecce Homo arch. Indeed, the triple archway of the Hadrianic forum, of which the Ecce Homo arch is the large center opening, bears a striking resemblance to the northern gateway to the city, the remains of which we have just examined, beneath the current Damascus Gate.

XIII

Byzantine Jerusalem

IN 324 C.E., THE ROMAN EMPEROR CONSTANTINE EXTENDED HIS RULE TO THE eastern empire, of which Palestine was a part. Precisely when Constantine became a Christian believer is hotly debated (he was not actually baptized until he was on his deathbed in 337, although the Edict of Milan, in 313, legalized Christian worship and returned confiscated church property). There is no question, however, that the empire was Christianized during his long reign. This, of course, had enormous repercussions for Jerusalem.

In short, Jerusalem became a Christian city. And it prospered and flowered. The city was no longer just a provincial outpost (Caesarea on the Mediterranean had been the capital of Judea during the late Roman period); Jerusalem once again became a religious center, this time the destination of thousands of Christian pilgrims who had to be serviced in hostels and churches and were enticed and nourished by the beauty of the city, both physical and spiritual.

The only part of Jerusalem that remained decrepit was the Temple Mount, the ruins signifying the desolation of a people who had brought monotheism into the world and who had worshiped their one God at this place.

For a flickering moment, this situation almost changed. In 361 C.E., Julian the Apostate became Roman emperor at the tender age of 30. Adamantly opposed to Christianity, he attempted to return paganism to what he believed was its rightful position. A devotee of Hellenism, Julian wanted to restore to his empire the glory of classical Rome. In his opinion, Christianity was something of a barbarian superstition. As part of his campaign to extirpate Christianity, Julian even

Byzantine houses excavated south of the Temple Mount. The silver-domed Al-Aqsa mosque sits on the southern end of the Temple Mount.

225

The Nea Church

For centuries, the great Nea Church built by Emperor Justinian in the 6th century C.E. was only something referred to in ancient literary texts. Israeli archaeologists found it in 1967. Now it can even be located on the Madaba mosaic map (p. 206): From the Church of the Holy Sepulchre continue south (right) on the Cardo Maximus to the end. There, on the east side of the Cardo, is a red-roofed structure (churches on the Madaba map have red roofs) that represents the Nea. Indeed, the Cardo may have been extended south in the Byzantine period to connect the Church of the Holy Sepulchre with the Nea. Although it was a monumental structure (the interior of the church was over 300 feet long), architecturally the Nea was a customary basilica, with a large forecourt, a nave with side aisles created by columns and a triple apse at the end. Portions of the two smaller side apses have been recovered in archaeological excavations. The portions in black on the plan (right) have been found; the rest has been reconstructed. The photo at right shows the northern apse during excavation. In the photo above, the southeastern corner of the church protrudes from the Old City wall.

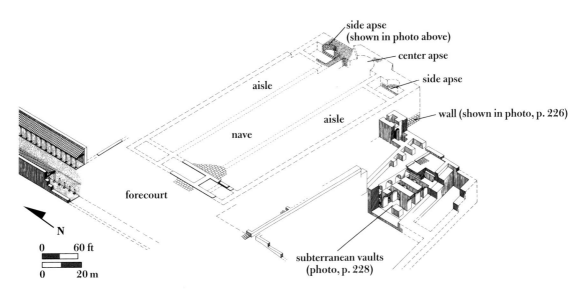

side apse
(shown in photo above)

center apse

side apse

aisle

aisle

wall (shown in photo, p. 226)

nave

forecourt

N

0   60 ft

0   20 m

subterranean vaults
(photo, p. 228)

In a huge, vaulted hall (opposite), which served both as a water cistern and as support for a wing of the Nea complex that extended over a slope (much as Solomon's Stables does for Herod's Temple Mount), excavators found a monumental inscription. Over 25 feet above the floor and enclosed in a tabula ansata (a rectangular frame with triangles pointed toward it on either end), this Greek inscription sits above a giant cross in high relief (above). It is a dedicatory inscription, telling the world that "this is the work that our most pious Emperor Flavius Justinianus carried out with munificence." The inscription is dated to the 13th year of the abbot Constantinius's induction, probably equivalent to 549/550 C.E.

removed all Christian clerics from positions as teachers of literature.

Julian also formed a natural alliance with the Jews, offering to restore the Jewish Temple in Jerusalem, where, as in pagan temples, animal sacrifices could once again be offered. He had no difficulty incorporating the Jewish God into his pagan pantheon; indeed, the only thing odd about the Jews was that "they believe in only one God. That is indeed peculiar to them and strange to us [pagans]."[116] The Jews naturally accepted Julian's offer to rebuild the Temple and proceeded with alacrity.

Julian, of course, was aware that by restoring the Jewish Temple, he would be giving the lie to the common Christian belief, as Eusebius put it, that "by the murder of the Lord, [Jerusalem] experienced the last extremity of desolation, and paid the penalty for the crime of its impious inhabitants."[117]

Alas, work on the Temple came to an abrupt halt in 363 C.E. when the young emperor was killed in a skirmish with the Persians in the east. He was succeeded by Jovian, a devout Christian, and the wheel of history turned back again. But an archaeological memento of the brief Temple project may have survived. On the western wall of the Temple Mount, beneath Robinson's Arch, a shallow inscription was etched into one of the Herodian ashlars. The inscription is a quote from Isaiah: "When you see this, your heart shall rejoice, and your bones shall flourish like the grass" (Isaiah 66:14). But whoever inscribed this quotation on the western wall changed one word of the original. Instead of "*your* bones," it reads "*their* bones."

Before recent excavations, this ashlar in the western wall of the Herodian Temple Mount was below ground. When it was exposed in the excavation, a Hebrew inscription from the Book of Isaiah was found on the upper part, probably carved in the 4th century C.E. during the hopeful but short-lived effort to rebuild the Temple under the pagan emperor Julian.

This chapter of Isaiah has been interpreted as a vision of the End of Days, which will mean not only the restoration of the Temple, but also the resurrection of the dead. Apparently, whoever engraved this quotation on the wall was saying that when you see the Temple restored you will rejoice, and you will see the resurrection of the dead (*their* bones). Although this is the commonly accepted interpretation of this inscription, the date is hardly secure; it could have been inscribed at any time from the 4th to the 7th century C.E. But the historical situation seems to fit best with the Julian episode.[118]

When the Temple Mount once again became a refuse dump, the area to the south was no longer prime real estate, and a dense though often elegant warren of Byzantine residences grew up there. We have already looked at some shining examples of Byzantine architecture—the Byzantine portion of the Cardo and the shrine Constantine built at the Holy Sepulchre. The city continued to expand and flourish for the next 300 years.

The peak of development occurred during the reign of Justinian (527–565 C.E.), when the part of the western hill known as Mount Zion was once again built up. The population of the city grew to about 60,000, a number exceeded in ancient times only in the Herodian period (when it was about 80,000). Jerusalem's population never exceeded these numbers until the 20th century.

A more nuanced look at the pottery under the Byzantine section of the Cardo excavated by Nahman Avigad shows that it was built in the 6th century, during Emperor Justinian's reign.

Justinian's largest project, however, was the Nea (Greek for "new"), or New Church of St. Mary, Mother of God, one of the greatest monumental churches in the world. Previously known only from ancient literary references, the Nea has recently been partially recovered (see pp. 226–229). The plan of this church is standard—a basilica with rows of pillars creating side aisles and a triple apse at the eastern end. What makes the Nea unusual is its size. The building was 375 feet long and 185 feet wide, making it the largest known basilica in Palestine.

Portions of the two side apses of the Nea have been excavated, but none of the central apse. The southeast corner of the church sticks out from under the present southern wall of the Old City west of Dung Gate. It is obvious from the size of the blocks, which dwarf the stones roundabout and the stones in the Old City wall, that the church was a mammoth structure. A segment of the walls of the church was found inside the Old City; they were more than 20 feet thick.

Because the ground adjacent to the church falls away, an underground vaulted structure was needed to support the platform on which part of the complex was built (in much the same way that Solomon's Stables supports the southeast corner of the Temple Mount). This vaulted structure rose to a height of nearly 35 feet. At least two of the vaults survive intact. High on one wall of this vaulted structure was a Greek inscription set within a molded frame, called a *tabula ansata* (a rectangle with a small triangle on either side pointing at and touching the rectangle). Below the *tabula ansata* is a large cross (see top photo, p. 229).

The inscription, in plaster relief and painted red, commemorates the building of the structure. It is not difficult to imagine the thrill the excavators felt when they found that the inscription actually mentions the Emperor Justinian (Basileos Ioustinianos) and the date the church was built (549/550 C.E.).

Located at the southern end of the Cardo (indeed, the front of the building reached the eastern edge of the Cardo), the Nea may explain the Byzantine extension during Justinian's reign: The extension connected the Church of the Holy Sepulchre in the north with the Nea Church in the south. Incidentally, the Nea Church is depicted on the Madaba map exactly where the archaeologists found it.

XIV

Moslem and Crusader Jerusalem

I N THE EARLY 7TH CENTURY, THE GLORY OF BYZANTIUM CAME TO AN END. AS had happened so often before, in Palestine two great world empires, east and west—this time Byzantium and Persia—clashed. Palestine once again became a battlefield, changing hands at least three times in the early 7th century C.E.

In 614, the Persians captured Jerusalem. They did not manage to hold it for long, but long enough to destroy most of the churches. The Nea was a special target of Persian destruction.

The next victory belonged to the Byzantine Christians. On March 21, 629, the Byzantine emperor Heraclius entered Jerusalem in a splendid procession at the head of his army. He entered through the Golden Gate, the same gate through which tradition tells us that Jesus entered the city. By what was regarded as a miracle, the true cross, which had been seized by the Persian army a little more than 14 years earlier, was returned to Christian care. Jerusalem was once again a Christian city.

The continuing confrontation ended, however, with exhaustion on both sides. Despite their ostensible victory, the Byzantine hold of Palestine was severely weakened. This left the country open to relatively easy conquest by a third force—the Moslem Arabs.

In 634, Arab forces attacked Gaza. Four years later, Jerusalem was in their hands. The local patriarch Sophronius surrendered the city peaceably in the spring of 638.

The Moslem caliph Omar, Commander of the Faithful, entered the city on

The Dome of the Rock is one of the great jewels of Moslem architecture. Built shortly after the Arab conquest of Jerusalem in the late 7th century, it has survived 1,300 years without substantial alteration.

foot (in contrast to Jesus, who entered on an ass, in fulfillment of a messianic prophecy in Zechariah)[119] because, he said, it was his servant's turn to ride his horse. The
Byzantine period in the east had ended. The Arab period, which determined the
dominant character of the region for the next 1,300 years, had begun.

Jerusalem now became a Moslem city. The Temple Mount, desolate during
the Byzantine period, became the focus of the city once again. It was soon
enhanced by a magnificent domed structure intended to outshine the dome of
the rotunda that marked the site where Jesus was buried.

The Dome of the Rock is, of course, one of the great jewels of Moslem architecture; the building, with its recently refurbished dome plated with pure gold,
still dominates the city. The original structure was built in the late 7th century
by the Omayyad caliph Abd al-Malik (reigned 685–705 C.E.). It was followed
soon thereafter, in the early 8th century, by the silver-domed Al-Aqsa mosque,[120]
on the southern part of the Temple Mount, which may have been intended to
outdo the Constantinian basilica in front of the tomb of Christ. (Unlike the Dome
of the Rock, however, the frequently rebuilt Al-Aqsa mosque is now much smaller
than the original.)

The Dome of the Rock is not only one of the most beautiful achievements
of Islamic architecture, it is also the earliest dated building extant in the Moslem
world. And it is unique. As one scholar has observed, "No contemporary build-

Al-Aqsa Mosque

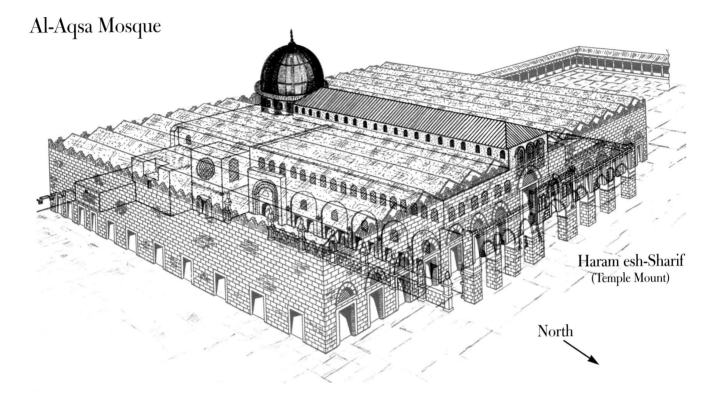

Haram esh-Sharif
(Temple Mount)

North

The silver-domed Al-Aqsa mosque sits on the southern end of the Temple Mount. As the drawing above shows, Al-Aqsa was originally a much broader structure. (The original structure is shown in brown, the current structure is outlined in blue.) Only the central part has survived. South and southwest of the Temple Mount were at least five Arab palaces (see p. 239) built over Byzantine residences, using stones thrown down by the Romans during the destruction of Jerusalem in 70 C.E. A bridge gave direct access to the Haram esh-Sharif, the Arab name for the Temple Mount.

ing in any neighboring culture offers a comparison with the Dome of the Rock."[121] The mosque has remained almost unchanged since it was built in 691 C.E., surviving for 1,300 years without substantial alteration.

Inside the octagonal building are two concentric octagonal ambulatories. Within these is a circular area surrounding es-Sakhra, the rock mass from which, in Moslem tradition, Mohammed, after a night ride from Mecca, ascended to heaven on his steed el-Burek. The hoofprint of el-Burek is still visible, impressed in the rock. In Jewish tradition, this is the site of Mount Moriah, where Abraham nearly sacrificed his beloved son Isaac (Genesis 22). In Moslem tradition, it was really Ishmael, the ancestor of the Arabs, who lay beneath the uplifted knife when God intervened.

The octagonal shape of the Dome of the Rock suggests that it was designed in conscious imitation of a Christian *martyrium* (memorial). *Martyria* are churches commemorating particular events in the life of Christ or other biblical figures; they customarily enclose equally on all sides the site of the event being memorialized. Both the original chapel enclosing the traditional site of the Nativity in Bethlehem and the house of St. Peter (where Jesus stayed) in Capernaum are, like the Dome of the Rock, octagonal structures. Precisely which events were intended to be memorialized here is uncertain (perhaps Mohammed's Ascent, or the near-sacrifice of Isaac/Ishmael). Nor are the dates known when the various traditions arose. But what seems clear is that

the Dome of the Rock, drawing on both Christian and Jewish traditions, was intended as a statement, as one scholar has written, "of the final truth of Islam."[122]

The new Omayyad rulers of Jerusalem (661–750 C.E.) also built a massive palace compound just south of the Temple Mount, in the old Byzantine residential section. So far, five major buildings in this palace complex have been at least partially excavated (see drawing, p. 239). The largest building enclosed a broad, stone-paved courtyard, which was discovered in Benjamin Mazar's excavation supervised by Meir Ben-Dov. The rectangular building was two stories high and more than 300 by 275 feet in area, which gives some idea of the magnitude, if not the splendor, of the palace. From the building itself, the excavators found lovely frescoes painted in bold colors, plaster reliefs and marble mosaics. Only floral and geometric decorations were used—no human or animal figures. The palace was probably built for the caliph to use on his visits to Jerusalem.

A bridge at the level of the roof of the building provided direct access to the Temple Mount, or Haram esh-Sharif, the Noble Enclosure or Noble Sanctuary, as it is known in Moslem tradition. On a more mundane level, the palace complex included at least seven bathrooms fitted with water-flushed toilets.

Many of the huge ashlars used to build the palace were reused stone blocks taken from the destroyed Herodian Temple Mount enclosure wall (see photo, p. 238) or perhaps from the Nea Church, which had also incorporated Herodian ashlars. For excellent building blocks, nothing could beat those old Herodian stones. Marble columns and even chancel screens from destroyed churches were also used in the Omayyad palace.

Paradoxically, ancient literary sources give no hint of the existence, let alone the magnificence, of this major Omayyad palace complex. The reason is now clear. The Omayyads were succeeded by their bitter enemies, the Abbasids, who revolted and displaced the Omayyad dynasty in 750 C.E. The Abbasid caliphs, and the historians under their patronage, went out of their way to obliterate all references to Omayyad accomplishments. The Abbasid caliph Al-Mamoun (in the 9th century) even tried to claim credit for building the Dome of the Rock. A long dedicatory inscription inside the Dome of the Rock identifies *Al-Mamoun* as the builder. For centuries, some investigators relied on this reference to date the building. A careful examination of the inscription, however, shows that the name of the Omayyad caliph who actually built the Dome of the Rock, Abd al-Malik, has been scratched out and the name of Al-Mamoun substituted. But whoever made the substitution forgot to change the date in the inscription; the inscription still says that the building was constructed in the 72nd year of the Moslem era (691 C.E.), that is, during Abd al-Malik's reign.

This inscription deserves special mention. Part of the mosaic decoration of the mosque, the inscription is set in a narrow strip inside and outside of the

Es-Sakhra, the rock mass in the center of the Dome of the Rock. In Jewish tradition, Adam was buried below; Abraham nearly sacrificed his beloved son Isaac here; and the Holy of Holies was located here. In Moslem tradition, it was Ishmael who was nearly sacrificed here; and the Prophet Mohammed ascended to heaven from this rock.

internal octagon formed by columns nearest the outer walls of the building. It is nearly 800 feet long and is the earliest example of Arabic script used as part of a decorative scheme, a feature of Islamic art to the present day.[123]

The text contains an anti-Christian polemic: "Believe therefore in God and his apostles, and say not 'Three' [that is, the trinity]…God is only one God. Far be it from his glory that he should have a son."

As one authority has observed, from the Moslem viewpoint, "the Dome of the Rock was an answer to the attraction of Christianity, and its inscription provided the faithful with arguments to be used against Christian positions."[124] The Dome of the Rock was one volley in what has been called an "ideological 'cold war' between the Christian and Muslim empires at the time."[125]

Just as the Abbasids tried to take credit for the supreme Omayyad accomplishment, the Dome of the Rock, they also banned from their history books references to the Omayyad palace complex south of the Temple Mount. Ironically, it took an Israeli archaeological expedition to bring it to light. In the words of the excavator Meir Ben-Dov, "[In the Omayyad palace complex south of the Temple Mount] for the first time since the days of David and Solomon, the seat of the royal palace had returned to the vicinity of the Temple Mount; and it was the heirs of David and Solomon who were privileged to find its remains."[126]

A wall (lower right) of one of the Arab palaces south of the Temple Mount is adjacent to the southern wall of the Temple Mount (upper right). The wall of this Arab palace looks much like a Herodian wall—because the Moslem builders reused Herodian ashlars that once formed part of the walls of the Herodian Temple Mount but were knocked down in the Roman destruction of 70 C.E.

In 1099, after a five-week siege, Crusaders under Godfrey de Bouillon conquered Jerusalem, rampaging through the city and murdering both Jews and Moslems. Once again, Jews (and this time Moslems as well) were barred from the Holy City. Jerusalem became the capital of the Crusader kingdom, officially called the Latin Kingdom of Jerusalem. The Dome of the Rock, which the Crusaders regarded as the "Temple of the Lord," the Solomonic Temple, was converted into a church named Templum Domini. A cross was affixed to the top of the dome.

The Crusaders took Al-Aqsa to be the "Temple [Palace] of Solomon," that is, the residence of Israel's illustrious king (after all, this was the area where his

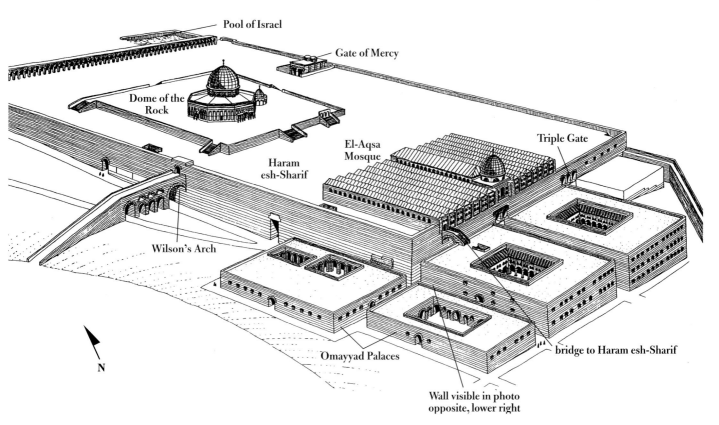

palace had been located); so they converted Al-Aqsa into a residence for the new ruler of Jerusalem. The building proved not to be very suitable for this purpose, however, and in 1128 it was turned over to an order of soldier-monks, who thus became known as the Templars. (Consistent with their other mistaken identifications, the Crusaders regarded the vaulted area beneath the southeastern part of the Temple Mount, built by Herod and now lying partially beneath Al-Aqsa, as the "Stables of Solomon," an inaccurate designation the area retains until this day. The Crusaders, however, did use the area as a stable.)

Crusader rule lasted nearly a century. It was a time of intense building. The two most outstanding extant examples are St. Anne's Church (see photo, p. 240), inside St. Stephen's Gate (the Lions Gate), and the Church of the Holy Sepulchre, the current facade of which is entirely Crusader. Both of these churches reflect typical Romanesque features of the 12th century.

Many Crusader churches have since been transformed into mosques or workshops.[127] The covered Crusader market, now restored on the line of the Cardo (but above the ancient Roman/Byzantine street), once again houses shops catering to tourists. But much more Crusader construction has vanished with time and destruction—monasteries, hostels, markets, as well as churches, all originally built to provide for the thousands of Christian pilgrims who flocked to the Crusader city.

Several extant towers on the walls of the Old City may date to the Crusader

In this drawing of Arab Jerusalem in the 7th–8th centuries C.E., the Dome of the Rock already sits on the Temple Mount, now called the Haram esh-Sharif. Al-Aqsa mosque covers most of the southern end of the Haram esh-Sharif. Arab palaces lie to the south and west. A bridge from the roof of the largest building leads directly to the Haram esh-Sharif.

period. One of the most prominent protrudes west of Dung Gate, marked on Crusader maps as the Tanner's Gate tower.

On July 4, 1187, the great Moslem general Saladin (Salah ed-Din), founder of the Ayyubid Dynasty, inflicted a stunning defeat on the Crusader forces at the Horns of Hattin, west of the Sea of Galilee (see photo, p. 242). Later that year, the Crusaders surrendered Jerusalem to Saladin peaceably. A cultured and humane ruler, Saladin once again permitted Jews, as well as Christians, to reside in the city. He removed the cross from the top of the Dome of the Rock, however, and transformed the Crusader Church of St. Anne into a Moslem school.

For two brief periods in the 13th century (1229–1239 and 1243–1244), later Crusaders regained control of the city, but it was soon recaptured by the Moslems. Foreseeing the possibility that the city might again be recaptured by Crusaders, the Moslem caliph ordered the walls of Jerusalem to be dismantled. In that way, if the Crusaders did recapture the city, they would not be able to defend it.

The Church of St. Anne, the best-preserved and finest example of Crusader architecture in Jerusalem, stands over the place where, according to one Christian tradition, Mary was born. In the foreground are excavations at the Pool of Bethesda, where Jesus cured the paralytic (John 5:2-9).

The city remained unfortified for several centuries, during the entire Mamluk period (1250–1516). As a result, the population declined, and the city was eclipsed both politically and economically. But it remained an important religious capital: Jerusalem became a center of Islam. Some of the most beautiful monuments on the Haram esh-Sharif date to this period.

The security situation continued to deteriorate throughout the Mamluk empire, and in the early 16th century Palestine was easily conquered by the expanding Turkish Ottoman Empire. In December 1516, the Ottoman sultan Selim I entered Jerusalem at the head of his cavalry, strewing coins to the cheering crowds that welcomed him. Between 1538 and 1541, the great Moslem ruler Suleiman the Magnificent rebuilt the complete circuit of the walls of Jerusalem on earlier foundations, and that is what we see as the Old City wall today.

The Ottoman period lasted until December 11, 1917, when the victorious British general (later viscount) Edmund Allenby entered the city on foot through

The remains of a tower, identified on Crusader maps as Tanner's Gate, abut the southern wall of the Old City. Beyond the tower is Dung Gate, through which refuse was removed from the city, thereby giving the entrance its name.

241

Rich Galilee farm-land lies in the valley leading to the distant Horns of Hattin, where Moslem forces under Saladin decisively defeated the Crusaders in 1187, allowing the Arabs to retake Jerusalem peaceably.

Jaffa Gate, a final victory in World War I. Palestine then became a British Mandate under the League of Nations. The British Mandate over Palestine ended with establishment of the state of Israel in 1948. In 1949, at the conclusion of bitter fighting between Arabs and Jews, the Old City remained in Jordanian hands. Jews were effectively banned from the Old City. In the Six-Day War, in 1967, Jerusalem was reunited under Israeli rule.

The Israeli poet Yehuda Amichai tells us that "the air over Jerusalem is saturated with prayers and dreams." He finds it hard to breathe. Then he adds:

> And from time to time a new shipment of history arrives
> and the houses and towers are its packing materials.
> Later these are discarded and piled up in dumps.

We have tried to explore some of these dumps, picking here and there to

242

see what we can learn. But mysteries remain. We can perhaps follow the thread of history, but the prayers and dreams upon which Jerusalem is built are beyond the reach of archaeology.

Notes

[1] See caption to pl. 11 in Kathleen M. Kenyon, *Jerusalem—Excavating 3,000 Years of History* (London: Thames and Hudson, 1967).

[2] In her latest pronouncement on the matter, Kenyon seems to opt for an offset/inset construction. Her reasoning is not clear, however. She says that "the wall to the south is too great for this [to be a gate tower]" (*Digging Up Jerusalem* [New York: Praeger, 1974], p. 84). She also allows for the possibility that this angle is the northeast angle of the city wall, marking its limit in this direction (ibid.). According to David Tarler and Jane M. Cahill, writing in the *Anchor Bible Dictionary* (s.v. "David, City of"), Yigal Shiloh found another jog, or offset, in the portion of the wall that he exposed, citing the plan in fig. 14 in Yigal Shiloh, *Excavations at the City of David I, 1978-1982: Interim Report of the First Five Seasons, Qedem* 19 (1984), p. 52. There is no discussion of this jog in this book. See p. 12. The presence of these two angles, in more than 200 feet of wall, does not seem enough evidence to declare it an offset/inset wall; the angles might be simply jogs in the wall, in order to change slightly the direction or location of the wall.

[3] As early as 1892, Father M.-J. Lagrange reasoned that earliest Jerusalem must have been on the eastern ridge. See "Topographie de Jerusalem," *Revue Biblique* 1 (1892), p. 17.

[4] Elisha Efrat in *Encyclopaedia Judaica*, s.v. "Jerusalem," subhead "Geography," col. 1513.

[5] Kenyon, *Jerusalem*, p. 19.

[6] William Foxwell Albright, "The Ṣinnôr in the Story of David's Capture of Jerusalem," *Journal of the Palestine Oriental Society* 2 (1922), p. 286.

[7] See Terence Kleven, "Up the Water Spout," *Biblical Archaeology Review* (*BAR*) 20 (July/August 1994).

[8] This is still the most common translation. The New Jewish Publication Society translation, however, uses "Jackals' Spring."

[9] Kleven, "Up the Water Spout."

[10] See Dan Cole, "How Water Tunnels Worked," *BAR* 6 (March/April 1980).

[11] Two of Shiloh's senior staff members who are working on the final report have written subsequent to Shiloh's death that "the discovery that Warren's Shaft incorporates a number of natural geological phenomena, all of which existed long before David's conquest of Jerusalem suggests, however, that the question of its relationship to the biblical *tsinnor* should be reassessed. Moreover, as similar subterranean water systems were operative in Mycenaean Greece as early as the 13th century B.C.E., the possibility that the technology for constructing such systems was introduced into the Levant during the L[ate] B[ronze] or early Iron I should not be summarily rejected" (Tarler and Cahill, "David, City of," p. 62).

[12] See Tarler and Cahill, "David, City of," which cites G.E. Mylonas, *Mycenae and the Mycenaean Age* (Princeton, NJ: Princeton University Press, 1966), pp. 15, 31-33, 40-43.

[13] See Dan Gill, "How They Met—Geology Solves Long-standing Mystery of Hezekiah's Tunnelers," *BAR* 20 (July/August 1994).

[14] The calcareous crust is created by ground water that contains carbon elements. See "Does Carbon-14 Prove When Warren's Shaft Was Dug?" *BAR* 20 (November/December 1994), p. 12.

[15] Captain Charles Wilson and Captain Charles Warren, *The Recovery of Jerusalem* (New York: D. Appleton & Co., 1871), pp. 190-192.

[16] Shiloh, "Jerusalem's Water Supply During Siege—The Rediscovery of Warren's Shaft," *BAR* 7 (July/August 1981).

[17] Although Macalister dated the construction of the structure to King David's time, he called it a Solomonic tower because it was supposedly rebuilt by Solomon. See R.A.S. Macalister and J.G. Duncan, *Excavations on the Hill of Ophel, Jerusalem, 1923-1925,* Annual of the Palestine Exploration Fund 4 (London, 1926), pl. facing p. 49.

[18] See Tarler and Cahill, "David, City of," p. 55.

[19] Tarler and Cahill, "David, City of," pp. 55, 56. In this they differ from Shiloh: "Kenyon and Shiloh both interpreted the substructural and superstructural components [of the Stepped-Stone Structure] as independent architectural units, dating to the LBII and Iron Age II, respectively...Subsequent evaluation of both the architectural and ceramic evidence from area G, however, indicates that the stepped stone structure and the stone and soil filled compartments beneath it are actually two components of a single architectural unit constructed in the 13th-12th century B.C.E."

[20] As Tarler and Cahill observe, "Kenyon interpreted the substructural compartments as platforms intended to provide level surfaces on which to construct 'civilized' buildings...Shiloh, in contrast, interpreted them as a means for expanding the level of the hillcrest, atop of which he located the 'Citadel of Zion'" ("David, City of," p. 55).

[21] Shiloh, *City of David*, p. 17.

[22] Kenyon, *Digging Up Jerusalem*, p. 100.

[23] G.J. Wightman, *The Walls of Jerusalem: From the Canaanites to the Mamluks,* Mediterranean Archaeology Supplement 4 (Sydney, Australia, 1993), pp. 28–29. See, for example, Nahman Avigad, *Discovering Jerusalem* (Nashville: Thomas Nelson, 1980), p. 24.

[24] Where the tribe of Simeon settled is confusing. According to one biblical account, the territory of Simeon lay "in the midst" of Judah (Joshua 19:1).

[25] Jerome Murphy-O'Connor, "The Cenacle and Community: The Background of Acts 2:44–45," in Michael Coogan, J. Cheryl Exum and Lawrence E. Stager, eds., *Scripture and Other Artifacts,* Philip J. King festschrift (Louisville: Westminster/John Knox Press, 1994), p. 296.

[26] Ibid., p. 299.

[27] Kenyon, *Digging Up Jerusalem*, p. 156.

[28] David Ussishkin, *The Village of Silwan: The Necropolis from the Period of the Judean Kingdom* (Jerusalem: Israel Exploration Society/Yad Izhak Ben-Zvi, 1993), pp. 298–299.

[29] See Hershel Shanks, "Is This King David's Tomb?" *BAR* 21 (January/February 1995).

[30] For a recent, extended discussion rejecting the identification of T1 as a tomb, see Robert Wenning, "Eisenzeitliche Gräber in Jerusalem und Juda," *Orbis Biblicus et Orientalis* (forthcoming, 1996).

[31] See Shanks, "Have the Tombs of the Kings of Judah Been Found?" *BAR* 13 (July/August 1987).

[32] See Gabriel Barkay and Amos Kloner, "Jerusalem Tombs From the Days of the First Temple," *BAR* 12 (March/April 1986).

[33] But see Wightman, *Walls of Jerusalem*, pp. 161–163, who argues that *spelaion basilikon*, usually translated "royal caverns," cannot mean "royal tombs." Josephus uses at least three other words when he refers to tombs. According to Wightman, what Josephus was referring to by *spelaion basilikon* was the large cave near the Damascus Gate known as Solomon's Quarry. "Essentially, what Josephus was trying to say was that these caves were unusually large" (p. 161). Father Jerome Murphy-O'Connor agrees. We have probably not heard the last of this debate.

[34] Before Herod's reconstruction, the Temple was extensively rebuilt by the Maccabees (Hasmoneans; see 1 Maccabees 4:38–58).

[35] See Barkay, "Measurements in the Bible," *BAR* 12 (March/April 1986), p. 37.

[36] For further details, see Volkmar Fritz, "What Can Archaeology Tell Us About Solomon's Temple?" *BAR* 13 (July/August 1987).

[37] See Amihai Mazar, "Bronze Bull Found in Israelite 'High Place' From the Time of the Judges," *BAR* 9 (September/October 1983); see also Shanks, "Two Early Israelite Cult Sites Now Questioned," *BAR* 14 (January/February 1988); and A. Mazar, "On Cult Places and Early Israelites: A Response to Michael Coogan," *BAR* 14 (July/August 1988).

[38] See Menahem Haran, "Altar-ed States," *Bible Review* 11 (February 1995).

[39] Carol L. Meyers, "Was There a Seven-Branched Lamp Stand in Solomon's Temple?" *BAR* 5 (September/October 1979).

[40] Meyers argues that various elements of the Tabernacle menorah show authentic Egyptian influence, appropriate for an early dating of the text. Although we have no seven-branch candlesticks from this period, Meyers likens the Tabernacle menorah to a tree of life and supports her argument that the Tabernacle menorah had seven branches with stylized tree of life depictions with three branches of the tree on either side of the trunk. This iconography disappears, however, in the Israelite period (ibid.).

[41] See Elie Borowski, "Cherubim: God's Throne?" *BAR* 21 (July/August 1995); and Tallay Ornan, "Symbols of Royalty and Divinity," ibid.

[42] A bend 134 feet north of the Straight Joint (observed by Warren) may mark the end of the Solomonic Temple Mount; see Leen Ritmeyer, "Locating the Original Temple Mount," *BAR* 18 (March/April 1992), p. 34.

[43] Ibid., p. 24.

[44] See Asher S. Kaufman, "Where the Ancient Temple of Jerusalem Stood," *BAR* 9 (March/April 1983).

[45] See Shanks, "Kathleen Kenyon's Anti-Zionist Politics—Does It Affect Her Work?" *BAR* 2 (March 1976); and "Yigal Shiloh—Last Thoughts," *BAR* 14 (March/April 1988).

[46] Some scholars believe that the siege of Jerusalem (described in 2 Kings 18:17–19:35) did not take place in 701 B.C.E. following Sennacherib's destruction of the cities of Judah, but rather was the result of a second refusal by Hezekiah some 13 years later to pay tribute to the Assyrian king. See John Bright, *A History of Israel*, pp. 267–271, 282–287 (Philadelphia: Westminster Press, 1959).

[47] Shanks, "Please Return the Siloam Inscription to Jerusalem," *BAR* 17 (May/June 1991).

[48] Simon B. Parker, "Siloam Inscription Memorializes Engineering Achievement," *BAR* 20 (July/August 1994).

[49] Gill, "How They Met," p. 64, footnote.

[50] See William E. Phipps, "A Woman Was the First to Declare Scripture Holy," *Bible Review* 6 (April 1990).

[51] See Josette Elayi, "Name of Deuteronomys Author Found on Seal Ring," *BAR* 13 (September/October 1987); and Tsvi Schneider, "Six Biblical Signatures," *BAR* 17 (July/August 1991).

[52] See Shanks, "The Fingerprint of Jeremiah's Scribe," *BAR* (forthcoming).

[53] For more on this hoard, see Shanks, "Jeremiah's Scribe and Confidant Speaks from a Hoard of Clay Bullae," *BAR* 13 (September/October 1987).

[54] See Avigad, *Hebrew Bullae from the Time of Jeremiah* (Jerusalem: Israel Exploration Society, 1986), pp. 27–28.

[55] See Schneider, "Six Biblical Signatures."

[56] See James B. Pritchard, ed., *Ancient Near Eastern Texts Relating to the Old Testament*, 2nd ed. (Princeton, NJ: Princeton University Press, 1955), p. 308b.

[57] For a different interpretation of this letter, see Yigael Yadin, "The Lachish Letters—Originals or Copies and Drafts?" in Shanks and Benjamin Mazar, eds., *Recent Archaeology in the Land of Israel* (Washington, DC: Biblical Archaeology Society/Jerusalem: Israel Exploration Society, 1984).

[58] These are traditional, not scriptural, dates. According to Jeremiah 39:2, the walls were breached on the 9th of Tammuz. Jeremiah 52:12–13 dates the destruction of the Temple to the 10th of Av. 2 Kings 25:8–9 says it was the 7th of Av.

[59] *The New Encyclopedia of Archaeological Excavations in the Holy Land*, ed. Ephraim Stern, 4 vols. (New York: Simon & Schuster, 1993), s.v. "Jerusalem," p. 709a.

[60] Barkay, *Ketef Hinnom—A Treasure Facing Jerusalem's Walls* (catalog; Jerusalem: Israel Museum, 1986), p. 22.

[61] Barkay, *Ketef Hinnom*, p. 31.

[62] A variation of this ancient blessing is found in Psalm 67:2.

[63] The excavator, Gabriel Barkay, suggests that there are other possibilities: They may have hung around the forehead (compare the command to wear these words "between your eyes" [Deuteronomy 6:8, 11:18; Exodus 13:9,16]) or they may have been enclosed in a case made of perishable material; see Barkay, "The Priestly Benediction on Silver Plaques from Ketef Hinnom in Jerusalem," *Tel Aviv* 19 (1992), p. 181. Several amulet cases have been found in Egypt and Phoenicia.

[64] James D. Purvis, in Shanks, ed., *Ancient Israel—A Short History from Abraham to the Roman Destruction of the Temple* (Washington, DC: Biblical Archaeology Society, 1988), p. 165.

[65] Avigad, *Discovering Jerusalem*, p. 62.

[66] See Magen Broshi, "Estimating the Population of Ancient Jerusalem," *BAR* 4 (June 1978). For additional discussion of population estimates and citations to the literature, see Tarler and Cahill, "David, City of," p. 65.

[67] The precise location of the Akra has been called "one of the most enigmatic topographical problems concerning Jerusalem in the days of the Second Temple" (Avigad, *Discovering Jerusalem*, p. 64). See also L. Ritmeyer, "Locating the Original Temple Mount," p. 36ff.

[68] See "*BAR* Interviews Amihai Mazar—A New Generation of Israeli Archaeologists Comes of Age," *BAR* 10 (May/June 1984).

[69] Shaye J.D. Cohen, in Shanks, *Ancient Israel*, p. 207.

[70] Josephus *Antiquities of the Jews* 15.11.5.

[71] Josephus *The Jewish War* 4.9.12.

[72] Josephus *Jewish War* 5.5.6.

[73] Baraita in Babylonian Talmud, *Sukkah* 51b; see also *Baba Batra* 4a.

[74] See Shanks, *Judaism in Stone—The Archaeology of Ancient Synagogues* (New York: Harper & Row, 1979), pp. 17–21.

[75] A recent suggestion of Howard Kee dating the inscription some time after the Second Jewish Revolt (132–135 C.E.) founders even more clearly on a historical basis—Jews were banned from the city after the Second Jewish Revolt.

[76] Frank Moore Cross, "Nahman Avigad—In Memoriam," *BAR* 18 (May/June 1992).

[77] Babylonian Talmud, *Pesahim* 57.1 = Tosefta, *Minhot* 13.21.

[78] See Shanks, "The Jerusalem Wall That Shouldn't Be There," *BAR* 13 (May/June 1987).

[79] For the latest, and very careful, volley, see Wightman, *Walls of Jerusalem*, pp. 159–181. Wightman suggests the Sukenik-Mayer Wall could be a barrier wall built by Jewish rebels just before the revolt began or a barrier wall built by the Roman Tenth Legion shortly after the revolt was suppressed.

[80] Josephus *Jewish War* 6.8–10.

[81] Avigad, "The Burnt House Captures a Moment in Time," *BAR* 9 (November/December 1983).

[82] Ibid.

[83] See Marvin H. Pope, "Hosanna—What It Really Means," *Bible Review* 4 (April 1988).

[84] See James Fleming, "The Undiscovered Gate Beneath Jerusalem's Golden Gate," *BAR* 9 (January/February 1983).

[85] See Myriam Rosen-Ayalon, *The Early Islamic Monuments of Al-Haram Al-Sharif, an Iconographic Study*, Qedem 28 (1989).

[86] See Joan Taylor, "The Garden of Gethsemane—Not the Place of Jesus' Arrest," *BAR* 21 (July/August 1995).

[87] See L. Ritmeyer and Kathleen Ritmeyer, "Akeldama—Potter's Field or High Priest's Tomb?" *BAR* 20 (November/December 1994); and Gideon Avni and Zvi Greenhut, "Akeldama—Resting Place of the Rich and Famous," ibid.

[88] Annas is twice referred to in the New Testament (Luke 3:2 and Acts 4:6) in what appears to be a different chronology from the one in Josephus. The latter is normally accepted as reliable in this regard. The conflict, as one authority suggests, "present[s] a problem not solvable with present evidence"

(*Harper Bible Dictionary*, s.v. "Annas").

89 Josephus *Antiquities of the Jews* 18.2.2, 4.3.

90 See Greenhut, "Burial Cave of the Caiaphas Family," *BAR* 18 (September/October 1992); and Ronny Reich, "Caiaphas Name Inscribed on Bone Boxes," ibid.

91 Although this is how it is commonly referred to, the correct Greek is *lithostroton*. See Shanks, "The Religious Message of the Bible—*BAR* Interviews Pierre Benoit," *BAR* 12 (March/April 1986), p. 64.

92 Murphy-O'Connor, *The Holy Land—An Archaeological Guide from Earliest Times to 1700*, 3rd ed. (Oxford: Oxford University Press, 1992), p. 37.

93 See Shanks, "Religious Message of the Bible," p. 64.

94 See Pierre Benoit, "The Archaeological Reconstruction of the Antonia Fortress," in *Jerusalem Revealed—Archaeology in the Holy City 1968–1974* (Jerusalem: Israel Exploration Society, 1975).

95 See Shanks, "Religious Message of the Bible," pp. 62–66.

96 Josephus *Jewish War* 5.11.4.

97 "A Perspective on Loss of a Biblical Site," *BAR* 12 (March/April 1986), p. 66.

98 Evidence of this quarrying as early as the 8th–7th centuries B.C.E. was also found by Broshi. See Broshi, "Evidence of Earliest Christian Pilgrimage to the Holy Land Comes to Light in Holy Sepulchre Church," *BAR* 3 (December 1977), p. 44.

99 Hillel Geva, in *New Encyclopedia of Archaeological Excavations*, s.v. "Jerusalem," p. 736.

100 Two scholars have recently suggested that this is a dome over the apse of the basilica and that the rotunda was merely a semicircular building. See Shimon Gibson and Taylor, *Beneath the Church of the Holy Sepulchre Jerusalem* (London: Palestine Exploration Fund, 1994), pp. 74, 77.

101 Some scholars believe the Romans built an actual pagan temple on the Temple Mount. See Dan Bahat, *The Illustrated Atlas of Jerusalem* (New York: Simon & Schuster, 1990), pp. 60, 66. Bahat relies on Cassius Dio who reports that "on the site of the Temple of God [Hadrian] erected a temple to Jupiter." For the variety of views as to what was on the Temple Mount and what was built on the later site of the Church of the Holy Sepulchre and which pagan deities were honored, see Gibson and Taylor, *Holy Sepulchre*, pp. 68–71.

102 Eusebius *Life of Constantine* 3.26.1.

103 Murphy-O'Connor, "The Location of the Capitol in Aelia Capitolina," *Revue Biblique* 101 (1994), p. 407.

104 Specifically, in the Russian (Alexander) Hospice, but elsewhere as well. See Bahat, *Illustrated Atlas of Jerusalem*, p. 66.

105 Eusebius *Life of Constantine* chap. 36.

106 Eusebius *History of the Church* 10.4.46.

107 Eusebius, "The 'Breviary' or Short Description of Jerusalem."

108 See Bahat, "Does the Holy Sepulchre Church Mark the Burial of Jesus?" *BAR* 12 (May/June 1986).

109 Ibid.; see also J.-P.B. Ross, "The Evolution of a Church—Jerusalem's Holy Sepulchre," *BAR* 2 (September 1976).

110 Murphy-O'Connor, *Holy Land*, p. 49.

111 See Broshi, "Earliest Christian Pilgrimage."

112 Gibson and Taylor, *Holy Sepulchre*, pp. 25–48.

113 See Yadin, *Bar Kokhba* (New York: Random House, 1971), pp. 124ff., 172ff.

114 See Menahem Magen, "Recovering Roman Jerusalem—The Entry Beneath Damascus Gate," *BAR* 14 (May/June 1988).

115 Jerome Murphy-O'Connor, based on finds of Father Louis-Hugues Vincent in the last century, believes this column stood outside the gateway, there being no real northern wall (only a gateway) of the city until the early 4th century.

116 Julian *Against the Galileans* 306a–b.

117 Eusebius *Life of Constantine* 3.33.

118 For varying readings, see Bahat, *Illustrated Atlas of Jerusalem*, p. 75; and Meir Ben-Dov, *In the Shadow of the Temple: The Discovery of Ancient Jerusalem* (New York: Harper & Row, 1982), p. 219.

119 See Matthew 21:5 and Zechariah 9:9.

120 Alas, the dome is now black; the silver dome was damaged in a fire set by a deranged Australian tourist nearly a quarter of a century ago.

121 Rosen-Ayalon, *Early Islamic Monuments*, p. 12.

122 Oleg Grabar, "The Umayyad Dome of the Rock in Jerusalem," *Ars Orientalis* (1959), p. 56.

123 Kufic script, rather than the present decorative Arabic script.

124 Graber, "Dome of the Rock."

125 Ibid., p. 60.

126 Ben-Dov, *Shadow of the Temple*, p. 321.

127 See, for example, Bahat, "A Smithy in a Crusader Church," *BAR* 6 (March/April 1980).

128 Yehuda Amichai, "Ecology of Jerusalem," in *Great Tranquillity: Questions and Answers*, trans. Glenda Abramson and Tudor Parfitt (New York: Harper & Row, 1983).

Select Bibliography

Avigad, Nahman. *Discovering Jerusalem*. Nashville: Thomas Nelson, 1980.

——. *Hebrew Bullae from the Time of Jeremiah*. Jerusalem: Israel Exploration Society, 1986.

——. *The Herodian Quarter in Jerusalem*. Jerusalem: Keter Publishing House, 1989.

Avi-Yonah, Michael, ed. "Jerusalem." In *The Encyclopedia of Archaeological Excavations in the Holy Land*, vol. 2. Jerusalem: Israel Exploration Society/Massada Press, 1976. English edition.

Bahat, Dan. *The Illustrated Atlas of Jerusalem*. New York: Simon & Schuster, 1990.

Barkay, Gabriel. *Ketef Hinnom: Burial Treasures from Jerusalem*. Jerusalem: Israel Museum, 1986.

——. "The Priestly Benediction on Silver Plaques from Ketef Hinnom in Jerusalem." *Tel Aviv* (Journal of the Institute of Archaeology of Tel Aviv University) 19 (1992), pp. 139–194.

Ben-Dov, Meir. *In the Shadow of the Temple: The Discovery of Ancient Jerusalem*. New York: Harper & Row, 1982.

Coüanson, Charles. *The Church of the Holy Sepulchre in Jerusalem*. London: Oxford University Press, 1974.

Deutsch, R., and M. Heltzer. *Forty New Ancient West Semitic Inscriptions*. Tel Aviv: Archaeological Center, 1994.

Geva, Hillel, ed. *Ancient Jerusalem Revealed*. Jerusalem: Israel Exploration Society/Biblical Archaeology Society, 1994.

Gibson, Shimon, and Joan E. Taylor. *Beneath the Church of the Holy Sepulchre Jerusalem*. London: Committee of the Palestine Exploration Fund, 1994.

Kenyon, Kathleen M. *Jerusalem—Excavating 3,000 Years of History*. London: Thames and Hudson, 1967.

——. *Digging Up Jerusalem*. New York: Praeger, 1974.

King, Philip J. "Jerusalem." In *Anchor Bible Dictionary*, vol. 3. Editor-in-chief, David Noel Freedman. New York: Doubleday, 1992.

Mazar, Benjamin. *The Mountain of the Lord: Excavating in Jerusalem*. Garden City, NY: Doubleday & Company, 1975.

Mazar, Eilat, and Benjamin Mazar. *Excavations South of the Temple Mount*. Qedem, no. 29. Jerusalem: Hebrew University, 1989.

Murphy-O'Connor, Jerome. *The Holy Land—An Archaeological Guide from Earliest Times to 1700*. 3rd ed. Oxford: Oxford University Press, 1992.

Rosen-Ayalon, Myriam. *The Early Islamic Monuments of Al-Haram Al-Sharif, an Iconographic Study*. Qedem, no. 28. Jerusalem: Hebrew University, 1989.

Shanks, Hershel. *The City of David: A Guide to Biblical Jerusalem*. Washington, DC: Biblical Archaeology Society and Tel Aviv: Bazak Israel Guidebook Publishers, 1973.

——. *Judaism in Stone—The Archaeology of Ancient Synagogues*. New York: Harper & Row, 1979.

——, ed. *Ancient Israel—A Short History from Abraham to the Roman Destruction of the Temple*. Washington, DC: Biblical Archaeology Society, 1988.

Shanks, Hershel, and Benjamin Mazar, eds. *Recent Archaeology in the Land of Israel*. Washington, DC: Biblical Archaeology Society and Jerusalem: Israel Exploration Society, 1984.

Shiloh, Yigal. *Excavations at the City of David I, 1978–1982: Interim Report of the First Five Seasons*. Qedem, no. 19. Jerusalem: Hebrew University, 1984.

Stern, Ephraim, ed. "Jerusalem." In *The New Encyclopedia of Archaeological Excavations in the Holy Land*, vol. 2. New York: Simon & Schuster, 1993.

Tarler, David, and Jane Cahill. "David, City of." In *Anchor Bible Dictionary*, vol. 2. Editor-in-chief, David Noel Freedman. New York: Doubleday, 1992.

Tushingham, A.D. *Excavations in Jerusalem, 1961–1967*. 2 vols. Toronto: Royal Ontario Museum, 1985–.

Ussishkin, David. *The Village of Silwan: The Necropolis from the Period of the Judean Kingdom*. Jerusalem: Israel Exploration Society/Yad Izhak Ben-Zvi, 1993.

Vincent, Louis-Hugues. *Jerusalem Underground: Discoveries on the Hill of Ophel (1909–11)*. London: Horace Cox, 1911.

Warren, Charles. *Underground Jerusalem*. London: Palestine Exploration Fund with John Murray, 1876.

——, and Claude R. Conder. *The Survey of Western Palestine, Jerusalem*. London: Palestine Exploration Fund, 1884.

Weill, Raymond. *La Cité de David*. 2 vols. Paris: Librairie Paul Geuthner, 1920–1947.

Wightman, G.J. *The Walls of Jerusalem: From the Canaanites to the Mamluks*. Mediterranean Archaeology Supplement, no. 4. Sydney, Australia, 1993.

Wilson, Charles, and Charles Warren. *The Recovery of Jerusalem*. New York: D. Appleton & Co., 1871.

Yadin, Yigael. ed. *Jerusalem Revealed—Archaeology in the Holy City 1968–1974*. Jerusalem: Israel Exploration Society, 1975.

Illustration Credits

Antikensammlung, Staatliche Museen zu Berlin—
    Preussischer Kulturbesitz: 50 (right)
Nahman Avigad: 82, 96 (right), 107 (top right), 108
    (bottom right and left), 109, 113, 165–166
Nahman Avigad, *Discovering Jerusalem*: 150 (bottom
    middle), 218 (top), 227 (top)
Gideon Avni: 171
Adapted from Dan Bahat, *The Illustrated Atlas of
    Jerusalem*: 5 (bottom), 71, 81, 121 (bottom), 172
Meir Ben-Dov: 130 (top right), 151, 156 (bottom), 160
Mme. Biasi, courtesy of Cabinet des Médailles: 98
    (top left)
Bildarchiv Preussischer Kulturbesitz, Berlin—
    Vorderasiatisches Museum: 2 (bottom right)
Werner Braun: 8, 24, 34, 37–38, 131, 135, 139,
    146–147, 153–154, 168, 226, 232, 240–242
British Museum: 101 (top)
British School of Archaeology, Jerusalem: 4 (top), 28,
    99
Brussels Museum: 2 (bottom left)
Carta, The Israel Map and Publishing Company, Ltd.:
    227 (bottom), 235
City of David Society: 103
Charles Clermont-Ganneau: 101 (middle)
Erez Cohen: 199 (bottom)
Adapted from Virgilio Corbo, *Il Santo Sepolcro di
    Gerusalemme*, vol. 2: 207 (left)
Judith Dekel/Ronny Reich: 41
Josette Elayi: 98 (top right)
James Fleming: 183
G. Franz/Gabriel Barkay: 118
B. Frenkel/Gabriel Barkay: 116–117
Yitzhak Harari/Yigal Shiloh: 18, 22
David Harris: 63, 100, 101 (bottom), 132, 134 (left),
    144 (left), 160 (top right), 163 (top), 170, 220
    (top)
David Harris/Nahman Avigad: 106
David Harris/Bible Lands Museum: 46, 50 (left)
Hebrew Union College—Jewish Institute of Religion: 70
Israel Antiquities Authority (IAA): 30, 31, 191 (black-
    and-white photos)
Collection of IAA, exhibited and photographed by Israel
    Museum, City of David excavation: 98 (bottom
    left), 107 (top left), 108 (top left), 110, 162
IAA/Tsila Sagiv: 97
Adapted from *Israel Exploration Journal* 17: 134
    (right)
Israel Museum: 96 (left)
Israel Museum/Gabriel Barkay: 114
Israel Museum, Teddy Kollek collection: 61
Israel Museum/Nahum Slapak: 78
Jewish Quarter excavations/Hillel Geva and Avital
    Zitronblat: 104, 111, 163 (bottom left), 164
    (top), 167, 174, 228–229
Adapted from Kathleen Kenyon, *Jerusalem: Excavating
    3,000 Years of History*: 95
Brian Lalor: 4 (bottom)
Erich Lessing: 53 (bottom left), 54, 56, 83, 88 (top),
    129 (right), 156 (top), 157 (left), 214
B. Lifshitz, *Aegyptus*, vol. 42, 1962: 216

Adapted from drawing by Gary Lipton: 27
Garo Nalbandian: *xvi*, 5 (top), 7, 10, 15, 19, 58–59,
    86, 90 (far left), 140 (top), 142, 145 (bottom),
    173, 180–181, 184–185, 187–188, 190,
    192–195, 197, 202, 204, 206–207 (right), 209,
    211, 230, 236, 238
Richard T. Nowitz: 36, 40, 42–45, 64 (bottom), 124,
    136, 198–199 (top), 201, 219, 222, 224
Oriental Institute of The University of Chicago: 49
    (top), 53 (bottom right)
Palestine Exploration Fund: 6, 21, 158
Adapted from *Qedem* 19: 123
Zev Radovan, Jerusalem: 26–27, 51–53 (top), 64 (top),
    76, 92, 94, 120–121 (top), 122, 128–129 (top
    left), 130 (left), 138, 161, 163 (bottom right),
    169, 176, 178, 182, 208, 212, 217, 221, 234
Ronny Reich: 191 (drawings)
Leen Ritmeyer: 48, 49 (bottom), 66–67, 73, 133, 144
    (top right, bottom right), 148–149, 150 (top,
    bottom right, bottom left), 155, 157 (right), 160
    (top left, bottom), 164 (bottom), 189, 218
    (bottom), 220 (bottom), 239
Nathaniel Ritmeyer: 145 (top right)
Beno Rothenberg: 93
H. Shafir/Yigal Shiloh: 13
Hershel Shanks: 68–69, 72, 85, 90 (top right, bottom
    right)
Adapted from Hershel Shanks, *City of David*: 91
Yigal Shiloh: 3, 77, 102, 112
Courtesy of Tel Aviv University: 119 (far left)
Lloyd Townsend: 74–75
Adapted from Louis-Hugues Vincent, *Revue Biblique*
    30: 39 (top left)
Adapted from Count J. Melchoir de Vogüé, *Le Temple
    de Jérusalem*: 145 (top left)
Charles Warren and Claude R. Conder, *The Survey of
    Western Palestine*: 140 (bottom)
Raymond Weill, *La Cité de David*: 39 (top right, both
    at bottom)
Baron Wolman: *ii–iii*
Adapted from Yigael Yadin, ed., *Jerusalem Revealed*: 127
Ada Yardeni: 98 (bottom right), 108 (top right)
Bruce and Kenneth Zuckerman, West Semitic
    Research/courtesy of the Israel Antiquities
    Authority: 119 (middle, far right)

    We would also like to extend our special thanks
to the following people who helped us on short notice
to find and obtain many of the subjects: our Jerusalem
correspondents Anita Ellis and Toby Shuster, Amalyah
Keshet at the Israel Museum, Sophie Durocher at the
IAA, Alon De Groot and Tami Shiloh, Avraham Biran
at Hebrew Union College, Shimon Gibson of the
Palestine Exploration Fund, Lisa Snider at the Oriental
Institute, Karl Heinz Putz at the Antikensammlung of
the Staatliche Museen zu Berlin, Kay Prag of the British
School of Archaeology in Jerusalem, Yehuda Ben-Arieh
at Hebrew University, Varda Nowitz, and interns Ophir
Lehavy and Amy Kushner.

Index

Abbasid dynasty, 237, 238
Abiathar, 47
Absalom, 47
Absalom's Tomb, 169
Adonijah, 47, 48
Adoni-zedek, 4
Aelia Capitolina, 205, 215-23
Agrippa I, 171
Ahaz, tomb of, 36
Akeldama, 186-87
Akiva (rabbi), 215
Akra, 125-26
Albright, William Foxwell, 12
Alexander the Great, 125
Alexander Janneus, 130, 135
Allenby, Edmund, 242
Altars
    at Beersheba, 52, 55
    in Tabernacle, 55
    in Temple, 52, 55
Amarna letters, 1
Amichai, Yehuda, 242
Amnon, 47
Amulets, 117-118
Anastasis (Resurrection) rotunda, 205, 208, 210
Annas, 187
Antiochus IV, 125-26
Antipater, 135
Apocrypha, 14
Al-Aqsa mosque, 234, 238-39
Aquila, 14, 15
Araunah, 32
Arch
    Ecce Homo, 183, 189, 194
    relieving, definition, 143
    Robinson's, 147, 152
    Wilson's, 152
Archaeological remains
    discovered during construction, 162
    lack of, 32
    uncovered by destruction, 161-62
Archaeologists. See also individual names
    maximalists and minimalists, 80
Archelaus, 170
Arcosolium, 169
Aristobulus II, 135
Ark of the Covenant
    moved to Jerusalem, 30-31
    moved to Temple, 57
    Temple built for, 31-32, 73
Arrowheads, 112
Asherah, 95, 96, 99
Ashlar, definition, 65
Assyria/Assyrians, 79, 81, 83-84, 105
Augustus (emperor), 61
Avigad, Nahman, 80, 93, 95, 102, 110, 153, 158, 162,
    165, 167, 175-76, 216, 231
Ayyubid dynasty, 240

Azaliah, 109
Azariah, 99, 113
Azekah, 109-110
Baal, 96, 99
Babylonia/Babylonians, 105, 109-10, 112-13, 115,
    117, 119
Babylonian Exile, 115-118
    return from, 119-20, 123
Barkay, Gabriel, 115, 117, 200
Bar-Kokhba, 215
Baruch, 105-6, 107, 108-9
Bathrooms, 103, 167, 237
Bathsheba, 6, 47
Ben-Arieh, Sara, 173
Ben-Dov, Meir, 237, 238
Benjaminites, 9
Benoit, Pierre, 173, 193
Bethlehem, 235
Bible
    divine origin, 97
    historical value, 6, 8
    Jerusalem first mentioned, 4
    oldest texts, 117-18
    Scroll of the Law found by Hilkiah, 96-98
Biran, Avraham, 68
Boaz (pillar), 51
Bone repositories/ossuaries, 115-16, 169, 189
British rule, 242
Broad Wall, 80, 81, 112
Broshi, Magen, 212
Bullae, 97, 99, 107, 108, 109, 113
Bulls
    at Bethel and Dan, 79
    in front of Solomon's Temple, 55
Burek, el-, 235
Burial artifacts, 116-18
Burial caves. See Tombs/burial sites
Burial sites. See Tombs/burial sites
Byzantine Christian rule, 206, 217, 220, 225-31, 233
Caiaphas, 187, 189
Capernaum, 235
Cardo Maximus, 205, 216-17, 220, 231, 239
Chalcolithic period pottery, 2
Cherubim, 56-57, 79
Christianization of Jerusalem, 225
Christians/Christianity. See Byzantine Christian rule;
    Christianization of Jerusalem; Crusaders; Jesus
Church of the Holy Sepulchre, 35, 196, 200, 202-3,
    205-6, 208, 210, 239
Church of the Redeemer, 203
City of David
    location of, 4
    origin of name, 13, 29
    as site of David's tomb, 36
    size of, 36, 122-23
Clermont-Ganneau, Charles, 102
Conder, Claude, 141
Conquests

Alexander's, 125
Babylonian, 105-13
Byzantine Christian, 233
Crusader, 238, 240-41
David's, 4, 6, 9
    Bible account, 12-13
    date, 11-12
    Fortress of Zion, 12, 25
    water shaft, 12-14, 23
Herod's, 135
Joshua's 4-6
Judahites', 9
Maccabees', 126
Moslem, 208, 210, 233-34, 240
Ottoman, 241
Persian, 233
Roman, 135, 171, 175-77
Constantine, 203, 205, 206, 225
    basilica and rotunda of, 205, 206, 208, 210
Controversies
    David's tomb, 40-45
    expansion of Jerusalem, 80
    Joshua, 5-6
    ship graffito in Church of Holy Sepulchre, 210,
        212-13
    Temple location, 70
    Warren's Shaft, 15-16, 20, 23
Corbo, Virgilio, 202
Cross, Frank Moore, 95, 165
Crucifixion, remains of victim, 179
Crusaders, 238-41
Cyrus the Great, 119
Dan, Tel, 69
David
    capital at Jerusalem, 29-30
    extent of kingdom, 31
    lack of archaeological remains, 32
    and *Millo*, 29
    moves Ark of the Covenant, 30-31
    purchase of Temple site, 32
    renames Jerusalem, 13, 29
    successor of, 47-48
    tomb of, 35-45
David's Tomb (named site), 35-36
David's Tower, 129
Defense of city, 12 14, 67, 110, 112, 129, 130, 173,
        175, 240-41
Deportation to Babylon, 115, 117
Deuteronomistic history, definition, 94
Dome of the Rock, 50, 65, 70, 71, 200, 234-35,
        237-38. *See also* First Temple (Solomon's
        Temple); Temple Mount
Dome of the Tablets, 71
Dragon's Spring, 14
Dung Gate, 239
Early Bronze Age, 2
Ecce Homo arch, 183, 189, 194
École Biblique et Archéologique Française, tombs at,
        42-45, 200
Egypt/Egyptians, 105, 109, 125
Ennion, 169
Eusebius, 205, 206, 208, 230
Execration texts, 1
Exegesis
    Millo, 29

tsinnor, 12-14, 15
Exile. *See* Babylonian Exile
Expansion of Jerusalem, 79-81, 122-23, 130, 217
Ezekiel, 56
Ezra, 120
Favissa, 92-93
Field of Blood, 186-87
Figurines, 93, 99
First Temple (Solomon's Temple)
    altar, 52
    Ark of Covenant moved to, 57
    Babylonian destruction of, 49, 175
    Bible description of, 49-57
    bronze bulls, 55
    cedars of Lebanon, 120
    cherubim, 79
    consecration of, 52
    David's purchase of site, 32
    decorations, 55-57
    feast at completion, 57
    as God's dwelling place, 94
    Holy of Holies, 50, 55, 56, 57, 71, 73
    incense altar, 55
    lamp stands, 55
    machtot, 52
    mechonot, 51-52, 57
    pillars, 51
    Solomon's building of, 31-32, 49-51, 57
    Western Wall, 60-61
    worship centralized by Hezekiah, 92
Fiscus Judaicus, 215
Fleming, James, 180-81
Fortress of Zion, 12, 25, 28
Foundation Stone, 73
Galilee, 215
Garden of Gethsemane. *See* Gethsemane
Garden Tomb, 196-97, 200
Gates/gateways
    Bab el-Amud (Gate of the Column), 223
    Damascus Gate, 183, 220, 223
    Double Gate, 97, 143, 147, 183-84
    Dung Gate, 239
    Ecce Homo arch, 183
    to Gihon Spring, 2
    Golden Gate, 70-71, 180-81, 183-84, 233
    Jaffa Gate, 242
    Lions Gate, 239
    Roman gate beneath Damascus Gate, 183, 220
    St. Stephen's Gate, 239
    for Solomon's entry procession, 48
    Triple Gate, 97, 143, 147
Gemariah, 109, 113
Geography of Jerusalem, 2-4, 8, 67
Geology of Jerusalem, 16, 18, 20
Gethsemane, 184, 186
Gibeon, 4
Gibson, Shimon, 212-13
Gihon Spring. *See also* Hezekiah's Tunnel; Warren's
        Shaft
    defense problems, 14
    "Dragon's Spring," 14
    gateway to, 2
    gushing of, 14
    influence on Jerusalem's location, 3-4
    irrigation source, 73

reservoir supply, 73, 76
site of Solomon's anointing, 47-48
Gilboa, Mount, 55
Gill, Dan, 16, 20, 23, 89, 91-92
Givat ha-Mivtar, 179
Godfrey de Bouillon, 238
Golden Gate, 70-71, 180-81, 183-84, 233
Golgotha, 196
Gordon, Charles George, 196
Greenhut, Zvi, 189
Hadrian, 194, 203, 205-6, 223
Haggai, 120
Hakim, 210
Hamrick, Emmett, 175
Hanan, 97-98
Haram esh-Sharif, 237, 239. *See also* Dome of the
    Rock; Temple Mount
Hasmonean period, 126, 129, 130, 135
Hebron, 143
Helena, 203, 205, 208
Hellenism, 125, 130, 161, 225
Heraclius, 233
Herod the Great
    building by, 137-38, 141, 143, 152
    character of, 137
    conquest of Jerusalem, 135
    death of, 170
    expansion of Temple Mount, 138, 141, 147
    rebuilding of Second Temple, 49-50, 60-61,
        137-38
    successors of, 170
Herodian period, 169-70
Herod's Temple. *See also* Second Temple
    building of, 49-50, 60, 137-38, 155-59
    Holy of Holies, 158
    Josephus's description of, 155
    Roman destruction of, 50, 175, 205
Hezekiah, 29. *See also* Hezekiah's Tunnel
    Assyrian siege preparations, 81, 83-85
    Hezekiah's Reform (religious), 92-93, 96
    name not in Siloam inscription, 87, 88
Hezekiah's Tunnel, 76-77
    construction, 88-89, 91-92
    as natural formation, 89, 91
    reason for constructing, 84
    route, 85-86
    Siloam inscription, 86-88
Hezir, 134
Hilkiah (Hilkiyahu), 96-99
Hill of Evil Counsel, 126
Hinnom Valley, 3
Hiram (architect of Temple), 51
Hiram (king of Tyre), 51
Holy of Holies. *See* First Temple
Horns of Hattin, 240
House of Bullae, 113
Household objects, 167, 169
Huldah, 97, 143
Hyrcanus II, 135
Incense shovels, 52
Inscriptions
    Dome of the Rock, 238
    ivory pomegranate, 95
    seal, 97, 107, 113
    Shebna's tomb, 102

Siloam, 86-88
Place of trumpeting, 153, 155
Isaiah, 230
Theodotus, 159, 161
Irrigation, 73
Isaiah, 81, 83, 92, 102, 230
Jachin (pillar), 51
Jaffa Gate, 242
Jason's Tomb, 134
Jebusites, 5, 9, 12-13, 23, 32
Jehoiachin, 109, 120
Jehoiakim, 105, 106
Jeremiah, 96, 105, 106, 109
Jeroboam, 79
Jerusalem Peace Forest, 189
Jesus
    arrest of, 186
    betrayal in Gethsemane, 186
    burial place, 196-97, 200, 202-3, 205-6, 208, 210
    condemnation by Pilate, 189, 193
    cross, 233
    Nativity site, 235
    route into Jerusalem, 179-80, 184
    Via Dolorosa, 189, 193
Joab, 13, 15, 23, 48-49
Jordanian rule, 242
Josephus, 45, 67, 129, 152, 155, 156, 175, 187, 194
Joshua, 4-6
Josiah, 96-97, 98, 99, 105
Judah ha-Nasi ("Rabbi"), 65
Judas, 186
Julian the Apostate, 225, 230
    restoration of Temple, 230
Justinian, 231
Kathros family house, 169, 175-77
Kaufman, Asher, 70, 71, 73
Kenyon, Kathleen, 1-2, 28, 29, 40-41, 48, 62, 80, 92,
    122, 129, 173, 203
Ketef Hinnom, 115
Kidron Valley, 3, 4, 73
King's Garden, 73
Kiriath-Jearim, 30
Kloner, Amos, 42, 45
Kochim, 134, 169, 202
Kollek, Teddy, 11
Lachish, 83, 109
Lachish Letter No. 4, 109
Lalor, Brian, 65, 152
Lamp stands, 55
Lemaire, André, 95
Levites, 9
Lions Gate, 239
Lithostrotos, 189, 193-94
Location of Jerusalem
    original city, 2-4
    reasons for, 2-4
    strategic importance, 8
Lower Aqueduct, 126
Lower City, 155
Lux, Ute, 203
Macalister, R. A. S., 25, 28, 129
Maccabees, 126, 129
Machtot, 52
Madaba map, 205, 206, 216, 223, 231
Magen, Menahem, 152

Al-Malik, Abd, 234, 237
Mamluk period, 241
Al-Mamoun, 237
Manasseh, 96
Mariamme, 137
Martin-Chave, (Sister) Brigitte, 194
Martyria, 235
Mattathias Antigonus, 130
Mazar, Amihai, 55
Mazar, Benjamin, 65, 81, 143, 147, 152, 153, 237
Mechonot, 51-52, 57
Menorah, 55, 157-58
Metsudat Tsion. See Fortress of Zion
Meyers, Carol, 55
Middot, 65, 157, 158
Mikva'ot, 167
Millo, 29
Mishnah, 65, 68, 157
Mohammed, 235
Monotheism, 94
Moriah, Mount, 235
Moslem rule, 233-43
Murphy-O'Connor, Jerome, 36, 47, 189, 193, 210
Nahum, 96
Names for Jerusalem
    Aelia Capitolina, 205
    City of David, 13
    Rushalimum, 1
    Urusalim, 1
Narkiss, Bezalel, 158
Nathan, 31, 47, 48
Nativity (site of), 235
Nea (New Church of St. Mary, Mother of God),
    231, 233
Nebuchadnezzar, 49, 109
Nehemiah, 14, 120, 122, 123
Netzer, Ehud, 173
New Church of St. Mary, Mother of God, 231, 233
Offering stands, 51-52
Old City, 2, 239-40, 241, 242
Omar, 210, 233
Omayyad dynasty, 237
Ornan, 32
Ossuaries. *See* Bone repositories/ossuaries
Ottoman Empire, 241-42
Palace compound (Moslem), 237
Palestine (name), 205
Persia/Persians, 119
Personal names, 98, 102-3
Peter (saint), 235
Pinkerfeld, Jacob, 35
Pomegranate, ivory (scepter head), 94-96
Pompey, 67, 135
Pontius Pilate, 171, 189, 193, 194
Pool of Siloam, 84, 85, 86, 87
Population, 122-23, 130, 231, 241
Pottery, 2, 116-17
Ptolemies, 125
Rabbi (Judah ha-Nasi), 65
Rabbinic Judaism, definition, 65
Rachel, 93
Reform (religious)
    Hezekiah's, 92-93, 96
    Josiah's, 96-97, 99
Rehoboam, 79

Religion/theology, Israelite, 93-94
Reservoirs, 73, 76
Residences, 161-62, 165, 167, 169
Revolts
    against Antiochus IV, 125, 126
    First/Great Jewish, 130, 169, 171, 175
    Second Jewish, 205, 215
Ritmeyer, Leen, 65, 67-70, 73, 184
Robinson, Edward, 14, 147
Robinson's Arch, 147, 152
Rome/Romans, 171, 175-77, 205, 215-17
Royal Stoa, 152
Rushalimum (Jerusalem), 1
Sacrifices, 52, 92, 152
Sakhra, es-, 235
St. Anne's Church, 239
St. Stephen's Gate, 239
Saladin, 240
Salome Alexandra, 135
Samaria, 79
Sanhedrin, 152
Seals, 97-98, 107, 113
Second Temple. *See also* Herod's Temple
    building of, 49, 120
    Herod as rebuilder, 49-50, 60, 137-38
    location, 73
    looting by Antiochus IV, 125
Seleucids, 125
Selim I, 241
Sennacherib, 11, 81, 83, 84
Seraiah, 109
Shebna, 102
Shechem, 29, 79
Sheshbazzar, 119-20
Shiloh, Yigal, 2, 15-16, 28, 76, 99, 108, 112-13
Sieges
    Assyrian, 81, 83-85
    Babylonian, 110
    Pompey's, 135
    Titus's, 171
Siloam Channel, 73, 76, 77
Siloam inscription, 86-88
Siloam Pool. *See* Pool of Siloam
Simeon Bar-Kosiba, 215
Six-Day War, 242
Solomon
    anointing as king, 47-48
    building of Temple, 31-32, 49-51, 57
    extension of city, 4
    killing of Adonijah and Joab, 48-49
    and *Millo*, 29
    successor of, 79
    tomb of, 36
Solomon's Pools, 126
Solomon's Stables (site), 61, 147, 239
Solomon's Temple. *See* First Temple
"Son," meaning of, 107-8
Stepped-Stone Structure, 25, 28, 29, 122
Strabo, 67
Struthion Pool, 194
Sukenik-Mayer Wall, 173, 175
Suleiman the Magnificent, 241
Synagogues, 159, 161
Syria/Syrians, 125
Syria-Palaestina (name), 205

Tainat, Tell, 51
Taylor, Joan, 186, 212–13
Templars, 239
Temple. *See* Dome of the Rock; First Temple
    (Solomon's Temple); Herod's Temple; Julian the
    Apostate; Second Temple; Temple Mount
Temple Mount
    during Christian rule, 206, 225, 230
    Hasmonean extension, 68
    Herod's
        building of, 60-62, 137-155
        Double Gate, 97, 143, 147
        enclosure wall, 138, 141
        place of trumpeting, 153-154
        Robinson's Arch, 147, 152
        Royal Stoa, 152-153
        Solomon's Stables, 61, 147
        staircase, 143
        Triple Gate, 97, 143, 147
        Western Wall, 60-61, 141
    included in city, 2, 4, 122-123
    Middot description, 65, 68
    during Moslem rule, 234-35, 237-38
    site purchased by David, 32
    size, 65
    Solomon's, 61-62
        archaeological remains, 62, 65
        location of, 61-62, 65, 67-73
    Straight Joint, 62
    traditions about, 206, 208, 235
Temples, 69, 51
Templum Domini, 238
Testa, Emmanuele, 212-13
Theodotus inscription, 159, 161
Theology. *See* Religion/theology, Israelite
Titus, 171
Tirzah, 79
Tomb of the Kings, 169
Tombs/burial sites
    Absalom's, 169
    Akeldama, 187
    Bene Hezir, 134
    burial artifacts, 116-18
    burial caves, 45
    Caiaphas's, 189
    David's, 35-45
    at École Biblique et Archéologique Française, 43-
        45, 200
    First Temple period, 99-100, 115-18, 200
    Garden Tomb, 196-97, 200
    Golden Gate mass grave, 181
    Gordon's Tomb, 197
    Hasmonean period, 130, 134
    Herodian, 169
    Jason's, 134
    Jesus', 196-97, 200, 202, 203, 205-6, 208, 210
    Judahite kings', 36, 37, 40-42
    location outside city, 81, 196, 200
    matriarchs' and patriarchs', 143
    Second Temple period, 134, 169, 202-3
    Shebna's, 102
    T1. *See* Tombs/burial sites, David's
    Tomb of the Kings, 169
    Zechariah's, 130
"Tower of David," 25

Tsinnor, 13-14, 15, 23
Tyropoeon Valley, 3, 161
Tzaferis, Vassilios, 179
Ugaritic cuneiform, 15
Upper City, 153, 161
Urusalim (Jerusalem), 1
Ussishkin, David, 42, 99
Valley of the Cheesemakers. *See* Tyropoeon Valley
Vespasian, 171
Via Dolorosa, 189, 193, 194
Vincent, Louis-Hugues, 193, 200
Vogüé, Melchior de, 141
Wailing Wall, 60
Walls
    Broad Wall, 80, 81, 112
    earliest enclosure, 1-2
    First Wall, 129, 172, 203
    Hasmonean, 129
    Herod's Temple Mount, 141
    Old City, 2, 239-40, 241
    Second Wall, 129-30, 172, 203
    Sukenik-Mayer, 173, 175
    Third Wall, 129-30, 172-73, 175, 203
    Wailing Wall, 60
    Western Wall, 60-61, 141
Warren, Charles, 14, 62, 67-68, 141
Warren's Shaft
    age of, 20
    climbing, 20-23
    discovery of, 14
    geology of, 16, 18, 20
    as natural formation, 16, 20
    Siloam Channel and, 76
    as *tsinnor*, 15, 23
    as water system, 15
Water channel/shaft. *See* Gihon Spring; Siloam
    Channel; *Tsinnor*; Water systems
Water systems, 16, 126. *See also* Warren's Shaft
Water's influence on Jerusalem's location, 3-4
Weill, Raymond, 36, 37, 40, 159
Western Wall, 60, 141
Wilson's Arch, 152, 161
Women's status, 97
Yerahme'el, 106, 107-8
Zadok, 47, 48
Zechariah, 120, 183
Zechariah's Tomb, 130
Zedekiah, 109, 110
Zephaniah, 96
Zerubbabel, 120
Zion (term), 12
Zion, Mount, 3, 35